Game On!

Tech.edu

A Hopkins Series on Education and Technology

Game On!

Gamification, Gameful Design, and the
Rise of the Gamer Educator

Kevin Bell

JOHNS HOPKINS UNIVERSITY PRESS   BALTIMORE

© 2018 Johns Hopkins University Press
All rights reserved. Published 2018
Printed in the United States of America on acid-free paper
9 8 7 6 5 4 3 2 1

Johns Hopkins University Press
2715 North Charles Street
Baltimore, Maryland 21218-4363
www.press.jhu.edu

Library of Congress Cataloging-in-Publication Data

Names: Bell, Kevin, 1968– author.
Title: Game on! : gamification, gameful design, and the rise of the
    gamer educator / Kevin Bell.
Description: Baltimore : Johns Hopkins University Press, 2017. | Series:
    Tech.edu : a Hopkins series on education and technology | Includes
    bibliographical references and index.
Identifiers: LCCN 2017009944 | ISBN 9781421423968
    (hardcover : alk. paper) | ISBN 1421423960 (hardcover : alk. paper) |
    ISBN 9781421423975 (electronic) | ISBN 1421423979 (electronic)
Subjects: LCSH: Education, Higher—Effect of technological
    innovations on. | Education, Higher—Computer-assisted
    instruction. | Internet in higher education. | Gamification. |
    Computer games. | Educational games. | BISAC: EDUCATION /
    Higher. | GAMES / Video & Electronic. | EDUCATION /
    Computers & Technology.
Classification: LCC LB2395.7 .B45 20107 | DDC 378.1/7344678—dc23
LC record available at https://lccn.loc.gov/2017009944

A catalog record for this book is available from the British Library.

*Special discounts are available for bulk purchases of this book. For more
information, please contact Special Sales at 410-516-6936 or
specialsales@press.jhu.edu.*

Johns Hopkins University Press uses environmentally friendly book
materials, including recycled text paper that is composed of at least
30 percent post-consumer waste, whenever possible.

Calling out one person in no way diminishes my appreciation of the large number of people who have supported and encouraged me through the production of this work. However, I dedicate it officially to my dad, Michael Bell, who taught in some pretty rough inner-city schools in the UK, motivating students that others had given up on. Contextualizing through his loves of literature, music, and (proper) football, he gamified spelling tests in the 1970s with leaderboards, promotions, and relegations, intrinsically motivating kids steeped in the highs and lows of supporting Newcastle United—the greatest team in the history of all sports *ever*.

Dad claims to understand next to nothing of my writings yet embodies the spirit and principle of the very best educators: those who inspire and change lives. Thanks fatha.

Contents

Acknowledgments

As is traditional, way too many people to list here, but I'll give it a go.

Two people went beyond the call of duty or friendship to help me with this work.

My dissertation chair, Dr. Laura Perna, provided unreasonably prompt and helpful feedback on the executive doctorate program at the University of Pennsylvania. A gamefully designed, intrinsically motivating goal of mine was to get my work to a level where I would get feedback on a draft with fewer than 100 comments, tweaks, or suggestions from her. It never happened. Even from Kazakhstan when *technically* offline, she spent precious time bringing her laser focus to bear, sending me significant (as in p-value less than 0.05, causing me to reject the null hypothesis) support. Thank you, Laura.

Robert Rosenbalm, because of geeky interest in the subject area and by being what I would simply call a great bloke, tirelessly and again, punctually, reviewed chapter drafts with an editor's eye, a pedant's accuracy, and a friend's sensitivity. His mantra for this work and the changes that were happening in my life at the time—"You got this"—became my comfort blanket, my mulligan, and/or my incentive to keep going. Thank you, Robert.

The book would be nothing without the input and reflections of the practitioners whose work and energy drove the cases. Massive thanks to some of the most inspiring and generous educators I have ever met—Drs. Neil Niman, Kevin Yee, and Gerol Petruzella and Fred Aebli and Greg Andres; I hope your work, even to a small degree via this book, gets you the recognition and unlimited quarters you all deserve.

I mention my dad, Michael Bell, in the dedication, and again here, for the balance and background he and my mum, Jean, provided: raising my brother and me with a blend of culture, academia, sport, music, love of reading, and a carefree, insulated start to our lives. Thank you both so much.

A shout-out to Cohort 12 at Penn, a supremely talented and intelligent group. Swimming in that gene pool was exhilarating, made more so by the unequivocal support, humo(u)r, empathy, and friendship provided along the way—many thanks and egészségére.

Professionally, Northeastern University was a solid base, and people there were great supporters of the doctoral work that led to this book. Thank you to (former dean) John LaBrie, (SVP/CEO) Philomena Mantella, and, for cheerleading and the occasional "pint," Peter Stokes, Bryan Lackaye, and Kat Hitchcock.

Finally, most importantly, thanks to my wife and family for allowing me the time and space to work on this book. Sorry I missed the occasional recital, show, or hiking trip, but I hope this work makes you a little bit proud. Diane, Shay, Téah, and Rhianna—thanks for making my life so full and apologies in advance for the *Gorf* refurbished video arcade cabinet unit that will arrive soon to celebrate book completion day.

Stay in touch, old friends and new:

Twitter: @kbell14; blog: kevinbell@wordpress.com; other social media channels. Or just come in person and see the kangas outside my office at Western Sydney University, where I serve at the DVC-A's discretion.

Game On!

Prologue

The year 1978 was interesting for many reasons. Two popes, Paul VI and John Paul I, died within six weeks of each other, while, just before the pontifical passing, both Ashton Kutcher and James Franco were born. The Bee Gees, collectively and solo (Andy Gibb), dominated the US charts with six number-one songs, but without doubt the most significant pop-culture event of the year was Taito Corporation's launch of Tomohiro Nishikado's arcade game *Space Invaders*.

By way of a tribute to a popular Japanese song of the time, Nishikado titled it *Space Monsters* before his bosses at Taito made him change it to スペースインベーダー : *Supēsu Inbēdā* transcribed into the Katakana used for imported western words in Japanese; *Space Invaders* in full-on western English. One, now somewhat debunked, part of the mystique around the game's popularity in Japan was that it caused a national shortage of the 100-yen coin, forcing the government to triple production. Note for readers born in the last 20 to 25 years: everyone used to go to arcades and put coins in slots in the antediluvian days before PlayStations and Xboxes were invented. While the 100-yen shortage story is exaggerated at best, and very possibly a downright myth, the hype made it over to the United States, where Bally's Midway division licensed the game a year later. By 1982 it had grossed $2 billion, a figure that adjusted for inflation comes close to $7.26 billion in 2016 terms. As a culturally similar comparison point, the highest grossing movie of the late seventies was a little flick by the name of *Star Wars*. George Lucas's first of ~~three~~, ~~six~~, ~~seven~~, <u>many</u> *Star Wars* adventures banked a cool $486 million. Impressive—but somewhat less so when compared to the success of *Space Invaders*. The movie made less than a quarter of the revenue of the arcade game. Bear in mind that each game interaction generated one single quarter—around one-tenth of the transaction charge ($2.53) of going to the movies in the late seventies. Maybe it didn't quite cause a shortage at the US mint, but that's almost surely enough quarters to take down the Death Star.

Before 1978, worldwide arcade options had been limited to pinball, pool, or the occasional feisty game of bingo. *Pong* and *Breakout* were the height of late-seventies technological sophistication. Atari's Nolan Bushnell developed the two-dimensional table-tennis paddle game *Pong* in 1972, while two guys he hired developed *Breakout* on a $750 budget. One of them, Steve Jobs, allegedly pocketed extra bonuses that were generated by his and the other Steve's (that'd be Wozniak) speed and particularly ability to code efficiently using a minimal number of transistor–transistor logic (TTL) chips. It's interesting to surmise whether this duplicity ever came up as they combined to found a company (Apple, Inc.) that would eventually be valued at over $700 billion (the first company to break that mark) in early 2015. In a serendipitous closing of this initial narrative loop, Ashton Kutcher, born in *Space Invaders'* year zero, portrayed Jobs in the 2013 movie featuring his name. It has to be said, the film, *Jobs,* generated a fraction of the revenue of either *Star Wars* or *Space Invaders*—perhaps by missing a key opportunity in failing to feature James Franco as Wozniak.

As a side note: First reported back in 2008, but still rumored to be on the way, Leonardo DiCaprio was primed to star as Nolan Bushnell in the movie *Atari*. According to the 2008 press release: "There's a lot of ground to cover: Bushnell co-founded Atari in 1972 on $500, hired Steve Jobs and Steve Wozniak as early employees, and sold the company six years later for $28 million to Warner Communication after inventing the Atari 2600 and the addictive arcade game *Pong*" (Hart 2008). Art imitates life.

Getting back to gamification, gameful design, and related ephemera, fast forward to 2014-15-16, as *Star Wars* once again leaps back into pop culture, this time as ™ property of *The Mouse* (Disney). Members of Generation X, those born between 1964 and 1981, are gaining responsibility and autonomy. Now midcareer, they provide an interesting anthropological study of the first video arcade generation to come of age. They have taken on roles in society with a degree of self-determination and authority, and yet they seem to maintain a desire to *play*, to make a difference, and—*dammit*—maybe even to save the world from the Gorfian Empire.

Narrowing to the world of academe, many of these Gen Xers have tenure now, while others are associate deans or vice provosts. As a result of their growing seniority they have job security and perhaps even a degree of autonomy to set their own agenda. Despite academic (leading to fiscal and beyond, by extension, to societal) success, likely enough to sate the appetites of non-earth-defending mortals, many of these *Space Invader* champions, *Pac Man* wizards, *Galaxian* gods, or Gorfian Space Avengers express disappointment with their lot. They are saddened to see students who seem listless or disengaged, do the minimum to get by, and lack basic intrinsic motivation for their studies. These defenders of the galaxy / guardians of the gradebook wonder if they might provide some sort of spark of motivation or illustration of how fun it can be to *achieve*. It is a challenge, as it has always been, for older educators, let's say mid-40s and up (Gen X), to get through to or connect with their much younger, culturally shifted students. In terms of trying to be *down with* the kids, or even relating to students in their late 20s / early 30s—what we could call "posttraditional" (older)—most instructors don't risk trying to relate through music or pop culture. One instructor's comment, "I have sweaters older than these kids," provides a succinct summary of the challenge of finding shared experience or even shared context for those from only narrowly different generations.

So, this is where we start to jump into the crossover world of game principles being applied to education and pedagogy. Is this the opportunity to achieve empathy through shared experience or shared experience through decontextualized (or recontextualized) teaching and learning? When witnessing the commitment that twenty- to thirty-somethings have to their phone screens, whether interacting socially or playing games, the question arises whether that commitment (the intrinsic motivation to interact, engage, and spend time on task) might be somehow transported to their education and their own futures. It is worth noting that this age group actually plays mobile games less than Gen X. They "over-index" (do more of it than other age groups) in sports, health and fitness, music, media and entertainment, lifestyle, and shopping. To put it another way, they are intrinsically motivated to interact more with apps and media that almost certainly have gameful elements built in beneath a nongame interface. They are engaging with apps and content in general, just not as much (compared to other groups) with mobile games. This is worth bearing in mind when we come back to the whole educational games / gamification / gameful design questions later in the text.

Nonetheless, the forty-something educators, perhaps still engaging on the sly with *Candy Crush, Hay Day,* or *Flappy Bird*, recall the heady cocktail of action and challenge that maximized their engagement when young. Gaming while hours flew by, for as long as the quarters (or 100-yen coins) lasted, a high score list securing their legacy in eternity or at least until someone reset the system. As touched on above, while their motivation to enhance education could be 100% altruistic, perhaps they are also channeling their own careerist angst or even boredom. Their positions are safe. They have paid their dues. Their first 20 years of workplace genuflection and conformity have bought them respect and the trust of their higher-ups, allowing them to experiment a bit. Their motivation may be to try stuff and kick the proverbial tires of their career vehicle. The chance of their getting "hauled to the dean's office" or even monitored (at least until something great—or terrible—happens) is minimal. The sanctity of the closed classroom door or even the perceived sense of self-direction in online/hybrid classes is encouraging them to reinvent and try things in a different, not-chalk-and-talk, manner. These instructors could certainly be accused of being self-indulgent or even narcissistic. Might they be doing these things to make their own lives and careers less formulaic? Does this constitute taking risks with their students' education? Surely it would be safer to stick to the tried and trusted. Then again, nihilistic texts like Arum and Roska's *Academically Adrift* (2011) have claimed that almost half of students in their sample (more than 2,300 students at 24 institutions were sampled) demonstrated no significant improvement in a range of skills including critical thinking, complex reasoning, and writing during their first two years of college. This suggests that the bar is effectively very low. In true *Pong* fashion, the ball is back in the educators' court. What damage can they really do? Why shouldn't they experiment with emerging theories for teaching and learning? Why not have a degree of fun? Why not even add uncertainty and risk to their (and their students') daily lives? Why shouldn't the "kids" get a window on the fact that we *used to be* cool way back when? Retro is in.

Given the ubiquity of social media and easily implementable technology, is it so wrong for these instructors to simply contemplate having fun in the remaining 20 years of their careers? If it doesn't really change stuff—no harm, no foul. If they happen to reinvent, disrupt, or evolve American and global higher education, then so be it.

Who knows, the force might just be with them—get some quarters, quick . . .

■ ■ ■ ■ ■ ■ ■ ■ ■ ■ ■ ■ ■ ■ ■

CHAPTER ONE

A Societal Imperative

THE IMPETUS FOR ONLINE EDUCATION

Before we dive headlong into how gamification (or one of its sub-branches) might impact higher education, the questions Where? and Why? rear their heads. To answer these questions, it is worth spending a few moments assessing how we arrived at this juncture where higher education is having to consider new formats for the delivery of their "product" in light of developing technologies and changing requirements as we near the end of the twenty-first century's second decade.

There are factors that have driven us to a place where many existential questions have emerged. Firstly, the emergence of for-profit schools between 2000 and 2005 seemed to bring a new "student as consumer" focus to the otherwise sleepy hollow of the admissions function within academia. Following that, the economic downturn from 2007 to 2012 caused a rash of conversations that focused on "value proposition" and "key differentiators" in places where that kind of phraseology had previously been absent. Finally, the 2012–13 massive open online course (MOOC) phenomenon drove academic institutions that had been still in a state of denial to accept the fact that *online* is not going away as a means of delivering education and, indeed, might have a key societal role to play. As the millennium turned (or soon after), universities—from smaller, fiscally challenged institutions desperate to diversify revenue streams all the way up to prestigious institutions—started, for one or all of these reasons, to question their own attitude toward online education. The MOOC experiments conducted by Stanford, MIT, Harvard, and others compelled many who had been hesitating to embrace any form of *online* to quickly join the party. When Teresa Sullivan of the University of Virginia was ousted by her board in June 2012 for her *incrementalism*, an arguably sensible lack of haste in jumping on the MOOC bandwagon or developing an alternative substantive digital strategy for her institution, many boards and presidents really began to pay attention.

Despite rising costs of attendance, governmental and societal pressure has grown in favor of a more inclusive intake from all demographics into some form of higher education. Multiple attempts to ramp up alternate credentialing, with the exception of coding boot camps, have so far failed to generate much interest beyond the focused attention of on-campus administrators looking for the next big thing. Despite many suggestions that there may be better ways of assessing viability of a job candidate, employers still gravitate toward the safe proxy of a college degree, particularly one from an institutional brand or name that they recognize. Isolated examples exist, Google being the most quoted, of companies that go beyond or even ignore traditional qualifications, using puzzles or intelligence tests to assess candidates. Despite that, the ticket to the middle classes and the lifetime earnings boost of a college degree (estimated at+$900,000 for a bachelor's degree over a high school diploma and close to an additional $400,000 for a master's degree according to a 2012 US Census Bureau report) remains a defined period of time in a class, a course, or a program that results in a walk across a stage and a handshake from someone wearing a large robe and, in all likelihood, a floppy hat.

If we accept the premise that opportunity and access to the means of procuring a diploma is a requisite of a civilized country, it becomes glaringly apparent that traditional campuses with limited facilities and dorm space cannot scale to deal with rising student numbers. The drive to increase the percentage of citizens completing higher education brings into play tens of thousands of previously unreached applicants from low socioeconomic status (SES) backgrounds along with first-generation and minority aspirants. As the makeup of the US melting pot evolves and, as some would say, the rich get richer, then the increasing proportions of the target demographic coming from these groups (low SES is a family income less than $36,000 in 2015 dollars) has led to some commentators asking how higher education will accommodate this "New Majority" in the coming years. Adding minority, ethnically diverse, and first-generation students to the low-SES population gets us above the 50% mark. These changing demographics sit unsteadily against a backdrop of rising tuition costs, a sense of over-the-top facilities (climbing walls or the campus lazy river), and either administrative bloat or rising faculty salaries, depending on which side of that divide one sits on.

Neil Niman, professor and chair of economics at the Peter T. Paul School of Business and Economics at the University of New Hampshire, refers to these challenges as the "coming perfect storm in higher education" (2014, 7).

His words align with those of management theorist Peter Drucker who calls them, more positively, "sources of opportunity," envisioning how they can spur and encourage innovation. According to Drucker in his 2006 book *Innovation and Entrepreneurship*, among the most common drivers for change in any sector are "changes in demographics that drive consumer behavior and production and distribution incongruities which arise as a result" (Soares 2013, 1).

The impending perfect storm of opportunity in higher education is clearly driving consideration of the following incongruities:

1. The rising cost of doing business in higher education is coming into obvious conflict with the need to tailor to increased numbers of poorer or less well subsidized students.
2. The admittedly disproportionately weighted, not so very common but perceived as significant, investment in luxurious peripheral facilities while learners want for effective academic/social support and mentoring. As Jane Wellman, an analyst at the College Futures Foundation, put it, "the symbolism of this is worse than the reality of it" (Woodhouse 2015). Louisiana State University's recent $85 million upgrade to its recreational facilities, including a lazy river shaped like the letters *LSU,* is emblematic of this trend. The project was funded from student recreational fees (the students are charged $200 per person at LSU, amounting to $1,080 over a four-year academic stay).
3. An increasing lack of student engagement and growing disenchantment, manifesting itself in lower rates of course completion and persistence to graduation.

Despite these warning signs, institutions persist with the same tools, technologies, and forms of instruction that many consider antithetical to student interests and preferences. The company Blackboard was founded in 1997 and, after two decades has not changed its basic functionality. While the platform's capabilities and features have certainly been augmented, the fundamental read-post-respond instructor strategy and training (as conducted by a majority of institutions) has, if anything, ossified. These ambiguities provide the opportunity, or the ominous warning, suggesting business as usual (traditional education) has to be reviewed against emerging technologies, developing innovations, and disruptive means of delivery. In his joint address to

Congress on February 24, 2009, President Barack Obama set a national goal for the United States to have the highest proportion of college graduates in the world by the year 2020. He emphasized a need to broaden the enrollment funnel, to get around eight million more young adults on track to attaining associate's and bachelor's degrees by 2020. What quickly became clear in the postgame analysis of these pronouncements was that, without some form of sustained attention and some different means of doing business, these targets had no chance of being met. The kind of growth and scalability President Obama was speaking of caused many to ponder the next round of challenges layered upon those listed above.

Firstly, despite facilities enhancement, most residential campuses have neither the finances nor the infrastructure to significantly expand the physical campus. Perfunctory dorm space development lacks the tour-guide-friendly charm of the revamped dining hall and the climbing wall, and so this new swell of student-customers cannot easily be accommodated on traditional residential campuses.

Secondly, many of the targeted students, being older and having more work experience, have families and jobs that prevent them uprooting to spend weeks, months, or years on a campus even if they wanted to.

Thirdly, even optimistic college completion rates mean that many of these new students are absolutely and depressingly destined to fail. As the National Center for Education Statistics report of 2013 relayed, the six-year graduation rate for first-time students attending full time and beginning their pursuit of a bachelor's degree in fall 2005 was only 59% (2013, 202). In the at-risk demographic groups described earlier, the rate plummets. It goes without saying that higher education only makes a difference when participants complete their studies. As completion rates fall, students who have dropped out with accrued debt but no degree are in far worse shape than those who never started at all.

Given the above, many observers have concluded that online courses simply have to play a major role in meeting these societal goals of producing a qualified workforce. Online circumvents the dorm space issue, is less disruptive for older working adults/parents, and, depending on the institution's development model, can be more affordable for participants. From the institution's perspective, online course development seems, at least at first blush, to be a means of diversifying an academic portfolio (allowing them to grow sustainably or at least not atrophy) without the need for extensions to physical facilities. A slightly wet blanket on this otherwise optimistic outlook is the fact that online courses tend to retain even more poorly in comparison to traditional face-to-face classes, particularly with inexperienced or fragile learners. A five-year study reviewing 51,000 students conducted by the Community College Research Center at Teachers College, Columbia University in 2011 found that 8% fewer students persisted in online courses to the end of their studies compared to those who persisted in traditional (face-to-face) courses. Despite this obvious need for caution, the societal goal of equity and increased access still leads many to conclude that online is the only viable option for many non-traditional students. Furthermore, it seems worthwhile to counteract the current two-tiered system, where the wealthy benefit from a comprehensive learning experience on a traditional campus leaving the disenfranchised to suffer through dated pedagogy and poor use of technology online. With social media becoming an omnipresent part of most students' lives, with the gameful design of apps like FourSquare and the rise of wearable technology like the Fitbit activity tracker (now mandated by Tulsa's Oral Roberts University of all its students), questions are increasingly being asked as to the logic and efficacy of persevering with outdated tools and jaded pedagogy for this engagement-hungry target audience. Backing up for a second, Jane McGonigal, game designer and author, in her text *Reality Is Broken: Why Games Make Us Better and How They Can Change the World* described how gaming tends to make people more optimistic and helps them develop a mindset that results in their being less likely to give up when, initially, failing at a challenge. She uses examples of her own convalescence from a head injury and how she defeated the challenges posed by her slow recuperation. Being more *optimistic* and *less likely to give up* sound like principles that could be quite excellent in an academic environment.

James Paul Gee, one of the earliest advocates of the potential gaming-education nexus, writes in his seminal 2003 text, *What Video Games Have To Teach Us about Learning and Literacy* (in what sounds like a moment of extreme irritation), that "better theories of learning are embedded in the video games children in elementary and particularly in high school play than in the schools they attend" (7).

He continues, "The theory of learning in good video games fits better with the modern, high-tech, global world of today's children and teenagers live in than do the theories (and practices) of learning that they see in school." Gee goes on to explain a further advantage of video games is that they provide integrated learning through contextualized interaction in what is, in fact, a "material, social and cultural world." This resonates for the contingency of traditional academics who are wedded to the internships or co-op experiences that are typically near impossible for the new-majority student to experience. Through use of contexts and "material, social and cultural worlds," can we create gameful experiences that provide opportunity for learning in contexts that are applicable to the workplace and the next stages of life in society?

The New Majority and the (Nuanced) New Agenda

Just as societal demographic changes were beginning to manifest in the student body, a further change, driven by philanthropic foundations, has come into play—that of asking new questions to institutions and their penchant for business as usual. Funders like The Bill and Melinda Gates Foundation and the Davis Educational Foundation have shifted their focus from an *access* agenda (2010–2013), which encouraged institutions to increase opportunity for all to get *into* further education, to the roughly 2014–16 *completion* agenda of making sure that as many entering students as possible *complete* their studies. This has accentuated the need for institutions not only to reduce costs and encourage diversity but also to make education, for their enrolled students, as "sticky" or close-to-addictive as possible. This institutionally acknowledges the sentiment that access for students of any stripe is futile, even counterproductive, if they merely start and then don't complete their studies. It is a weak point of the current higher education system that, in most cases, an accumulation of 110 credit hours (10 shy of a bachelor's degree at many institutions) results in precisely zero qualifications with marketable value. This alignment of the access/completion challenge wedded to the new majority students, who must be supported while lacking many of the intrinsic motivators that we typically take for granted (supportive families, a history of higher education, affordability in some shape or form), further supports the drive to disrupt and try something different. In the language of many funding opportunities, the evolving target demographic is underrepresented minorities (URM). This new designation in its entirety includes:

- minority students whose race/ethnicity is African American, American Indian/Alaska Native, Hispanic/Latino, or Native Hawaiian/Pacific Islander;

- students from low income or low socioeconomic status whose combined parental income is less than or equal to $36,000;
- first-generation college attendees whose highest parental education level is a high school diploma or less; and
- women in science, technology, engineering, and mathematics (STEM) fields, given their underrepresentation in those industries.

The STEM example actually provides one of the clearest illustrations of the challenges for these new students and the institutions belatedly trying to support them. A 2014 *Condition of STEM* report from the testing company ACT showed that while 59% of mainstream *majority* students are deemed college-ready in science, only 25% of the underserved are deemed similarly ready. In reality, the situation is actually much worse. The bulleted characteristics listed above have been shown to have a cumulative negative effect when combined. In other words, students who check two of the risk boxes (for example, low SES *and* first generation, or minority *and* low SES) score 20% lower on benchmark tests than those with only one risk factor. Students who meet all three of these risk criteria score 34% lower, producing the sobering statistic that fewer than 16.5% of first-generation, minority students from a low-SES background are deemed college-ready for the study of science.

As the clock begins to run down on the second decade of the millennium, a majority of states are seeing rising numbers of students from backgrounds with significant risk factors. Even more challenging, their population comprises students combining multiple risk factors. Loading the dice even further from a motivational perspective, these populations frequently have one reason to study: the resolute and genuine attempt to better themselves against multiple extremely stressful disincentives. These disincentives may include two or more jobs, a family to care for, the stress of challenging circumstances, or even the peer pressure from their own community not to persist. Even just taking the figure above indicating likely completion rates as a base, fewer than one in seven is likely to complete their studies. As higher education has started to ponder whether alternative means of credentialing or disruptive models might be feasible, co-author of *The Innovative University*, Clayton Christensen, discussing emerging models that might facilitate URM access and perhaps success, clarifies that students from these backgrounds are not making selections that come down to preferences between Harvard, Yale, or Stanford. These students are going to be predominantly enrolled in online courses so that they can fit in their studies between jobs or after their kids are down for the night. As Christensen puts it, "The next option is nothing."

From an instructor's perspective, this new student demographic shift presents new and unique challenges and typically ones they have not been trained to cope with. In addressing these challenges with no (or minimal) extra resources and support, an instructor most likely has one shot to engage these fragile learners and to get them through. Given the challenges students from URM backgrounds face, the costs they incur, and the logistical load they carry, if they fail, they typically do not (or cannot) come back. The vast majority of faculty, already with increasing demands on their time and skill-set, having added instructional design, technical troubleshooting, and the need to accommodate increased numbers of students with specific learning challenges, are now being asked to step up further to retain these at-risk students by any means necessary. The main, perhaps the only, consolation of this frankly depressing background is that in a seemingly hopeless situation every possibility is worth exploring. Perhaps this even includes trying to make games out of learning.

James Paul Gee, referenced earlier, was one of the pioneers in aligning specific aspects of teaching and learning with key features of successful video games. In addition, he recognized that these aspects or elements might well be applied to help engage those who, at the time of his writing, were referred to as fragile learners (particularly first-generation students). He references three elements addressed by game designers from which he feels educators could learn. They seem somewhat obvious, but they provide a solid initial framework when contemplating next steps:

1. The learner must be enticed to *try,* even if he or she already has good grounds to be afraid to try.
2. The learner must be enticed to *put in lots of effort* even if he or she begins with little motivation to do so.
3. The learner must *achieve some meaningful success* when he or she has expended these efforts.

Gee's working theory was that some barriers for learning might be surmountable if students can reach a state of engagement, being somehow hooked and committed, at least until they reach a level of sophistication where the subject matter itself becomes motivating. Unlike many second-, third- or even fourth-generation students fortunate enough to access higher education from middle-class backgrounds (or in my case, because I grew up in the United Kingdom, where higher education in the mid-to-late 1980s was basically free), emerging URM populations typically do not have the intrinsic motivators or the grit that comes of a statement like "I always knew I wanted to attend Stanford" or even "I come from a long line of lawyers" (substitute doctors/engineers/accountants). Gee's fragile (or URM, in the modern nomenclature) students—the first to venture on this high-risk of failure path—will rarely, if ever, be overheard stating, "My mum was a Husky (or a Cardinal or Panther—even a Terrier) so **I'm going to be** a (Husky/Cardinal/Panther/Terrier). In the absence of these kinds of intrinsic motivators, the need to be encouraged and supported is accentuated. The possibility of meaningfully endorsing and strengthening, even by artificial constructs, their commitment might just get them over the hump and to a place where they feel that they "belong," from where they have a fair chance at persistence and ultimately success.

Student services such as advising and financial aid are valuable and necessary tools in support of all students. From the instructor's perspective, getting back to the aging *Space Avenger,* the idea of trying to get students engaged by using game experiences is germinating. If *Space Invaders* could, in a galaxy and a time not that far, far away, get *them* out of bed and to the video arcade, then might it get and keep students in their classrooms, or online and engaged? Even the younger set of faculty, for whom the home-console world facilitated a feet-up, stay-at-home philosophy, were still saving the world while caught up in the game's narrative, rules, and challenges and still focused and seeking higher levels. Do games or (I'm going to shift at this point to) *gameful design* perhaps provide a means of getting contemporary students over the academic fear barrier, past the "I can't do this" or "Why did I even try?" mindset to participating with reduced fear of failure (a gameful element), feeling a sense of progression or journey (another gameful element), and getting back to either playing or feeling playful in class? In the most ambitious scenario, activities are developed where students get close or closer to what is termed a *flow state,* the Holy Grail scenario where engagement and challenge intersect. When experiencing flow, also known as being "in the zone," the journey of intriguing, well-structured involvement is so immersive and vital that it produces a sense of time flowing by. Imagine the phrase, "Wow! I spent X hours doing that." Flow state is often idealized in stories of elite sportsmen and athletes but also can be experienced by more sedentary puzzle solvers and even, here's the hope, engaged students when activities are well structured and challenging. See also Invaders (Space), Sudoku, Warcraft (World of), marathon running (when fit) and, our goal, well-designed learning challenges.

Most US instructors, as a subset of most educators on the planet, fall a little short of the resources, particularly fiscal, needed to build flamboyant multimedia simulations or complex games. They have neither the budget nor the programming support or in-kind technical team at their disposal. For most in the rewarding (just not financially so) world of academia, immersive simulations of highly programmed, highly sexy and/or violent shoot-em-up games are not on the agenda. Having established that these obvious hooks of eye candy and gore are off the table, we, as educators, have to perhaps get more psychological and analytical to see if we can engender a picture of engagement from quite a limited palette. In some ways, it may even be a blessing to not have the million-dollar multimedia budget. Where big budgets are blown on complex, interactive "educational games" the inevitable outcomes are: (a) the games are not very educational, (b) the education is not actually much fun, and (c) the inability to edit or "tweak" the simulations gives them a very limited shelf life.

Some faculty, typically but not exclusively those with some technical background, are aware of these concerns and are looking creatively at plug-and-play social/low-threshold technologies and asking themselves if there might be a way to bootstrap the development or piecing together of engaging learning resources. Cobbling together low-tech, simple activities featuring quaintly simple hooks and motivators that make participation less of a chore, along with this goal of incrementally leveling the playing field for all students, we get back to the question, soon to be really explored, as to whether these mid-forty-somethings, the well- intentioned *Space Invader* geeks (nerds before the word existed) might be able to actually relate to and hence engage in this much more diverse, much more fragile, learner community.

Some of us clearly think it worth a try.

Engagement/Time on Task

The most viable means of improving student course outcomes, in turn correlating with increased course completion, is to increase student engagement or time on task. George Kuh, one of the more prominent experts in the area of student retention, looked at how student engagement increases when students have a background in, or know more about, a subject. He references the value of practice, feedback, and collaborative problem solving. Student momentum tends to build, he posits, as they come to understand a subject on a deeper level and become more motivated to continue to learn and further explore. The primary challenge, and biggest potential, it seems, for gameful design is in this minefield between the faltering, nervous baby steps of a new learner (especially a new URM learner) and a student's more confident strides a class or two into a program, where she or he will likely show the more informed engagement patterns of a burgeoning subject matter expert.

Play/Games

Given this alignment of impetuses and the logical notion to give it a go because we have nothing to lose, *play,* in the most general sense of the word, is steadily entering our face-to-face and virtual classrooms. The arcade game instructors are playing with intrinsic motivators that they experienced as first generation gamers in the late seventies and early eighties. Some institutions, such as Southern New Hampshire University (SNHU) and Arizona State University (ASU) are exploring competency-based models that can reduce costs in online courses through automation of feedback and support. These models employ technology to help unbundle the traditional faculty role and consciously support student desire for immediate, informed feedback (as they would get from, say, a game). The economies of scale, as well as the automation and efficiency of these models, provide the potential for institutions to offer online courses at significantly lower tuition rates, thus extending access to still larger numbers of underserved and low-SES populations. In a rare positive reinforcement loop, the large numbers of these students attracted by slick and professional marketing, no longer the exclusive purview of the for-profits, allows institutions at scale (like SNHU in the national market) to reduce incremental course delivery per student costs to close to zero. There is the concern that these kinds of semiautomated courses, termed competency-based education (CBE), with their heavier reliance on student self-directed study and automated feedback, might exacerbate the low completion rate issue. Given the likelihood that this type of low-tuition disrupted model will attract fragile learners often lacking in confidence, and the stated aim to this effect of SNHU president Dr. Paul LeBlanc (a Clayton Christensen devotee), intrinsic motivators and experience and attrition could indeed be a big problem. LeBlanc and his team (disclaimer: I was a founding member of the original SNHU Innovation Lab), refusing to shy from the market and genuinely aiming to support and enhance the lives and livelihoods of URM, low-SES, and minority populations, have looked at any and all means of encouraging these learners. As SNHU's Executive Director for College for America, Kris Clerkin, stated in a personal interview:

> We've already incorporated elements of this [gamification] into the new User Inter-face (UI). We backed off a grant involving some quite complex games, but gamifica-tion is definitely on the radar—we think there are lots of things we could do. There are simple things we are already incorporating—the progress meter, measures of activity where we measure everything students are doing in the environment that we reward them for. Basically, measures of engagement we can reward them for, we're moving towards mobile, part of that is just alerts when various things happen; if they're off track or need encouragement, when students get their first "not yet" for a competency. We feel that we've just started down this path—we're just starting and we feel that there's a lot we can still do.

Technologies

In 2010, LeAnne H. Rutherford of the University of Minnesota described the potential of interactive technologies to encourage students to engage with course materials and take an active role in learning (Deneen 2010). This, she demonstrated, led to elevated retention of core course concepts and under-standing. The 2010 US Department of Education report *Evaluation of Evidence-Based Practices in Online Learning* also marked time on task (or engagement with the materials) as the key determinant affecting student success. Success, in this case, was measured as course completion in hybrid and online classes. It certainly seems a reasonable assertion that higher engagement should be possible when we recall how stupidly engaging something as simple as *Pong* was. A perfunctory learning management system (LMS) in 2015 had the capac-ity to store the data of 10,000 *Space Invaders* machines of the basic 1978 vari-ety. "Spacies" (1978 UK slang) was fun despite pixelated graphics and limited interactivity. It was fun because it was a well-thought-out game. The premise was immediately graspable (more gameful design hints), and the controls were usable after milliseconds of thought or observation of the greasy-headed lad in the line before you. The feedback of "BOOM, you're dead—the Earth is invaded," was instant and unambiguous, while the reward, "YOU SAVED THE EARTH" (at least until the next attack wave), was tangible. You had collaboration ("Go on, Jimmy, shoot the bonus spaceship at the top"), you had competition (leaderboard top score: "KB-rools," 97,452 points), and you had the need for concentration. The *Space Invaders* game was, and this statement is not as redundant as it sounds, gamefully designed. Basic tenets were in place, elements that have been in place in good games, good sports, and good books since time immemorial. The application of these tenets to good education is, in many ways, long overdue.

If we accept the premise that online (to say nothing of traditional education) is not going far enough to engage and support learners, particularly the new mix of fragile, nervous, inexperienced, and underprepared learners, then how should we proceed? We've confirmed that practically no one has *World of Warcraft* money or that kind of development time ($63 million and 4.5 years, if you're wondering). Throw in marketing budgets for major game developers or development projects and you are well over a quarter of a billion (with a *b*) dollars. My sense is that as educators we are unlikely to win in a full-on simulation/interactive/full-narrative/ first-person reality game head to head with these competitors. Nor should we try.

So, what is an impoverished educator to do? As practitioners, administrators and faculty, despite the budget envy, surely we should be exploring all avenues that may lead to even incremental support of student engagement and academic success. Gameful design takes elements of what makes games, or other forms of engagement, intriguing, boils them down to a fundamental level, and then applies them to educational experiences. Sensible practitioners reflect and build on things that good instructors do as second nature. They challenge their students, they provide prompt and supportive feedback, they try to reduce students' fear of failure, and they encourage cooperation or teamwork. These are all gameful design principles.

While some instructors make the case for tangible, replicable game elements (implementing leaderboards, rewards, badges, and levels in their courses), other more pedantic theorists consider these elements to be extrinsic to the actual game experience as they chase the goal of more consistently valuable and powerful intrinsic motivators.

There are no simple right answers, but the flip side of that is there are no really wrong answers either. Millennial students tend to deeply appreciate and be supportive of any efforts to meet and engage them. While almost everyone from the Gen X population is sure that Millennials are playing games (usually on their phones) ALL the time, they aren't. They are disproportionately engaging with gamefully designed apps and actually play online games less than we do (that is, if you're 30–45). If you're not, then enjoy youth, as it fades quickly—right around 39 and a half.

In online courses most students have experienced what we'll call read-post-respond (perfunctory) discussion boards fueled by horrible PowerPoint slides and unreadable (on screen) PDFs. They are *very* eager, even borderline desperate, to try anything as an alternative. Remember that retro, basic-is-cool, and even drafty creative ideas can fly. Napkin sketches are what set Steve Jobs, Bill Gates, and (probably) Mark Zuckerberg on their way. The song "Louie Louie" was written by Richard Berry on toilet paper in a club's men's room. Back as far as 1814 at Chesapeake Bay, Francis Scott Key wrote the lyrics to "The Star-Spangled Banner" on the back of a letter, having seen the flag still there "by the dawn's early light."

Unlike set texts and didactic lecturing, online courses provide a continuing illustration of what works and what doesn't via the footprints that student participants make through the system. As analytics become more central to institutions' strategic work, gameful redesign of coursework provides a wonderful opportunity to meet students where they are at, especially supporting those whose confidence and engagement are unfairly low. As one of my cases states, it can even provide a way to democratize participation. In a good game, everyone participates, not just the smart, confident students. Gamification or gameful design, when well done, has the effect of personalizing the student experience. It puts the student at the center of learning. I have heard this referred to as a "Copernican revolution": the student who was formerly orbiting at a distance around a dazzling and worrying mass of materials is now at the center of the universe, with smaller sets of materials and options orbiting around them. This mirrors what has happened with traditional TV scheduling being supplanted by on-demand. We are no longer beholden to receiving content or entertainment solely on the networks' terms. Given the potential for commercial-free binge watching (with personal preference ranging from one episode a month to near-OCD viewing patterns, watching three screens at once), the scheduling has become viewer-centric. As C. Scott Rigby describes, this centrality, or this notion of "me being in control," accentuates the ability to meet the core psychological needs of mastery, autonomy and relatedness. Mastery energizes and motivates (Ryan and Deci 2000), autonomy provides choice and freedom from control, and relatedness ensures that we feel that we *matter* to ourselves and to others (Rigby 2014). Let's just accept that education is suffering from a significant amount of deferred maintenance. While we should certainly be building on inherent strengths, we should also be exploring the Copernican revolution and what it means to our instruction. We should try putting the student at the center of their studies, encouraging their autonomy and choice, and facilitating their engagement through narrative, competition, cooperation, or challenge. As Niman, who you will meet again in his brilliant case study, stated, "We have not engaged students in a way that has made their educational experience a personal one with demonstrable benefits and a clear rationale for how it is going to make them more successful."

So put on your game face, and we'll see what we can do to fix that in the coming chapters.

■ ■ ■ ■ ■ ■ ■ ■ ■ ■ ■ ■ ■ ■

CHAPTER TWO

How Did We Get Here?

THE MATURATION OF ONLINE EDUCATION

Before diving headlong into practitioner cases, it is worth spending some time understanding the state of online course development and deployment in higher education. As one of the few to have had a job title that actually included both those terms, I feel I have to somehow justify a position I held for almost exactly four years (2012–2016): executive director of curriculum development and deployment of Northeastern University's College of Professional Studies.

The massive open online course (MOOC) explosion of 2012 brought a tsunami of attention to online instruction of all varieties. Discussions about online education finally and firmly landed in the worlds of the "Ivies" and highly ranked research universities. While initial massive interest was tempered by findings that MOOC completion rates appeared to be extremely low (substantially lower than for other forms of online and traditional education) for many, MOOCs provided a kind of validity to online education that had, to that point, been lacking. Prior to that time, online environments had been (a) inaccessible without tuition (the unknown fueled suspicion) and (b) championed almost exclusively by for-profits, lower-ranked institutions, and community colleges. Before 2010, most institutions dabbling in online had been compelled to diversify revenue streams because other aspects of their campuses either were not working or could not scale. The assumed "lack of quality" argument so often proffered by the more elite institutions was thrown into doubt by the fact that Harvard, MIT, and Stanford were now getting their feet wet with online offerings. The lure of the rock star experience (with tens of thousands of students) appealed to egos and consequently institutions, and faculty that had never previously considered delivering anything online suddenly showed interest in mounting what appeared to be a momentum-gathering bandwagon. My own experience was that faculty who previously had no interest now suddenly perked up. They wondered why my

team, with our budget for course development right around 10% of that being spent on MOOCs, didn't feature such polished multimedia, why we *still*
had to launch from a learning management system where things like grades
were being kept FERPA-proof (that is, adhering to the privacy requirements of
the Family Educational Rights and Privacy Act), and why, ultimately, they
couldn't engage and maintain a student audience with minimal (MOOC-
like) faculty presence, feedback, and encouragement. MOOCs shifted quickly
from a blessing to a curse and then, soon after, to an irrelevance as we continued trying to build 15-week, participation-focused, online experiential (I
know, somewhat oxymoronic) courseware and content. My takeaway from
where we are at with respect to the MOOC phenomenon:

- As we've been through the hype and the post-hype letdown, now is
  the time to coldly evaluate what is/was great about the MOOC
  concept and what else is out there (technology- and pedagogy-wise)
  that could be added to the mix to meet institutional goals.
- MOOCs, at least originally, were not tasked with effectively addressing
  community building, secure assessment, or persistence/completion.
- There are means to meld elements of MOOCs with work that has
  been done over the last 15–20 years by instructional designers and
  innovators in the field. It should not be an either-or situation.
- Administrators, developers, and faculty should pay attention to the
  target audience for their classes (demographic, prior exposure to
  higher education successes/failures, etc.) when we decide on institutional strategy.
- Fragile/post-traditional learners will not persist in a MOOC environment without comprehensive support and a boatload of intrinsic
  motivation addressed as part of the course build. "We can scale
  content; we can't scale encouragement" (Siemens 2011a).

The primary takeaway lesson is that for the twenty-first-century student
hooked on social media, where instant "likes" equate to instant gratification,
their penchant for immediate feedback represents a growing challenge for
purveyors of online education. The obvious solution to this, increasing faculty
presence, is not viable at most institutions, while the near-universal desire to
scale and cater to larger populations exacerbates the challenge. Although
MOOCs shone a light on this disconnect, the sense that demand for contact
and engagement had long outstripped the faculty supply of the same was an

issue well known to students and administrators in "traditional" online education for a number of years. From full-time faculty members with multiple concurrent duties to adjuncts teaching multiple sections, most find it hard to maintain a viable and supportive presence through web-based systems between classes. At institutions like Western Governors University and Southern New Hampshire University, either a more pliant governance system or, in the latter case, focused and resolute leadership has resulted in what has been called an unbundling of the faculty role, to allow a significant proportion of these high-touch students' needs to be served by (candidly, more affordable) alternate mentors, advisors, or graders.

As differentiated models of online education have propagated, from MOOCs through adaptive to self-directed courses and beyond, many campuses have supported the establishment of new positions. These new staff members typically have to find the middle ground between ambitious administrators and experienced, sometimes change-resistant faculty.

Instructional Design

The concept of instructional design developed primarily from the World War II need to assess learners' abilities to succeed in military training programs. Bloom's Taxonomy (1956) articulated a basic set of terminology that evolved through the work of Skinner (1971) and others, developing into the lexicon and core concepts of the profession that persist to the present day. With the development of online training, courseware, and programs of study, the principles transitioned and developed to the degree that the majority of current-day instructional design practitioners are involved in the development of online learning. In the 1980s and 1990s, personal computers, games, and simulations started to appear, and *the web*, with its use of hyperlinks and digital media, became recognized as having a role to play in the field of e-learning. The ability to quickly locate and link to online resources enhanced the value of educational tools and added to the complexities of the online product. As technologies evolved, the potential of online learning for corporate (and then academic) purposes became increasingly apparent. With resources and formats becoming more varied and nuanced, practitioners started to collect and monitor metrics in attempts to determine which factors were integral to the design of engaging courses. Foci evolved from initial basic course usability and navigation, through target audience fluency in online terminologies, to considering level of challenge (difficulty) of learning content. This combining of emerging concepts like grit and self-efficacy proved to be an important consideration for student success.

The developing complexity and recognition of a key skill set typically missing from campuses prior to the last decade or so has made the instructional design skill set quite sought after and marketable. In 2014, the website Recruiter .com rated the job of instructional designer as "new and emerging," projecting rapid growth with the 2010 employment of 128,780 expected to grow to 165,000 in 2018 (a 3.5% annual rate of growth). Along with, and concurrent to, this hockey stick upturn as a general career choice, in larger institutions the role has diversified into more specialized subcategories. These include *production specialists* (with a focus on materials development), *learning architects* (honed on tenets of cognitive science and pedagogy), *online curriculum/assessment specialists* (correlating promised outcomes and objectives with actual materials, activities, and summative assessments), *graphic/multimedia support,* and *LMS specialists* charged with making sure all the component parts speak to each other.

The increasing complexity of available technologies, such as discussion boards, audio threads, and multimedia elements, to create personalized and adaptive systems has further emphasized the need for effective instructional design. Newer iterations of the LMS have made the basic posting and hosting of materials quite simple so that the majority of faculty can manage themselves after a brief training or orientation, thus freeing up the instructional designers for more complex and nuanced work.

The early instructional designer's role, sometimes considered more of an educational technology support role, assisted the experienced classroom instructor in doing whatever he or she felt might capture face-to-face presence best. The efforts clearly had limitations, for when instructors try faithfully to transfer their face-to-face instruction directly to an online format, often classroom capture via streaming video, they miss opportunities to make better use of the online environment. In most progressive institutions, instructional designers have been able to move past perfunctory technical (help desk) support of academics to more appropriate discussions of online pedagogy, assessment, and best practices for online instruction. Illustrations of this shift from a focus on technical functionality (what can I do with the LMS?) to better pedagogy (how can I teach, as well or better, using the LMS and related tools?) are seen in the transitions from early attempts to simply

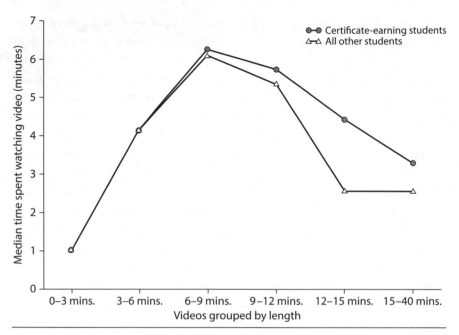

Figure 1. edX video engagement findings, 2013. Analysis by Philip Guo, pg@cs.rochester .edu.

replicating live classroom experiences to using better practices for content formatting. Early efforts included capturing of hour(s)-long lectures by video. Didactic lecturing is tough to stay with in person; online, as evidence now shows, it is pretty much unwatchable, with viewer attention long gone by the six- or seven-minute mark, as figure 1 shows. Well-structured content in contemporary online courses is referred to as "chunked"—sized (based on accrued evidence of what works) so that the consumer—student—can grasp a concept before he or she is asked to go and *do* something with the knowledge. The emphasis in later iterations also shifted to the challenges of building community online, increasing engagement, and constructing more easily retained content.

Wallace "Wally" Boston, CEO of American Public Education, Inc., notes that his instructors and instructional designers don't make video or audio files of more than four minutes (2014). As research and the trend-monitor have come around to emphasis on what is variably called "student-centered learning" (SCL), "active learning," and "the learner at the center," the shift away from the lecture, particularly in the online environment, has gathered steam.

The humility needed for some instructors to lean on expertise provided by (usually) younger and (predominantly) female staff has constituted a culture shift at many institutions. Several observers have reflected on the challenge for the traditional instructor, who assumes mastery of both teaching and instructional design despite having little to no training in either of these fields. Dr. Richard Clark of the University of Southern California refers to the "expert blind spot," articulating the challenge for high-level experts (faculty) to remember the small steps that all novices, including themselves, needed when they first approached concepts as beginning learners. The information that is transmitted to the student should be both suitably leveled (appropriate level of challenge) and suitably sized, or chunked, to allow steady, more incremental progress in learning. M. David Merrill's work on component display theory and mental models in human-computer interaction described the need to deconstruct established instruction habits and consciously design to leverage the potential of electronic communications media generally and online instruction specifically (Carroll & Olson 1988; Merrill 1983).

Development Models

As we crest the many challenges in delivering effective, pedagogically robust teaching and learning, both in a classroom and at a distance, further possibilities and further challenges are opening up. At most institutions, along with online growth has come the realization that to develop and deliver effective online courses that encourage engagement, there must be further investment in design expertise. Some institutions have moved to external vendors that have taken on the cost of course development, marketing, and many other risks of launching courses. These vendors, Embanet and Everspring among them, look to negotiate multiyear revenue shares of up to 80% of tuition income. Other institutions have insourced to leverage institutional focus by committing faculty to work alongside instructional designers, online pedagogy experts, and technologists. The advantage to an institution with in-house development is that once materials and technology have been developed, online instruction becomes scalable with incremental costs per learner and potentially large profits.

For instructional designers and those in related fields, the search is on to implement principles that will encourage fragile online populations to stay engaged. The societal impetus to engage larger numbers of learners with limited prior academic success is a real and substantial challenge for all in academia. Having previously addressed the low-hanging fruits of design concepts that support users on the web (generally usability, content architecture, and accessibility), attention is shifting to elements that they might weave into instructor-provided content. This may draw on cognitive science, adaptive learning, learning analytics, and gamification, which I use here intentionally as the umbrella term under which a Monty Python–esque range of subgenres exist (see "People's Front of Judea"/"Judean People's Front"). An embrace of the term and the concept of gamification at least provides inspiration for design teams to move beyond basic course design and encourage creativity and experimentation with some of these newer concepts. As some practitioners have described, it is time to move on to wherever we should be now. If early HTML was online 1.0 and the LMS with basic plugins was 2.0, then surely it's time to see what constitutes 3.0. Research shows that courses centered on discussion boards that are structured to support requirements for students to simply read, post, and respond may, in fact, limit active learning (Moorhead, Colburn, Edwards, & Erwin 2013).

Gamification melds and unifies many of the best practices and potentials of other pedagogical approaches, as will become apparent in the forthcoming chapters. Karl Kapp simply defines gamification as "the use of game mechanics to make learning and instruction more fun" and expounds on this definition to describe the concept more viscerally. "Think of the engaging elements of why people play games—for the sense of achievement, immediate feedback, feeling of accomplishment, and success of striving against a challenge and overcoming it" (Kapp 2012, xxi–xxii). He further describes gamification as "motivation to succeed" with the "reduced sting of failure."

When considering the potential of online classes to increase access for underserved communities, the "post-traditional" learners that Louis Soares, vice president of the Center for Policy Research and Strategy at the American Council of Education, describes in *Post-Traditional Learners and the Transformation of Postsecondary Education* (2013) must not be neglected. Soares predicts that these students will have disproportionate participation in online (a.k.a. affordable) courses. Kathryn Ecclestone, professor of postcompulsory education at the Westminster Institute of Education, worries that these fragile learners need specialized, multifaceted care of their emotional well-being and the kind of encouragement and support that are not feasible in large-scale online classes (2008). Into this conundrum, just perhaps, steps some of the work and findings of early gameful designers.

If a concept such as gamification has the potential to affect student engagement positively through practitioner feedback, it could benefit the students who struggle most with learning and persistence in online education. It is certainly worth exploring gamification and its constituent parts to see whether these early practitioner efforts merit further, more measured, experimentation. Although there are many ways to approach gamified courses in terms of how they interface with the user (simulations, video games with educational settings, or even clickers in the face-to-face classroom), it is more beneficial to review the underlying mechanics and how they can be applied to online courses. It is instructive to examine how a practitioner implements specific game elements in courses with the aim of increasing student engagement. Jesse Schell of Carnegie Mellon University has referred to this concept of increasing user stickiness or propensity to stay on page as the "psychology of engagement" (2010).

Why Now?

We are living in a time of flux and possibility in online education. The field has matured to the extent that there is a growing body of evidence mapping out criteria that positively impact student learning outcomes and a sense of entrepreneurial possibility is in the air. The US Department of Education's 2010 meta-analysis of 99 studies comparing online and face-to-face classes concluded that "Students in online conditions performed modestly better, on average, than those learning the same material through traditional face-to-face instruction" (xiv).

The report also identified a number of elements typically implemented in the design phase of online course development as having an influence on learning outcomes. The elements included use of multimedia, active learning (where the learner has to take actions such as clicking on items to reveal content), and student time-on-task.

The report's most notable takeaway was that time-on-task is a critical factor with respect to learning outcomes irrespective of format. Online learning's potential simply may be the fact that it is more conducive to the expansion of time-on-task than is face-to-face instruction. To expand time-on-task in face-to-face classes, instructor time, classroom space, and students' ability to physically attend at set times all have to be considered. In online classes, the uploading of late-breaking news or current, interesting readings or activities by the click of a mouse can achieve the same result with far fewer ramifications.

Despite these clear conclusions, a degree of inertia persists within academia with regard to implementing designed elements—even those shown by a preponderance of evidence to make an online course or program more likely to increase student engagement. At times, faculty members' passion and confidence in their own teaching experience make them unwilling to explore new concepts for teaching and learning. On the instructional design side of the equation, evidence supporting specific aspects of course design has started to align as research in the field develops.

Early instructional design centered on learning styles and multiple intelligences (Gardner 1983) before developing via the field of cognitive science (Clark 2005; Mayer 2003), and then expanding to noncognitive student characteristics and more recent concepts such as intrinsic motivation, gamification, and learning analytics. With the recent development of analytics software in online classes, it has become easier to track student behavior and quantify which course elements produce more student engagement and, per the US Department of Education report, better learning outcomes. With data in hand, faculty and administrative design staff should be better able to develop effective online lessons supported by direct research into what is really working. Before digging further into definitions of key elements in the gamification literature, it is essential to understand some of the basic tenets of student engagement. The hope of practitioners and theorists alike is that gamification may be a means to implement concepts and techniques broadly in online courses to lead to an uptick in student engagement.

Measures of Engagement

Engagement long has been identified as an essential precursor of student success in face-to-face and online classes. Chen, Gonyea, and Kuh say that engagement is positively linked to a number of desired outcomes, including high grades, student satisfaction, and perseverance (2008). Despite that clarity, and despite the opportunity provided by online courses where student access and behavioral data are readily available, there is no universally accepted definition of what constitutes engagement. One serviceable definition is that engagement is the "quality of effort students themselves devote to educationally purposeful activities that contribute directly to desired outcomes" (Krause & Coates 2008, 493). Other studies define engagement in terms of interest, effort, motivation, and time-on-task and suggest that there is a causal relationship between engaged time (the period of time in which students are completely focused on and participating in the learning task) and academic achievement (Bulger et al. 2008).

In his report on the National Survey of Student Engagement, admittedly focused on traditional classroom study, George Kuh (2009) quotes the work of Chickering and Gamson (1987), who list principles required to foster student engagement. Their work, *Seven Principles for Good Practice in Undergraduate Education*, emphasizes student-faculty contact, cooperation among students, active learning, prompt feedback, time-on-task, high expectations, and respect for diverse talents and ways of learning. The general conclusion from the literature is that engagement is a complicated blend of active and collaborative learning, participation in challenging academic activities, communication between teachers and students (and between students), and involvement in enriching educational experiences and communities (Chickering & Gamson 1987; Clark 2005; DeTure 2004; Kuh 2009).

The ability to quantitatively measure student engagement in online courses is dependent on the data-capture capacities of technology in which the course is situated (Rankine, Stevenson, Malfroy, & Ashford-Rowe 2009). Most of the companies still in the LMS market, such as Blackboard, Instructure, and Desire2Learn, offer metrics of some kind, but the available data, until very recently, were rudimentary and time-consuming to extract and interpret. Captured LMS data can and have been used to approximate student engagement and the evaluation of learning activities (Dawson & McWilliam 2008). Yet LMS data can only approximate actual student engagement. Simple metrics, such as frequency of student logins and grade point average (GPA), have been the most commonly observed measures. MOOCs and some of the newer adaptive learning providers in particular are promising much more granular and potentially significant metrics.

There is the danger that data might provoke inaccurate conclusions. Technologically savvy students might download documents and review them multiple times, while a less tech-savvy student might repeatedly go back to the LMS without actually reading much. From the perspective of the captured data, the tech-savvy student has visited the documents once during the term whereas others, choosing to click on the documents at every visit, erroneously appear more engaged. In reviews of student engagement, this kind of ambiguity will have to be borne in mind as metrics are considered. The uncertainty of the data in this area is one of the reasons that early studies tended to focus on interviews and qualitative data when trying to assess the merits of a variety of treatments.

Building Engagement Into Online Courses

A number of theories inform our understanding of how aspects of instructional design can increase student engagement. The field itself is in a fairly constant state of flux given the rapid pace of technological change and the academic press's fascination with the next big thing. Some concepts have become established in the field and are a common part of the lexicon (usability, information architecture), some technologies that seemed to have great potential have faded from consideration (virtual 3D worlds like Second Life), while other aspects have had narrow yet persistent support among their fans (open education resources). A viable proposition is that adaptive learning allied with leading work in cognitive science and learning analytics could be a game-changer in the connected world of instructional design and higher education. With the basic tenets of those fields marked out, it could be instructive to assess the point at which they intersect to consider whether they might come together under a banner heading of gamification.

Cognitive Science

Self-efficacy, a central element of cognitive science, describes the belief in one's capabilities to organize and execute the courses of action required to produce given attainments and has long been proposed as a determinant to learner success in online courses (Bandura 1997). Data from a number of studies show correlations between student low self-efficacy and failure to persist in online courses (DeTure 2004; Schrum & Benson 2001). There is a sense that the effect of low self-efficacy, while important in traditional/face-to-face classes, is exacerbated in online classes, where it (self-efficacy) is more difficult to recognize and harder to correct through support (DeTure 2004). The positive relationship between computer familiarity and computer self-efficacy was empirically verified by the work of Compeau and Higgins (1995), while Staples, Hulland, and Higgins (1999) found that those with high levels of self-efficacy in remote computing situations were more productive, satisfied, and able to cope when working remotely.

Cognitive science theory extends beyond self-efficacy to look at how much and in what way students can assimilate and retain materials most efficiently and effectively. The prime challenge is determining how cognitive skills and strategies make it possible for certain people to act effectively and complete tasks that others struggle with and fail. Studies suggest that students are more likely to gain deeper and lasting conceptual understanding from materials or content designed with cognitive science principles (such as how information is represented, processed, and transformed) in mind (Baggett 1984; Mayer 2003; Mayer & Moreno 2002). Online courses that are designed based on cognitive science principles assist students in managing their cognitive load, or focusing their cognitive resources during learning and problem solving, thus leading to better learning outcomes (Chandler & Sweller 1991). Sweller, Van Merriënboer, and Paas's later work on cognitive load theory in particular discusses how learning is limited by the capacity of working memory (1998).

Both Sweller and Clark outline a number of strategies instructional designers can use to help students manage cognitive load so that learning is made more effective, more efficient or both (Clark 2005; Sweller, Van Merriënboer, & Paas 1998). Cognitive task analysis connects most clearly with the world of instructional design when practitioners carefully format materials with specific attention to what is called "chunk" size, defined as the amount of content that is organized into one part. The size of chunks, neither too large nor too small, is positively related to a student's ability to assimilate knowledge. The importance of appropriate chunking was demonstrated in Moreno's work, which showed that participants who studied a carefully segmented, or chunked, version of a classroom video reported lower mental effort and perceived the learning materials as less difficult than participants using nonsegmented versions of the same material (2007). The benefit of effective chunking was most pronounced in the case of novice learners, who were less capable of adequately processing information unless it was packaged thoughtfully. Long and short-term memories differ in fundamental ways, with only short-term memory demonstrating temporal decay and chunk capacity limits (Cowan 2009). When working memory is overloaded or "extraneous content provided," a barrier comes down and prevents anything passing over to long-term memory (Sweller, Van Merriënboer, & Paas 1998). If the content is effectively chunked, the learner can better process conceptually distinct clusters of information and better retain them (Mautone & Mayer 2001; Mayer & Moreno 2002; Pollock, Chandler, & Sweller 2002).

Part of the attraction of games and gamification may be that they effectively chunk learning (of game features) so as to steadily reveal new features, skills, and techniques to the user who practices and assimilates them. Another developing phenomenon that is worth framing before digging into the detail and nuance of gamification is adaptive learning. Adaptive learning extends the principle of chunked knowledge, directing different students to different chunks based on their aptitude or study preferences with the goal of encouraging engagement through appropriate challenge and personalized paths.

Adaptive Learning

Adaptive learning describes the provision of multiple paths through materials and supplemental materials that are personalized and tailored to individual users based on choice and prior performance. For-profit companies such as Knewton, Cerego, and CogBooks are leading a charge to implement systems that resonate with gamers in that user choice leads to system consequence. Macroadaptivity is based on prior behavior of large numbers of users and is best illustrated in the corporate world with Amazon's "People who bought book x, also liked book y." Microadaptivity is tailored to an individual user's prior personal selections and successes. If a user performed better on self-check tests and quizzes after accessing video content, a microadaptive system would record this and, wherever possible, serve up video as opposed to text-based content. Advocates see the potential to make coursework more attractive or "sticky" to students, keeping people motivated to persist. This approach aligns with online course development priorities seeking to increase engagement, time-on-task, and, consequently, learning outcomes.

A frequent criticism of traditional classroom instruction, and at times of the instructors themselves, is that instructors teach to their own learning style (Stewart, Jones, & Pope 1999), defined as "a set of factors, behaviors, and attitudes that facilitate learning for an individual in a given situation" (Reiff 1992). The singular style of most classroom instructors, transferred directly to static-design web-based instruction, frequently has produced monotonous courses, some salvaged with persistent instructor presence, others not. The pace of improvement in online learning has been slowed by inexperienced instructional designers and instructors failing to apply appropriate instructional strategies or to monitor student progress when developing online classes (Inan & Lowther 2007; Palmer & Holt 2009; Schrum & Benson 2001; Song et al. 2004).

Adaptive learning has the potential to track what is and isn't working, producing evidence to promote student learning outcomes. Song and Keller suggest that enriched learning experiences occur when the design of instruction considers student motivation and preferences (2001). Growing interest in the concept is demonstrated by foundational and corporate funding opportunities such as the Adaptive Learning Market Acceleration Program grant opportunity commissioned by the Bill and Melinda Gates Foundation and the Adaptive Learning Research Grant Program offered by Adapt Courseware. The hope of these funders is that, when implemented correctly, adaptive learning systems will increase student performance, motivation, and attitudes while concurrently decreasing learning time and usability problems (Brusilovsky, Sosnovsky, & Yudelson 2009; Dogan 2008; Papanikolaou et al. 2003; Tsandilas & Schraefel 2004; Tsianos et al. 2009).

Learning Analytics

A final perspective that might inform the understanding of gamification of online courses is learning analytics, defined by Siemens as "the measurement, collection, analysis, and reporting of data about learners and their contexts for purposes of understanding and optimizing learning and the environments in which it occurs" (2011b). The term has been increasingly applied to the field of education as practitioners start to understand the information that can be gathered from an LMS. As numbers of students taking online classes have grown, with a recent bump through the massive enrollments associated with MOOCs, the opportunity to analyze data about student behavior is of great value. Proprietary LMS companies are promoting new analytics suites, with access to on-demand information aimed at improving academic success and student retention. Learning analysts use this quantitative output to assess student behaviors and learning trends.

The Blackboard LMS, in particular, has been very vocal in touting the new dawn that this ability to collect and analyze data heralds. On their website, they state that clients participating in a field trial of their new analytics suite in 2013 reported "great success in gaining insight into student activity, identifying outstanding course designs that promoted active student engagement, [and] fostering a culture of discovery and investigation about the future of online and blended learning" (Blackboard 2013). While these proclamations come across more as a sales pitch than solid quantitative research, the claim that their tool is able to directly measure the impact of online course design and online teaching techniques on student engagement and learning outcomes merits attention. Learning analytics can potentially measure even incremental gains wrought by the application of cognitive science and adaptive learning systems. If gamification is a banner cause able to unite these areas, driving adoption and focused analysis, then we might be seeing (no pun intended) a real game-changer.

Gamification

Educational gamification, accentuating and embracing the visceral elements of gaming and drawing from social cognitive and adaptive learning perspectives, has the potential to move the dial on student engagement, time-on-task, and student outcomes (US Department of Education 2010). Prensky (2001) and Asgari (2005) believe that gamification is a broad, comprehensive, accessible, and even visceral term with the potential to align previously distinct schools of thought within the instructional design community. Gamification encompasses insights gained from the work of cognitive scientists, adaptive learning, and learning analytics, and it seems to have promise to improve student engagement in online courses radically. As Jesse Schell reflected during his keynote at the Design Innovate Communicate Entertain (DICE) Summit in 2010, design is moving from the perfunctory to a new focus on immersion in aspects that approximate fun rather than merely functionality. "There is something that's happening in culture right now—a shift just as sure as the Industrial Revolution was a shift. We're moving from a time when life was all about survival to a time when it was about efficiency into a new era where design is largely about what's pleasurable" (Schell 2010).

The value of this shift was claimed at the For the Win Conference held at the Wharton School in Philadelphia back in August 2011. Gabe Zichermann, gamification author, entrepreneur, and blogger, stated then, "It's the meaning we will enrich, educations we will improve, health we will foster and lives we will lengthen through the application of gamification design that will be among our most important legacies" (2011). Gamification likely would have not made an impact at all had the progenitors of cognitive science, learning analytics, and early online learning analysts not led the way by suggesting that there was work to be done in enhancing online education.

Educational games, gaming theory, game mechanics, and gamification have all had numerous evolutions and a few false dawns during the last couple of decades. The field developed as gaming extended its reach beyond the console, initially to corporate training, then to health care, then finally on to education. Heralding a shift in focus away from clickers and avatars,

Kapp defined gamification as "a careful and considered application of game thinking to solving problems and encouraging learning using all the elements of games that are appropriate" (2012, 15–16). Gee, who provides a lot of the energy in the area of gaming implemented in the educational milieu, explains why learning should be more like gaming. "Learning is, or should be, both frustrating and life enhancing. The key is finding ways to make hard things life enhancing so that people keep going and don't fall back on learning and only work with what is simple and easy" (Gee 2003, 6).

The first manifestation of gamification in the "serious" world (as was true of the field of instructional design itself) was military, where war games have been used for centuries to train personnel without loss of life. Many consider *Chaturanga*, played in India in the seventh century, to be the first war game, with pieces representing foot soldiers, elephants, and chariots moved on a playing board much like the modern chessboard. Fast-forward to the present day, with the average American child between the ages of 8 and 18 playing seven hours of video games each week, and it is clear that video games do capture students' attention and interest (Gentile & Walsh 2002; National Institute on the Media and the Family 2002).

A reasonable working hypothesis is that elements intrinsic to games can be factored into materials development to improve student learning outcomes (more recently and now, more typically, referred to as gameful design). Materials structured with game principles in mind could enable students to work with big ideas contextually, as well as symbolically, so they learn how to apply abstract ideas in qualitative and meaningful ways (diSessa 1982). Safe, "it's only a game . . ." experimentation with big ideas and symbols may help students develop domain-specific schema (ways of thinking) that they can start to use to develop and demonstrate the particular nuance and mindset more typical of domain experts than of novice learners (Ambrose 2010). Evidence presented by Greeno, Collins, and Resnick (1996) and others suggests the potential for users to become active rather than passive participants in shaping their role and actions to promote engagement and time-on-task. When students become active participants in the knowledge- assimilation process (Greeno, Collins, & Resnick 1996), the "focus of learning shifts from covering the curriculum to working with ideas" (Scardamalia 2000). This form of system response is analogous to that of adaptive learning (addressed earlier) where student action produces a system reaction tailored to reinforce, support, or redirect behavior.

There are still distinct factions under the gamification banner. One side is enthused by the simulation or game design side of the research, whereas the other focuses on the psychological underpinnings of gaming. Fully-fledged, immersive game development is far beyond the scope of many design teams. While exact figures are hard to locate, *World of Warcraft* has been quoted at around $63 million to develop (digitalbattle.com) with perhaps three times that amount for marketing and upkeep in its first four years of existence (kotaku.com). With *World of Warcraft* as the competition, most efforts to produce action versions of education have fallen flat and are generally received by students as watered-down games and by academics as watered-down education. Irrespective of the visuals and technical sophistication, low-tech activities can provide intrinsic motivation by incorporating game elements such as optimal level of challenge; appropriate goals; uncertain outcomes; clear, constructive, immediate feedback; and elements of curiosity and creativity (Brophy 2004; Cordova & Lepper 1996; Malone 1981).

One example that could be explored in a low-tech context would be the way that game designers encourage a player's acceptance of failing as a step toward learning. Education stigmatizes failure, and whether it does so consciously or not is a moot point. A former president of a midsized college in the northeastern United States captures the costs of failure, stating in a personal conversation that, at her institution, only 10–15% of students who needed one remediation course completed associate's degrees. Students who failed again and needed a second remediation course, in her experience, *never* graduated despite repeated attempts in class sizes with a high-touch average of just nine students per instructor. Compare that to the motivation that game failure provokes. Again, quoting Gee, "When the character you are playing dies in a video game, you can get sad and upset, but you also usually get pissed that you have failed. And then you start again, usually from a saved game, motivated to do better" (2003, 82).

Which response should we be cultivating: abject failure and misery or annoyed, pissed even, resolution to beat this damn thing?

Prior Studies

Studies since the early 1990s, when the phenomenon first started to gain attention, suggest the promise of gamification and provide guidance for present-day focus. Though the systematic application of gamification to conventional online learning is a relatively new concept, since the 1990s a number of studies have analyzed the effects of games used as instructional tools. A 1992 meta-analysis reviewed 67 studies conducted over 28 years comparing game-oriented learning against the same content delivered by conventional instruction (Randel et al. 1992). They found that 56% of individuals in the game-oriented groups showed no difference in learning outcomes between games and conventional instruction, while 32% had higher learning outcomes (demonstrated via measurable tests) from the game format. The authors concluded that subjects where content is very prescriptive and not particularly open to interpretation (e.g., math) are more likely to show beneficial effects for gaming (Randel et al. 1992). Wolfe's 1997 analysis concluded that game-based approaches produced greater knowledge-level increases over conventional case-based teaching methods. A more recent meta-analysis concluded that subjects' confidence in their grasp of core course concepts was on average 20% higher in courses with game elements, declarative knowledge (defined as "knowing what") was 11% higher, procedural knowledge ("knowing how") was 14% higher, and overall student retention was 9% higher when simulations were used (Sitzmann 2011). Ke (2009) reviewed 89 research articles that provided empirical data on the application of computer-based instructional games. She found that, of the 65 studies specifically examining the effectiveness of computer-based games on learning, 52% returned a positive impact and 25% had "mixed results," where an instructional game supported some learning outcomes but not others. In only one study of 89 did she find that conventional instruction was more effective than computer games.

Gamification is an inexact term used for successful implementation of many game-related elements. As such, developers (and other interested parties) who are interested in digging further into the concept need to understand constituent elements. How are courses gamified? By what definition and composition?

We'll look into these questions throughout the cases and analysis that follows. Bear in mind as you proceed, a degree of deconstruction is necessary before course development can begin. When building a gamified or a gamefully designed course, implementing elements that bring together thinking from cognitive science, psychometrics, and adaptive learning, the developer/instructor (whether one and the same person or two individuals) must not neglect the need to build in a way to stimulate user enjoyment. If learning is always a task to be endured, then many will not persist. The final element to consider, the lubricant to make the progress smooth, is flow. In the literature of games and gamification, flow is frequently referenced (see, e.g., Kapp 2012; Schell 2008; Zicherman 2011). Flow provides foundation and context as well as an ultimate goal for the construction of effective engagement in gamified courses.

Flow

Mihaly Csikszentmihalyi (1990) builds on the concept of extreme engagement, referring to "flow" as the point at which engagement makes effort feel compelling and achievement feasible. The "game-psychology" faction led by Prensky (2001) and academics such as Asgari (2005) argue that, while the visually striking elements of simulations—or "novelty effects"—initially may provide competitive enjoyment or stimulation, the best types of engagement come from learners' enjoyment of "more effective learning experiences, ones that put them in control and encourage active participation, exploration, reflection, and the individual construction of meaning" (Galarneau 2005). Papert (1997) refers to the principle of "hard fun" as the enjoyment derived from a challenging but meaningful learning experience, an experience that James Paul Gee (2003) described as "both frustrating and life enhancing." As Csikszentmihalyi describes it, flow represents "times when, instead of being buffeted by anonymous forces, we feel in control of our actions, masters of our own fate," with a "sense of exhilaration, a deep sense of enjoyment that is long cherished and that becomes a landmark in memory for what life should be like" (1990). These moments, contrary to many assumptions, are not relaxed, idle periods; they are challenging and require focus. "The best moments usually occur when a person's body or mind is stretched to its limits in a voluntary effort to accomplish something difficult and worthwhile." Csikszentmihalyi describes eight components as critical in engendering flow. The task at hand must be *achievable*—the person involved must believe that she or he can achieve it with some degree of effort. In addition, the person must *concentrate*. The task must have *clear goals,* and there must be *feedback,* both immediate and continual. The participant should feel a sense of *effortless involvement* with *control over actions* having immediate and purposeful results. Finally, when experiencing flow (a.k.a. being "in the zone"), *concern for self disappears*. The only thing the participant is thinking about is the activity, and she or he experiences a notable *loss of sense of time* such that hours feel like minutes (Csikszentmihalyi 1975). In recent revisions Csikszentmihalyi adds one final element: "the experience is an end in itself" (1990, 71). As people seek enjoyment, what they really seek is to be in a state of flow. This goal of optimum engagement is even more valuable than a prize at the end (Reeves & Read 2009).

Other theories inform understanding of flow but are less widely cited than Csikszentmihalyi's. Malone's (1987) theory of intrinsically motivating instruction describes three key elements that make a game motivational: *challenge*—goals with uncertain outcomes, *fantasy*—an environment that evokes mental images of things not present to the senses, and *curiosity*—an optimal level of informational complexity. Lepper, a contemporary of Malone, contributes Instructional Design Principles for Intrinsic Motivation. His four principles are *control*—providing learners with a sense of agency over the learning activity, *challenge*—setting goals of uncertain attainment and an intermediate level of difficulty, *curiosity*—highlighting areas of inconsistency, incompleteness (or even inelegance) in the learner's knowledge base, and *contextualization*—highlighting the functionality of the activity (Lepper 1988).

Little is known from available research about how these states of flow or intrinsic motivation can be effectively and intentionally built into an online course or the impact of these elements on the engagement and time-on-task of online students. Further research is also required to understand the effects on outcomes for underserved or developmental subgroups that typically have found sustained institutional study (traditional, face to face, and online) challenging.

Defining Game Elements or Getting to Gameful Design

Constructing (or reconstructing) an academic course with embedded or intrinsic game elements first requires specifically defining what those elements are. In the literature, there are many attempts to categorize and separate elements that make up a successful game. One of the more accessible lists is based on what has been called the "elemental tetrad" (Schell 2008). Schell came from a video gaming background and identifies how key aspects of successful, recreational games could be applied to online courses. He describes the importance of the following elements:

- *Mechanics*—the procedures and rules of the game. The goal of the game and how players can and cannot try to achieve it.
- *Story*—the sequence of events that unfolds as players play the game. It can be linear and pre-scripted or emergent and branching.

- *Aesthetics*—how the game looks, sounds, smells, tastes, and feels. The aesthetics should reinforce the other elements of the game to create a truly memorable experience.
- *Technology*—from paper and pencil to lasers and rockets. The technology chosen for a game allows it to do certain things and not do others. The technology is the medium in which the aesthetics take place, in which the mechanics will occur, and through which the story will be told.

All of these elements are of equal importance and must, according to Schell, interact seamlessly (2008).

Other authors break game components into more specific categories. Kapp references 12 distinct elements, with some overlap to the list above.

Aligning his definitions with those of Schell, Kapp says, "Gamification is using game-based mechanics, aesthetics and game thinking to engage people, motivate action, promote learning and solve problems" (2012). Kapp, among others, recommends that essential components of a well-designed game include abstractions of concepts in which the game environment provides an alternate rendering or approximation of reality, whether it be hypothetical, imagined, or fictional. Pretty much all of the literature focused on this field stresses that games must have goals to add purpose, focus, and measurable outcomes and rules (defined as operational or how the game is played), foundational (underlying formal structures), implicit/behavioral (defining the social contact between players), and instructional (what you want the learner to know and internalize after playing the game). Added to these fundamental aspects, Kapp also encourages building conflict, competition, and cooperation into a game, asserting that good game design includes elements of all three, intertwined to provide an engaging environment. Time or time constraints also can be included by creating conditions where time is a key factor, increasing tension and demanding focus as it expires, or where time is compressed to show outcomes more quickly (typical in games where civilizations are built up or crops farmed). The most often trivialized and perhaps misunderstood element of gamification is what Kapp calls reward structures, which include badges, points, or a leaderboard. Kapp argues that all need to be thoughtfully implemented as integral parts of the game rather than treating gamification as an add-on.

Feedback in video games is almost constant—designed to evoke the correct behavior, thoughts, or actions—and Kapp includes feedback in his categories. Feedback is the place where gamification most closely aligns with cognitive science, behavioral training, encouragement, and direction. Hunicke, in a speech at UX Week in 2009, described what gamers call "juicy feedback" as tactile, inviting, repeatable, coherent, continuous, emergent, balanced, and fresh (2009). Schell (2010) describes "juicy" more metaphorically as a ripe peach—just a little nibble of which gives you a good flow of delicious reward.

Kapp also stresses the need for defined levels in an effective game. Levels keep a game manageable and allow for building and reinforcement of skills while serving as motivation. Storytelling adds meaning, provides context, and guides action. One of the more common stories is that of the "hero's journey," first described by Joseph Campbell in 1949 and developed by Christopher Vogler in 1992. The hero's journey represents a quest with challenges and hardships on the way before a final, immensely rewarding conclusion. Elements of the structure of the hero's journey might well be applicable to an online class even if the epic, evil-conquering aspect is not. Kapp's final three elements indicate that developers need to think about the game/gamified course's curve of interest, defined as how a game can hold a learner's attention by plotting the level of interest through time. Aesthetics (appropriate and aligned visuals, showing the designer's attention to detail) help create an immersive environment that contributes to the overall game experience. The elemental replay or do-over gives participants the permission to fail with minimal consequences. Failure in an effective game equates to an additional level of content, as it makes the player reconsider his or her approach to a game. The act of failing multiple times makes the act of winning more pleasurable.

The potential of these elements for increasing student engagement with courses is apparent. Good teachers may feel that they incorporate some of these elements to varying degrees in their traditional classes. One would certainly hope to see overlap between tenets of effective teaching no matter the format. The search for elements of instruction leading to enhanced student engagement suggests that gamified instruction and good, effective instruction do not have to be distant relatives.

Potential Application to Online Courses

Having analyzed the literature and broken down the concept and constituent parts of games and gamification, a question that arises is whether these elements are feasible inside a restrictive LMS and governance-bound academic courses. As suggested above, a number of elements already may be built in—either consciously or unconsciously—to what evidence suggests are "good" online courses ("good" in that they engage students and produce effective learning outcomes). The MOOC phenomenon has shined a spotlight on the capacity of instructional design to develop student engagement at a higher level in lieu of an unscalable instructor presence. In traditional online courses, adjunct faculty are increasingly pressured by well-intentioned administrators to maintain close to 24/7 connectivity to provide what amounts to almost "immediate corrective feedback." MOOCs, typically featuring full-time faculty and massive enrollments, cannot rely on faculty connectivity and effort to be the sole means of maintaining student engagement.

The industry is almost at the stage where it can assert that principles of cognitive science and adaptive learning can contribute to developing student engagement. A more intriguing question is whether gamification might provide a more comprehensive, generalizable, and applicable overview of the possibilities for engagement.

The following chapters present practitioner experiments in this emerging realm of gamification or, more specifically, gameful design. In review of these examples we can ask questions about the incorporation of gamification in courses, including

1. How are principles of gamification / gameful design incorporated into selected courses?
2. What forces contribute to and limit the implementation of gamification into the selected courses?
3. What are the potential effects on student engagement of gamified online courses?

For each of the five reviewed courses, I interviewed the project lead (defined as the main person in each case conceiving of the idea and driving its implementation). Where possible, I also interviewed instructional designers or developers involved in the build of the course and then faculty or the instructor, who typically also played one of the other roles already mentioned. I interviewed students when they were available and, if time and access permitted, interviewed administrators at the institutions. Participants were selected based on their availability and centrality to the project.

Given my initial thinking that gamification / gameful design might lead to increased student engagement, I conducted the analyses as a form of explanation building—an iterative process beginning with a theoretical statement, refining it, revising the proposition, and repeating this process. In analyzing my interview data, I used coding schemes to explore consistencies and inconsistencies within the interview narratives. My review included eyeballing—the ocular scan method—proofing for words that stand out as unusual or commonly occurring. This extended to what Bogdan and Biklen call the intraocular percussion test, "where you wait for patterns to hit you between the eyes" (1982, 153).

I found that the chosen examples are all practitioner-driven, faculty-led projects that were at first either off-radar or only loosely supported by their host institutions. They show the value of "giving it a go" and demonstrate that students appreciate any worthwhile effort. While not constituting unequivocal successes, they justify supporting future initiatives and provide ideas for development.

■ ■ ■ ■ ■ ■ ■ ■ ■ ■ ■ ■ ■ ■ ■

CHAPTER THREE

The Fairy Tale MOOC

The University of South Florida (USF), motto Truth and Wisdom, is an American metropolitan public research university located in Tampa, Florida. Established in 1956, it was the first independent state university conceived, planned, and built during the twentieth century. It employs 6,133 academic staff (over 1,700 instructional faculty) and enrolls close to 50,000 students, with approximately 36,000 of those at the undergraduate level. A member institute of the State University System of Florida (the fourth-largest in the state), it is made up of 14 colleges and offers more than 80 undergraduate majors and more than 130 graduate, specialist, and doctoral degree programs. Classified by the Carnegie Foundation as a top-tier research university, it has a proud history and placed 10th overall among all universities worldwide in 2011 in the number of US patents granted, according to the Intellectual Property Owners Association. Alumni include Pam Iorio (mayor of Tampa), Tony LaRussa, Lauren Hutton, and Hulk Hogan.

USF's 2014–15 undergraduate tuition costs were $211.19 per credit hour for in-state students and $575.01 per credit hour for out-of-state students, translating to total annual tuition of $6,410 for in-state and $17,324 for out-of-state students. As of fall 2014, the student diversity profile of the university consisted of 55% White, 12% African American, 21% Hispanic, 7% Asian/Pacific Islander, and 0.16% American Indian. Four percent of students reported two or more races, and 1 percent did not report.

Kevin Yee is Director for Teaching and Learning Excellence at USF, having moved over from the University of Central Florida in 2012, switching between his discipline, German (he holds a PhD in German Language and Literature from the University of California, Irvine) and his vocation supporting and leading technology-facilitated instruction. At USF, he offers faculty workshops and consultations, performs classroom observations, serves as events coordinator for university-wide conferences, and coordinates outreach and training for adjunct faculty and graduate teaching assistants, among many other duties. He continues to teach in the world languages program and the honors college, and he has delivered graduate-level courses on course design and learning management system (LMS) pedagogy in online and hybrid formats.

Prior to launching his fairy tales course, Yee pulled together a list of principles of video games that he felt were relevant to gamification in an educational environment:

Display Progress
- Reward effort, not just success;
- Reward after fixed intervals (e.g., every five tokens) but also randomly;
- Offer momentary rewards ("great job" flashes on screen) or persistent rewards;
- Provide rewards in the form of badges—people are natural collectors;
- Use progress bar if not using a badge list; *and*
- Show progress summary not only when initially accomplished, but in a global spot that is easy to access later (and visible publicly to other participants).

Maximize Competition
- Motivation through innate competitiveness;
- Leaderboard; *and*
- Beware FERPA issues.

Calibrate Difficulty Carefully
- "Balance" issues—neither boring nor anxiety-inducing;
- Early, easy wins, then ratchet up difficulty;
- Add skills incrementally;
- Return to early skills with spaced repetition; *and*
- Boss levels.

Provide Diversions
- Mini-games reset the attention clock;
- Reward exploration via Easter eggs (example: humorous alt text on images);
- Your word choices: "quests" rather than "objectives";
- Allow for nonlinear (or branching) progress toward the goal; *and*

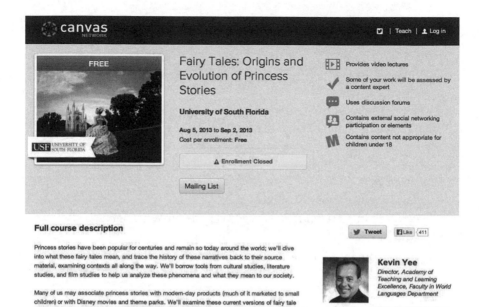

Figure 2. Screenshot from the Canvas-based Fairy Tales: Origins and Evolution of Princess Stories MOOC. © Kevin Yee, University of South Florida; reproduced with permission.

- Where practical, embed games and other content rather than link away.

Employ Narrative Elements
- Start with a hook (high concept, "elevator pitch");
- Determine a central conflict that drives the storyline;
- Think in terms of setup, buildup, and payoff;
- Do not tell a story so much as construct a mystery; *and*
- Imagine characters, backstories, and use as many details as possible.

Yee took his theory into practice via USF's first massive open online course, or MOOC. Fairy Tales: Origins and Evolution of Princess Stories (figure 2) was developed by Yee and offered over four weeks between July and August 2013. With an initial enrollment of 1,200 students (and about another 200 who joined midstream), a cohort of 107 (8%) completed the course, with completion defined as submitting all assessments. Students were permitted to join the course at any time during the offering.

USF **USF Human Resources**
@USF_HR

🐦 Follow

(via @USFNews) Fairy Tales and Princess
Stories: USF's first Massive Open Online
Course begins Aug. 5. bit.ly/1aYRwRz

← Reply ⇄ Retweet ★ Favorite ••• More

12:35 PM - 19 Jul 13

Figure 3. Tweet from University of South Florida Human Resources promoting the Fairy Tales MOOC. © Kevin Yee, University of South Florida; reproduced with permission.

Fairy Tales was a MOOC developed by the instructor himself on the Canvas platform with no major support or promotion from any of the recognized MOOC providers like EdX or Coursera. The USF communications department issued the following press release to support the launch:

> TAMPA, Fla. (July 19, 2013)—A free online course offered by the University of South Florida, "Fairy Tales: Origins and Evolution of Princess Stories," affords anyone in the world the opportunity to explore online learning. As the university's first MOOC (Massive Open Online Course), the four-week class starts Aug. 5 and explores the meaning of fairy tales and their relationship to modern society.

And tweeted about the new offering (figure 3).

Yee leveraged his personal networks and used word of mouth to promote the project with a target of enrolling manageably large, rather than massive, numbers. Part of the reason that he wanted to develop and deliver the course was that, given his need to be knowledgeable about teaching and learning in any and all formats, he considered the project overall as job training. To an extent, his work was intended, as he put it, to "kick the tires" of both the Canvas platform and the whole process of managing an open-enrollment MOOC with larger numbers than would be typical for USF faculty. With the massive surge of interest and (academic) press hype over MOOCs, he anticipated requests in the near future for support from his faculty peers. For his pilot version he had no specific target enrollment but built the course to be scalable for anywhere between 50 and 50,000 participants. His initial hope was to reach five figures, but he fell short of that with the overall registration of 1,400.

Yee's perfunctory experimentation with the technology and scale of a generic MOOC might have had some interesting results of itself, but his interest in the concept of gamification compelled him to meld those two aspects, which, in turn, more than doubled his own learning outcomes. His long-standing interest in gamification as a mnemonic tool stemmed from his college days in the late eighties when he realized that he was retaining more details of the role-playing games of the day, such as *Zelda*, than of his studies. One strong reminiscence about a game that he was playing in the late 1980s brought back sharp memories of the game, "the story line, the invented histories and all that stuff," compared to subjects that he formally studied, about which he could remember very little. This experience made him suspect that games had potential for use in education. He came to realize, as he puts it, "not an overly academic assertion . . . that because games are fun you care about them, and when you care about them you are more likely to remember the things you hear, the things you go through."

After gaining his doctoral degree in German in 1997 and working for a number of years as an adjunct professor, Yee shifted to work for a company headquartered in Southern California named Interplay, a developer, publisher, and licensor of video game software. While at Interplay, he worked on interpretation and cultural flavoring of American-produced video games for release in foreign countries. Then in 2001 he returned to the world of academia, first as an adjunct teaching German and humanities and then, starting in 2007, in faculty development. Over all that time he maintained his interest in games and gamification but put the interest on hold against his more immediate life duties, staying employed being primary, and the feeling that the technology was not yet evolved enough to help him achieve his goals. His interest in gamification as a possible enhancement to traditional forms of education was rekindled prior to his work on this MOOC, particularly through his observations of the development of smartphone technology and the ubiquity of games in retail and social media generally. One key trigger event was him observing his wife's interest in the location-sharing iPhone application FourSquare. Yee described how these observations helped him realize that gamification principles had firmly made the leap to the corporate world. In thinking about smartphone usage of gamification principles he realized that there was nothing particularly new about gamification, but the way that it was penetrating a wider swathe of society was significant. Describing his wife's use of FourSquare he opined:

This is that technology where you check in and you tell your friends and the system where you are located . . . you get some rewards, you get discounts in places where you go a lot and eventually you get bragging rights in the form of mayorship when you're the one that checks in there the most. So, that recognition that there's something in it for you to keep doing what are rote tasks, that is what I think has attracted business's attention and now more and more people are talking about what is gamification and how we can use it.

Progressing from reflections on married harmony through to a similar line of thinking with regard to parenthood, Yee saw these principles again in kindergarten instructors' distribution of gold stars and "most helpful student" awards aimed to maintain order and attention among their charges. His final day-job reflection, when the planets really aligned for him, was when he saw instructors in traditional (face-to-face) higher education situations dividing their classes, holding competitions, and keeping track of scores for the day. In these cases, the activities were rigidly finite; in his opinion, the instructors missed an opportunity to provide longer-term, sustained motivation for the students. The cumulative effect of seeing his wife, his children, and students at his workplace all dabbling in the world of gamification was stimulus enough for him to begin planning his course. Given the concurrent rise in popularity of MOOCs and Yee's academic technology role, he designed a course so he could, in an informed manner, advise other USF faculty members on what works and what doesn't in MOOCs generally. He saw an opportunity to experiment with engagement normally not seen in online classes, explaining, "What I was trying to get here was identified best practices; this was not an attempt to be scientific about my approach. It was an exploratory attempt to see what does and doesn't work from a practice point of view of gamification, not so much from the metrics."

He did find himself having to reassure some faculty regarding the fear that they might be automated out of their careers. As Yee puts it, "I think there's always a role for your subject-matter experts to stay plugged in." Continuing, "most faculty have not been replaced, the LMS has become another tool to use when thinking about the constant pedagogical issues of classroom management . . . of scaffolding material correctly and carefully for this audience— the LMS just helps with that and gamification can do some of the same things." In doing so, his core questions became solid:

How do we get students motivated?
How do we get students caring?

How do we get students reading and properly processing, putting all the
things in place they need to succeed?

He felt that gamification addressed all of the above without needing to
replace the faculty member.

Why Gamification?

Yee described seeing gamification becoming prevalent in many aspects of
society and, as he termed it, "penetrating today's life." When pushed further,
he reiterated his wife's use of FourSquare and other gamified apps on her
smartphone but admitted that many of his reflections came retroactively as
he was in the process of developing the MOOC. His more succinct version,
with observations relegated to the subliminal, was that he simply decided
that the time was right to blend his passion and his career. As he embarked
on the project he acknowledged that the complexities and ambiguities of academia presented challenges in higher education that were perhaps not as obvious, or missing entirely, in corporate FourSquare or training gamification
projects. He was very sensitive to potential Federal Education Rights and Privacy Act (FERPA) issues, and given that the entire course build-out and implementation was on his shoulders alone, he knew that he needed to develop
safeguarded and simple means of ensuring compliance.

Yee reflected that, in early gamified courses such as his own, many willing
experimenters had to play multiple roles, particularly at less-resourced institutions. The need to play multiple roles is partly due to the paucity of available
resources but also because these experimenters are creating and implementing
courses and course elements beyond the current support framework at their
institutions. This mapped to his own experience as the project lead, concomi-
tant with the responsibilities and skills he needed to develop, build, and
maintain the course while also updating it and acting as the class instructor.
Even as there was no evidence of Yee being anything less than transparent
and communicative at his institution, he also represents the edgy "hacker-
instructor" who seems to revel in being a little under the radar.

The meta-questions that initially motivated Yee and that he developed as
ongoing drivers for his work were:

How do we get students motivated to stay engaged with courses and
course materials?
How do we get students to care about their studies?

How do we get students to read and properly process academic courses? How do we put all the things in place that will help them succeed?

In considering how he might increase student motivation, he posited that a pop culture phenomenon called the Easter egg had potential to increase student engagement with materials. Easter eggs, in the geeky gamer sense, are typically intentional jokes, hidden messages, or features in a computer program, movie, book, crossword, or other work that only dedicated participants are ever likely to find. The earliest frequently referenced example of a hidden in-joke buried away in an obscure section of the code (in other words, an Easter egg) was in the 1979 Atari 2600 game *Adventure*. The game's main programmer, allegedly annoyed at the lack of official recognition for his development role in the game, secreted the message "Created by Warren Robinett." Players could find this message if they directed a gray dot into a hidden room in the game. Even further back, the Fairfield Channel F console, launched in 1976, featured a number of hidden messages. 1978's *Video Whizball* (a version of *Pong*) displayed the coder's name (Bradley Reid-Selth) on screen if the player carried out a series of complex moves at the end of the game.

Yee's sense of the potential for Easter eggs came three or four months before taking this task on, when he had just finished reading the novel *Ready Player One* by Ernest Cline. As the book blurb relays, "In the year 2044, reality is an ugly place. The only time teenage Wade Watts really feels alive is when he's jacked into the virtual utopia known as the OASIS. Wade's devoted his life to studying the puzzles hidden within this world's digital confines—puzzles that are based on their creator's obsession with the pop culture of decades past and that promise massive power and fortune to whoever can unlock them." Throughout the novel, the players solve puzzles and reveal Easter eggs by virtue of an understanding of 1980's cultural references. As a child of the '80s, Yee was obviously hooked on the narrative, but what it really underlined for him was that people *lived the material* in service of unearthing the Easter eggs. This suggested potential for the world of academia, where much of an instructor's challenge is in getting students to really engage with the materials. Yee was also fascinated at the level of challenge that the text provided. He determined to make the Easter egg challenges harder and less obvious than just lying on the surface.

The emerging question of what actually constituted gamification encouraged Yee to experiment with a range of elements while feeling safe in the knowledge that the concept generally was yet to solidify into a definitive model or set of rules. He reflected that he allowed his own personal whims and interests to guide him in coalescing the principles of what made games and activities interesting. He effectively shoehorned these elements and principles into his own compendium-teaching model. This flexibility and laissez-faire attitude encouraged him to explore a variety of elements, with the idea of experimenting to see what worked. His desire to experiment with the format was, in part, his reaction to the media frenzy about MOOCs (described by John Hennessey, then president of Stanford, as the coming "MOOC tsunami" [Auletta 2012]). Yee's dual role at USF, encompassing not only his own teaching but also the training and support of other instructors university-wide in pedagogy and technology, fueled his suspicion that USF faculty would soon beat a path to his door seeking guidance as to how to implement a successful MOOC. He was motivated to have a range of experiences and some quasi-research-based findings to share with them. His hope was that the experience and his learning would be useful for him to support faculty who might subsequently be interested in delivering a MOOC.

Yee decided to build out his course on the Canvas LMS that USF had moved to a year or so earlier so that he would learn through his own trial and error what worked and what did not. He built the course with the idea that with minimal adjustment and only basic technical expertise it could be repurposed to run again with alternate subject matter. This notion of reusability or re-purposing was part of Yee's philosophy as a developer and supporter of faculty activities. He felt that a more open platform, rather than overdesigned simulations or more game-y games, would be of more or wider use to the institution. As he put it, "It's one thing to get a million-dollar grant to build a custom video game environment that teaches accounting, but that's not going to help your chemistry teacher."

If it had not been for this secondary goal, Yee claims that he would have tried to publish his MOOC on the more visible and richer Coursera platform, which would have given him exposure to a much wider audience and likely have resulted in more course registrants. It is worth reiterating that this was not simply a MOOC for his own edification but rather a learning experience for him, as a faculty developer and also as a pioneer paving the way for future USF MOOCs. His prescience in sensing other USF instructors' interest seems to be validated by the USF press release announcing Yee's MOOC, which concluded, "A second free MOOC will begin Sept. 9, 2013 entitled, 'Forums for a Future,' which discusses current societal issues that will impact the future of the world. Anyone at USF interested in offering a MOOC should contact . . ." The parameters framing Yee's work were that, while he was eager to experiment with his personal interest in gamification, a lot of the course build had to be simplistic and replicable by an instructor with limited technical skills. Yee, with no formal gamification training, used simple HTML coding and a good degree of creativity to build basic game elements into the Canvas-based MOOC, allowing him to test theories and game principles that he had seen in his nonacademic career. His thought process boiled down to whether the gamified elements could promote engagement and student motivation.

His desire to keep to a low-tech implementation actually short-circuited some of the tracking capabilities of Canvas and reduced his ability to record student data on individual pages or learning objects. He built HTML pages in Adobe Dreamweaver and uploaded them to Canvas, which rendered them only as files without the regular tracking capabilities of the Canvas system. He did this to maintain the aesthetic elements that he created using cascading style sheets. He described balancing process as an ongoing "war between design and functionality," including it in his personal debrief for the gamification elements. Given his interest in gleaning better information from his student data, Yee noted this inability to granularly track student progress in the course as a critical lesson learned and a possible amendment for his second run of the course.

Elements of Gamification

In identifying the key gamification elements of his MOOC experiment, Yee focused first on the concept of competition. In explaining his perspective on the value of competition, he connected it to the notion of reward as a means of motivation, "People are more invested when there is competition, and I think it's important to show progress somehow. You can't just have competition that goes nowhere—then you're just on a treadmill."

Yee's emphasis on competition and challenge formed the critical underpinning of his fairy tale MOOC. Competition and challenge provided a large part of the impetus for students to engage with the academic, mostly text-based materials. His plan was to document and display the fruits of this competition on a fairly rudimentary student leaderboard built using HTML with

JPEG images that he would paste in manually whenever he wanted to assign a badge. The leaderboard for Yee was emblematic of academic-specific challenges not apparent in other participatory environments.

> When you are an educator, you are thinking about other elements to this that are not necessarily in every gamification model for businesses out there; FERPA, for instance. I can't just put people's scores out on a leaderboard, so you have to end up gamifying or badge-ifying things that are not worth points in the class so the list of things that I am gamifying include stuff that's not weekly grades. It's more likely to be things like "the first discussion post of the week" or the "best challenge tech of the week." I've challenged them [with that one] and they put up products basically. "The best question or best answer on the discussion board," "The most amount of perfect scores on Easter egg quizzes for their team," etc.

The MOOC design concept meant that courses and course elements had to potentially accommodate tens of thousands of people. Yee's fairy tale MOOC ultimately enrolled around 1,400 users, of which only a few more than 100 persisted through to completion of the final exam. He was firm in saying that he intended the design to be able to support up to 50,000 users. Wanting to build in engagement and scalability, Yee implemented what he called the "Harry Potter proxy protocol," whereby individual effort yields rewards for the whole house, as in the book/movie of the same name. Students were grouped alphabetically with the hope of producing the dual benefit of developing team spirit among the participants while reducing an instructor's need to assess and reward on an individual basis. This Harry Potter proxy protocol was based on the principle known as the "dependent hero contingency," where consequences are delivered to a group based on the performance of one member or a subset of members, as researched in the work of Litow and Pumroy in 1975. The approach was intended to provide subtle peer pressure without the demotivation (for some) of full-on competition by replacing it with a gentler co-desire not only to not let down, but also to impress, teammates.

This bunching of feedback and reward to teams rather than individuals also had the course management effect of diminishing the impact of the large numbers in the MOOC platform, thus reducing instructor load. Even with that reduced load, however, Yee reported that he was unable to keep up with the awards or even the initial design work of the numerous badges he had intended to award (see examples in figure 4 below). As one student constructively commented in the student survey responses, "The badge system

Figure 4. Sample badges, developed but not implemented, in the USF MOOC. © Kevin Yee, University of South Florida; reproduced with permission.

would have been great, and maybe it would help the professor to have an assistant assigned just to do that job."

Easter Eggs

The rationale for Easter eggs is that people have to engage with and go through the content numerous times to locate more difficult eggs. This strategy is basically employing a trick. The Easter egg hunt is a fun activity but could produce academic results by promoting increased immersion in the content. Many people do question whether hunting for Easter eggs actually entails engaging with the content or merely looking between, over, or above the content when searching for clues. The content in Yee's course tended to be simple text but could also encompass other formats that students had to access repetitively, such as watching videos multiple times or listening to audio files over and over. Yee intentionally built in Easter eggs using an array of simple coding techniques, including subliminal messages that flashed every few seconds in a webcam lecture, the gradual revelation of a hidden URL, the title tag of a picture providing a secret URL to visit, and URLs hidden in background images (deliberately faded) set on repeat. Yee felt it vital that the sections of the course featuring the Easter eggs were carefully embedded in the course content rather than hyperlinked out. As he states, "People are more likely to click on these diversions when they're right there in front of them." He also noted that "People reacted in different ways—one user clicked back 37 times to one document—a three-page story. She was looking for Easter eggs, but there were none in that document." Yee even had an awesome *Fight Club* rule for Easter eggs on the discussion boards. It read "First rule for Easter egg hunts—no-one discusses Easter eggs on the discussion boards."

Of the 16 students submitting comments to the USF survey (as mentioned earlier, 36 students completed the ratings) on all aspects of the course, 10

(62.5%) commented on the Easter eggs. Eight of these 10 comments were positive. Representative comments include:

> The course was made more fun by the fact that we had virtual Easter egg hunts.
> I was quite surprised of the effect on the Easter eggs by myself (and others); it really worked.
> The Easter eggs were awesome as a gamer I LOVE Easter eggs in games.
> The game aspect was definitely interesting. The Easter egg hunt was wonderful!

As the "37 times" quote from Yee above illustrates, the course data captured the behavior of some students who revisited course content multiple times in pursuit of Easter eggs. The Easter eggs irritated a few students (2 of 16 completing surveys), and there was no way of knowing whether any students who dropped the course before submitting surveys were also turned off by the activity or its degree of difficulty. Yee felt, from his rudimentary tracking of course statistics, that students might have dropped off at certain places in the course specifically because of frustration at their inability to find a certain Easter egg.

> The data is not specific enough to say exactly where they fell off—to one specific item or one specific Easter egg. I will say that one specific Easter egg generated a ton of email from students who couldn't find it. It was obscure enough that a ton of people sent me emails. There is a possibility that people dropped off as that was too hard. I went into this thinking Easter eggs are bonus content—who cares if you can't find it, but it could be that people cared enough about the Easter eggs that it made them stop coming to the class in general.

Narrative Elements

Yee intended to include a narrative element in the course whereby the participants would receive motivating thematic text, in addition to badging awards, describing their progress in the world of the fairy tale MOOC. His operating metaphor was the carnival game where you throw a ball and it lands in a scoring hole giving you three points, four points, five points, or zero points, and your horse moves along the back wall of the carnival booth the requisite number of spaces. What Yee intended was that the group earning the most badges would have "awesome things happen to their team in the storyline that week" (akin to their horse moving many spaces), whereas the group earning the medium amount of badges would have "a medium thing happen to them that week in the storyline." As he put it, "the story would lurch towards some conclusion that I would not prearrange."

The narrative element was another part of Yee's original plan that he was not able to implement fully. Part of the challenge that he saw in developing the narrative was the complexity of a branching storyline accounting for every contingency. Even with only four weeks of branching, a system with four or five possible outcomes for each team each week could amount to more than 200 independent outcomes, with each possible path involving creative, instructor-developed narrative twists pending each group's performance. Despite attempted simplifications, Yee realized that, given his other work/life obligations, he would be unable to commit the needed time to generate worthwhile narrative and cancelled it as a course element prior to the start date. Taking a positive from this shortcoming, the narrative-free course provided a more focused environment for him to test out the elements he did implement (Easter eggs and team competition). Nonetheless, eliminating the narrative elements reduced the breadth of his experimentation. One student who had discussed the narrative aspect with Yee concluded, "I do wish the competition aspect had worked out, but if I had to choose between the individual challenge of the eggs and the team competition, I would go for the individual challenge each time."

Challenge

When generalizing on what makes a game bad or good irrespective of delivery format, the instructor returned to the idea that presenting the appropriate level of challenge is essential. "What makes a game bad is if it's got balance issues—if it's unbalanced. If it's too hard, it's anxiety inducing, if it's too easy, it's boring. You need exactly the right difficulty, early easy wins and then you ratchet up the difficulty and you use the skills one at a time. It's very much like education, you learn something, you master it and then you go onto the next thing." His student survey comments seemed to accentuate the critical aspect of what Yee called the "Goldilocks" effect of making challenges "not too easy, not too difficult, but just right." One student indicated in her responses to the USF survey that the activities were, at times, too challenging, "Finding all of the game elements was a little frustrating. I was unable to locate one [Easter egg], but I believe that it is more due to my way of thinking than the difficulty of the task." Another student remarked, "I had a lot of problems with the Easter eggs. Still can't find them. Will have to look at the cheat sheet!"

In addition to the above, Yee included technical challenges to entice students to try new things. In the first week, for instance, he encouraged students to develop a short video explaining why they were interested in taking the course. Many students shared that this was their first experience developing multimedia and that it had been a challenge for them. One student's survey response reflected positively on the role of the technological challenges, "[I] loved that Dr. Yee incorporated new technology into the course. With each of the technology challenges I learned something new and hopefully I can apply my new knowledge to my current or future job."

When reviewing the issue of challenge in the MOOC, Yee concluded that all instructors—but particularly those working on gamified courses—must consider balance issues and make activities neither boring nor anxiety-inducing. Instructors and course developers should offer early, easy wins and then ratchet up the difficulty. In terms of using challenge to increase student information retention, he suggests adding skills incrementally, returning to early skills with spaced repetition, and implementing "boss levels" (a gaming term that describes a challenge analogous to that of traditional final exams). Boss levels are summative *ultimate* challenges introduced once students have bought in, are committed, and (the developer is confident) will spend substantial amounts of time trying to "defeat an enemy" utilizing all skills and experiences to that point learned in the game/course.

Outcomes

Of 1,400 course starters, 400 persisted beyond the first week of the course (defined as attempting the second assessment), and 107 completed the final exam. Of the group of completers, 36 completed surveys that were distributed in the final week of the course through the Canvas platform. Yee's survey featured 10 fixed-response questions asking students to indicate their agreement on a rating scale of 1to 5. There was also one section for additional commentary introduced thus, "This course is being studied for its application of game principles to education. Please provide any additional comments about the course you feel are relevant to this study." The survey also included six optional demographic questions.

The 36 respondents were predominately female (82%), the age spread was wide (figure 5), and the majority of participants were college educated

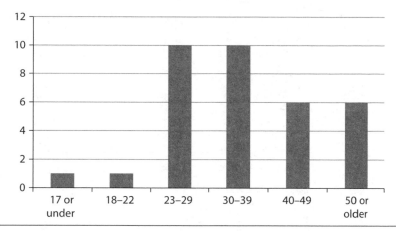

Figure 5. Age of participants in the USF Fairy Tales MOOC (*n*=36). *Note:* Data gleaned from student surveys conducted by Kevin Yee of USF; used with permission.

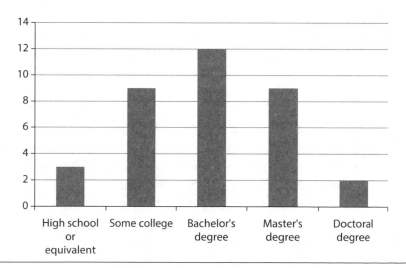

Figure 6. Academic background of participants in the USF Fairy Tales MOOC (*n*=36). *Note:* Data gleaned from student surveys conducted by Kevin Yee of USF; used with permission.

(figure 6). Two-thirds (68%) of the respondents were participating from North America and 24% from Europe. There was a wide range of declared incomes (figure 7) in the smaller subset (*n*=22) disclosing that information.

The course, as a whole, was rated as very enjoyable (4.44 out of 5), and the inventiveness of the instruction methods was appreciated (4.15 out of 5). Those students completing the survey claimed to have learned a lot (4.26).

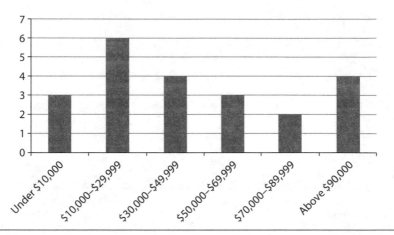

Figure 7. Family income of participants in the USF Fairy Tales MOOC (*n* = 36). *Note:* Data gleaned from student surveys conducted by Kevin Yee of USF; used with permission.

The response to the question of whether they learned more in this course than in "most other online courses" was rated lower, although still toward the positive (3.26).

Faculty Role

Yee acknowledged that the time it takes a faculty member to plan out a gamified course is likely to be more substantial than for a typical online course. Bearing in mind that Yee is an experienced designer and deliverer of online courses, his comments are instructive. "Development was a minimum of 40 hours—probably more like 80 hours of effort. Keep in mind that I'm fluent in HTML and a power user of the LMS so a regular faculty member would spend probably twice as much time. Implementation was honestly only 2–5 hours per week. Next time I do this that will be higher."

His main regret from the experience was his inability to fully support and implement his gamification elements. He emphasized the need for faculty and developers in gamified/online courses, but in MOOCs particularly, to think carefully about manual processes in courses that need consistent attention on the instructor's behalf. Yee's hope is that early pioneers will work with their successors in mind to build and develop scalable, replicable models so that not everyone is starting with a blank slate. As Yee notes, "Scalability is very much part of my daily vocabulary as a faculty developer, and I built what I did with the MOOC with this in mind."

Yee also commented on the need for sustained faculty visibility to users in the course as something that is essential irrespective of format (traditional online vs. MOOC) and its degree of gamification (from none to extensive). The amount of faculty presence is a common concern in traditional online courses. Gamification may, Yee feels, exacerbate this problem by adding other elements to update besides the common challenges of responding to discussion board posts, grading assignments and hosting synchronous sessions. Yee candidly reflected on his own inability to maintain a consistent presence in the class and how this ultimately hurt the class dynamic and, more likely than not, student completion. "Normally speaking, what I would have done was have way more interactive videos every week talking about what their discussion board posts had been and giving very customized individual feedback. I think that it, as much as anything was why they stopped checking in after week one. We had had a full third of people there week one and then they didn't finish week two and I think that's because I didn't give them a lot of sense that I was present in the class between weeks one and two."

Although Yee cannot directly prove, based on the system data he could get from his Canvas build, that his gamification/gameful design efforts increased student engagement, the student enjoyment and repeated reading of content suggests that conclusion. Student survey responses show that many of those students who stuck around to the end loved the Easter egg component of it. As Yee concludes, "For the people it [the gamified course/game elements] worked on, it worked very well. What we can't say is that it worked on everybody." He recognized that a logical next step would be to move to a 1x2 research design, splitting the class and offering the same content to both but with one group receiving gamified elements. As described earlier, the nature of his first attempted build (including the way he built out his content in the Canvas system) hampered data collection. "What's not captured in the data is how many people kept reading week by week but stopped filling in the quizzes. And you could maybe guess at it with class-wide statistics data looking at how many people saw the pages."

It seems likely that a revised version of Yee's course with more instructor time to connect and update the game elements as well as enhanced tracking ability would be a valuable exercise given what look like promising initial ideas. Yee's fairy tale MOOC illustrated the potential for a creative instructor who is willing to take a few risks to implement technically simple game elements into a course. Participants' survey comments described the course as engaging and reported that the course encouraged interaction with what could otherwise be quite standard text-based content. In Yee's opinion, for those for whom the course worked, it worked very well. He suggested that gamification might especially benefit academically lower-level students. Yee expands on this in his review of the MOOC, "I didn't come to gamification with a target population in mind, yet . . . it may be that fragile learners might be induced to find and file away education differently . . . have a different approach and attitude to education if it were to grab their attention in a different manner."

Yee extended his thinking to a more philosophical level when contemplating how gamification might be used to modify traditional academia and whether this is actually a good thing to do. He speculated that gamification might pander to the superficiality of some of today's students rather than calling them on it by bringing them up to our concept of education. Philosophically he continued, "It's an open question as to whether I'm doing more harm than good by meeting that student halfway, or more than halfway, in our various definitions of what education means." While addressing the question of gamification's potential to support students who have traditionally struggled to engage with higher education he commented, "It could be that a fragile learner could be more easily met by this—it's a different political question whether you want a fragile learner to be met by this—perhaps a special education teacher or something could be done with certain intents very well. It probably does lend itself particularly well to certain contexts better than others."

Student Comments

I learned a lot about the fairy tales, which I never think a lot before. And at the same time, I know a lot of history about those stories and authors. It is great!

I was quite surprised of the effect on the Easter eggs by myself (and others); it really worked. Too bad the badges didn't work, but I guess this group of students was more interested in the search than in status. Always good to check!

The Easter eggs were awesome as a gamer I LOVE Easter eggs in games.

I really enjoyed being able to jump in to a course like this with using the topic of fairy tales. The only thing I had trouble was with finding all the hidden Easter eggs. I enjoyed being able to learn and use other websites to do projects.

Finding all of the game elements was a little frustrating. I was unable to locate one, but I believe that it is more due to my way of thinking than the difficulty of the task.

I did not find any Easter eggs. I had no idea where to start or what to look for.

The game aspect was definitely interesting. The Easter egg hunt was wonderful! I do wish the competition aspect had worked out but if I had to choose between the individual challenge of the eggs and the team competition I would go for the individual challenge each time.

I liked it I learned a lot about the other fairy tales besides the Disney ones.

Had a lot of problems with the Easter eggs. Still can't find them. Will have to look at the cheat sheet! Loved that Dr. Yee incorporated new technology into the course. With each of the technology challenges I learned something new and hopefully I can apply my new knowledge to my current or future job.

The course aided in the exercise of critical thinking and application of multiple paradigms to a single question.

It was made more fun by the fact that we had virtual Easter egg hunts. The badge system would have been great and maybe it would help the professor to have an assistant assigned just to do that job.

The badges could have been fun, but there should have been announcements when badges were posted and more explanation about them (i.e. if there is a best comment give a link to the comment). The Easter egg hunt was fun until I got to the last module. I cannot make the one (I suspect two) work with the hidden text no matter how many permutations I try, and I don't own a smartphone or anything that would read a QR code. Plus, the file with Easter egg spoilers won't load either, and now it is no longer fun.

I enjoyed being able to use a lot of new web sites that I didn't know about to do projects.

It should be nice if we got [all] those game elements we were promised.

I love it, it has been wonderful.

For non-native English is difficult following videos without subtitles and most activities are dedicated to people who control speaking in this language.

Yee's candid experimentation, his can-do attitude, and his infectious enthusiasm were certainly huge assets. As we'll see with other experiments in subsequent chapters, the students who provided feedback were extremely supportive of his efforts. His MOOC retained around twice as many students as was typical at the time, and I, personally, learned a lot about fairy tales— some of it quite nasty (one sister in Cinderella actually cuts off her big toe and part of her heel to try and fit into the glass slipper in the Brothers Grimm version).

Where Are They Now?

In mid-May 2016, I spoke with Dr. Yee to see where he had got to with the fairy tales project. My questions were: How has the project evolved? Has it grown or atrophied at the institution?

BELL—So as time has passed, what happened with your project, the Fairy Tale MOOC? Did it run again? Did you tweak it? What happened with the interest, both yours and institutionally? Where you are at with gameful design, gamification?

YEE—So as you know, mine was a little higher than normal completion rates for a MOOC, and that was useful. First, some backup for why I had offered that particular MOOC. The topic wasn't new to me, nor was gamification as an idea. Our university had not done any MOOCs at the time (around 2014), and people were worried that MOOCs were about to sweep or take over. I wanted to be in a stronger position to protect the university, and I feel that there is no substitute for doing something yourself and seeing what happens. So that was sort of the major motivation for me rather than the research specifically into the gamification side. Also, I had done a MAGNA seminar on gamification at one point [MAGNA is a for-profit player in faculty professional development]. So I had a fairly established faculty-facing, hour-long presentation as to what gamification means for me and the principles that I prescribe to it. I have my own six principles for the things we want to steal from games.

That is a long way of explaining that I didn't pick up the MOOC beyond that second run because it's not a priority for what we do. Now I'm a faculty member I'm [on call twelve months a year] . . . my main job is to know things and do things so that we can help faculty become more effective, it's not to teach MOOCs. So I haven't returned to it for that. Now, in terms of gamification, I do teach about once a year, but lately what I've been teaching is an honors class with only about 20 students. Honors students are already motivated. This last year I was teaching the topic [not fairy tales but] Disney World. The title of the class was Deconstructing Disney World. With a topic like that they really don't need the external motivation that gamification provides because there's enough inherent motivation in it, so it wasn't my first thought to do it.

Now there is, however, an answer for how it has transmogrified in my brain or how I have started to do things differently with gamification. I have started to use some of those principles in what we do in faculty development; the ways in which we not only engage faculty but keep them interested in our longer events. We have a two-day event called Summer Teaching Symposium (STS). We don't offer a stipend, a cash stipend, for people to come to this, so it has to be useful or they won't come back, and, to some extent, it has to have some fun elements to it. So we have kind of evolved into a position where we make the event not just a staid instructor-level very formal sort of "Go to workshops [and] learn from this and that." It has much more of a fun vibe, so your nametag when you get it comes with games built into it. There's a picture of a particular kind of chocolate in the corner. Then there's code in the corner down here that says *A* and then *17-2* or something like that, and then over in the other corner there's a word written, like *frost*. And they all represent different games that are to be used to interact with each other during the course of the two days. So the person with *frost* has to find someone else's nametag (they're all custom) with a word that can go with *frost* to form a combination word. *Frost* and *house* wouldn't go together, but someone with *frost* could go with someone with the word *bite* to make *frostbite*. When they meet a person where the names are compatible, then they interview each other about their best teaching trick—that sort of thing.

I don't know that it follows necessarily my principles of gamification to force students to do work that is otherwise boring to them, but what it does do is it generates interest in the event and keeps things fresh. Again, it being a faculty event, I wouldn't do it that way with students, I don't think. So there's a fair amount of that, and it turns out the very next year's STS topic is going to be gamification. This year was the flipped classroom—how you flip classrooms, why you do it, what are the problems you have, and how you surmount those—all of that stuff.

BELL—Are you taking a lead in that—the gamification? Or is that something that has come up organically at the institution?

YEE—No, the event is ours. I'm the director of the office, so I think you can probably safely say it's just an executive decision by me that this last year was going to be the flipped class and that next year will be gamification. So the reason why? I don't know, I guess there are a couple of reasons why. First, it's something that we, or at least I, have a lot of experience in doing, and most faculty don't know what it is or how to do it. So it becomes a topic that is kind of ripe for a two-day intensive look at it with lots of breakouts. And, of course, the event itself will be gamified . . . just as the flipped classroom event was flipped . . . We have a fairly well produced trailer for what STS 4 will look like. There's a Harry Potter element to it, so that we ended up using music from one of the *Harry Potter* trailers and overlaid images of students basically not being plugged in and texting and all those other things. We're suggesting that there are principles of games that we could steal that would make things more interesting in the classroom. The Harry Potter connection is how we will gamify the event. We are going to sort our faculty into four Harry Potter houses and provide "five points for Gryffindor," etc., when they do something good in one of these breakouts.

BELL—That was one of your key principles, wasn't it? The dependent hero contingency— the Harry Potter principle of engendering, whether it's peer pressure or team spirit or whatever?

YEE—Yes, I think for me the Harry Potter idea (and you might as well just use the actual Harry Potter—right?) came about more from a logistical point of view because there is not automation in the LMS. Actually, Blackboard may have it now. We've been on Canvas for a while, and Blackboard does have badges of some sort built in. But because of the lack of automation in the LMS level, the generic principle is one of proxy. You do something good your whole team benefits, because I'm not keeping a gigantic table with 300 people's scores.

BELL—That makes sense. So back to the MOOC experiment—you said you ran it twice in quick succession. Did you tweak anything between runs? Did you ramp anything up or scale it down?

YEE—I actually have to report that term, and this is why there was no third MOOC. I ended up getting even busier with the day job than I was even first time around. The first time around, what happened was it was only a four-week MOOC, and about three weeks into it I started running into logistical challenges. I didn't have enough hours in the day to do the gamified parts of it, and so a couple of the badges were just not awarded . . . or I guess they were, but they were done very late in the cycle each time. And so I felt like I wasn't really making as much of a presence in the discussion boards as I had wanted to, and it ended up becoming a stealth experiment into how much you could automate a MOOC. By the second time around I did it I had even less presence week to week, and still things ran. The Easter egg hunts still continued. People still reported like they did with the first one that they were intensely interested in finding all the Easter eggs, and that really drove them to read things multiple times. So all of that continued, but sort of the house challenge—where the first person who posts a question this week gets a badge or whatever, that kind of thing—the second time around some of those things just did not get awarded because I just was not finding the time within the workweek to do it. So out of that guilt I did not try to run it again.

BELL—So your MOOC stalled a little. You do have the faculty development piece. The class you are teaching you say you don't see the need to implement. Do you have any other plans to implement anything gamified on your campus?

YEE—No. You know, if this were a phone call in two years' time—that would be a year after we do our STS event on gamification—I would be willing to bet there will be some faculty on campus who are trying to develop some version of this. Unfortunately, I don't have much I can share with you now just because . . . we have a million things we try to push, and there a million things I try to make myself an expert on, and gamification is only one of them. If I was a nine-month faculty member I probably would have taken that topic or a similar one and said, "this is my niche," and kept publishing on it, but that's not my situation.

BELL—So obviously with your work you are generating a good degree of interest on your campus. Have you been seeing or hearing concerns over trivializing or from faculty that when you gamify your course it makes my (traditional) course seem even more boring by contrast. Have you had any of that kind of pushback?

YEE—Yes. When I give my regular one-hour workshops on gamification—which I have done over the years—there are three main concerns that I hear most frequently. One is about trivialization, one is about lack of universality—what you just said—like "if my colleague doesn't do this," and the third, which is the deadliest of them, is that we are not actually addressing core motivation. What we're doing is actually tricking the students into doing something. If you were to look into industry definitions of gamification it would be something along the lines of (take Four-Square) where if you get people to check in to here they become mayor, so there's something in it for them. In the meantime, Starbucks can now offer you a coupon for being nearby, that sort of thing. So the industry definition of gamification is often about taking a boring or routine process and making it fun. But that implies that what we're teaching them in the classrooms is boring or routine, and gamification doesn't really fix that. To some extent it's a critical flaw to what we do as gamification.

So what does it mean? Well I don't purport to have all of those answers, but what it might mean is that gamification serves to create some initial interest after which, theoretically, they have bought in to the actual inherent content itself. Now they might sense a reason for memorizing something like all the bones in the body in biology because it's become interesting in and of itself; the game was a means to an end. My background is actually in languages—I have a PhD in German—so when I teach German classes we have always, since the beginning of time, done some version of games within classes to make things more interesting. So the way you memorize certain prepositions can be done to the tune of, say, "Twinkle, Twinkle Little Star." So that conversion of a game gets you somewhere towards them knowing it and remembering it, and now they care about these other, bigger things within the discipline. That's a little bit different from doing a semester-long Harry Potter type thing.

You know, I meet some faculty who are willing to give that ground where they say, "So what if it's purely extrinsic?" Let's say it is. There's nothing intrinsic about it, but they come to class and they end up learning something as a result of it . . . even though I haven't turned them on to the world of calculus, but they got through it and they enjoyed the class and [it received] good evaluations and they actually learned something. And maybe they don't like it, or maybe they like it for the wrong reasons, but at least they got through my class.

BELL—And you don't hold to the trivialization argument either then, for similar reasons, I guess? It doesn't matter why they are engaged so long as they are?

YEE—No, that's a really good question, and I think that cuts to the heart of a style question. I don't see that as trivialization—as kindergartenization—that it seems beneath us as faculty members at a college level, that we would resort to doing this through a game lens. Why don't we just approach this as adults? The bigger problem is not so much the faculty pushback on that as it is faculty recognizing that there will be a subset of students who will push back on that. Gamification actually speaks to the lowest common denominator of students, the ones who will be the least likely to be engaged. To some extent it really is an imposition to the people who are already engaged for intrinsic reasons. You know, "Now you have to go through this game element." "Well, what game element? Can we please talk about the bones in the body and how they interact with each other?"

BELL—At least one of my other practitioners said almost the same thing, that it's a hook to get students to the level of engagement to where they are hooked by the subject area.

YEE—Well, to use the flipping analogy as well, there are degrees of implementation here. So with the flipped classroom you can flip five minutes and then create five minutes' time during the lecture to do something different—you didn't do very much. So the game version of that is stealing . . . one of my principles is to leverage competition. Students are, generally speaking, looking for a chance to be competitive with each other, literally just for the hell of it. You don't have to give them prizes or anything, just, like, "This half of the class won today," they eat that up. So can you turn . . . that moment when you are getting a review into a game where they have to call out the right their answers based on what side of the room they are on. That's stealing some of the principles of gamification without making it a semester-long thing. You know, it makes today a little raucous, makes today maybe a little bit less staid and boring, but it's not a big jump from what people already do now. Sort of microimplementations of gaming.

BELL—So clearly your interest is still there. What would it take to make this really catch fire at USF?

YEE—You never really know in faculty development what it will take. So what you hope is that the message itself will resonate enough that people will start doing it. That's why we have it [in the STS], is that we hope faculty will just say, "We've heard of this flipping thing and at the STS I find out that it's not too hard and there are ways to get it wrong but it's generally quite safe to try," so they nibble at the edges. So what you're talking about is culture change, and there's a body of literature around culture change, and much of it suggests it's hard, it takes a long time, it happens via individual champions, and sometimes it's political, yes. So, politically, to do it at the first-year experience class would mean that the person in charge [of] the first-year experience class would have to be convinced that it's a good thing. That would be a single attempt to convince someone. I think in our case, we're going to start at the STS because that's where the faculty themselves are. We're actually restructuring these days . . . the units like student affairs and undergraduate studies will be combining to some extent, so the first-year experience class may be being looked at again. That might be an opportunity there to raise my hand and to say, "Let's look at this gamification thing again," so you just never really know what's going to catch on—or which of the various methods.

You mentioned money—does course redesign pay? Sometimes, but we've tended not to incentivize around money out of my office for a couple of reasons. It creates expectation, and it's also, to some extent, the wrong metaphor. I think faculty should be revisiting their classes all the time, and they shouldn't need to be paid to do that. It's a little bit like giving faculty members five dollars every time they brush their teeth—they shouldn't be paid for doing that.

BELL—Any other reflections? Anything else you are seeing that you think exciting?

YEE—I've been reading Karl Kapp and Michelle Dickey, so whenever brochures come out with books I do tend to review and try to stay aware of them. We're going to start planning now based on the literature and revised research—we have 11 months to plan and prepare for the next STS.

BELL—Do you still play games? What are you playing at the moment?

YEE—I'm playing a Steam game right now called *Dungeon Defender II,* and I've been playing *Battlefield 4* on the Xbox when the kids are not awake (because it's not a kid-appropriate title). *Dungeon Defender II* is, like many STEAM games, free to play. It's multiplayer and it's kind of a tower defense meets platform game. So you have things you have to shoot—your enemies—because your towers are not strong enough to do it by themselves, and so it's multiplayer, multipath tower defense with shooting. And you switch character roles so you're different classes (and you can switch in the middle of a level)—might be good for these kinds of flying things, or these towers are strong but this has the best ranged attack, whatever this stuff is. It's actually—my 13-year-old started playing it, and now I play it with him—it's a family thing that we do.

BELL—That's great, so you're keeping your sense of fun and youth . . .

YEE—Yeah. One of the things I did recently, actually, was to bring into my office my games . . . the ones I rocked out on back in the day. It's become part of the positioning or the branding of the office is that, you know, I've got experience in the gaming industry, so I'm going to leverage that.

BELL—Well, thanks so much. It's great to catch up and great that you're still working on this and thinking about this.

YEE—Yes, it's lower-level and more on the faculty development side of things, but that is the main job, so that's where I have to keep it for now.

BELL—I had a great experience working with you, and I can report that it worked on me. I can report that my retention of fairy tale history and genesis is still strong. My daughters thank you. Keep in touch.

■ ■ ■ ■ ■ ■ ■ ■ ■ ■ ■ ■ ■ ■ ■

CHAPTER FOUR

The Hero's Journey

In bucolic Durham, New Hampshire, the picturesque campus of the University of New Hampshire (UNH) provides a scenic backdrop to some innovative programming and instruction. The UNH catalog describes economics as

> the study of how societies organize themselves to produce goods and services and to distribute those products among the members of society. In the modern world, a combination of market forces, public policies and social customs perform these basic economic tasks. Economists use concepts, models and data to analyze efficiency of resource use, fairness of economic outcomes and development of global and national economies.

The department chair and instructor, Neil Niman, has gone beyond the typical bounds of a standard economics class (figure 8). He provides a snapshot illustrating underpinnings to his philosophy of narrative gamification, quoting Lydia Plowman's paper "Narrative, Linearity and Interactivity: Making Sense of Interactive Multimedia," "Narrative isn't just a shaping device: it helps us think, remember, communicate and make sense of ourselves and the world. The role of narrative is not therefore simply aesthetic; it is central to our cognition from earliest childhood" (1996, 96). For a variety of reasons, and to a variety of ends, as presented in this chapter, Niman runs with this concept to address the challenge of helping (self-declared) nontechnical/math-phobic students succeed in his class.

Background

UNH was founded and incorporated in 1866 as the New Hampshire College of Agriculture and the Mechanic Arts, a land grant subsidiary of Dartmouth College in Hanover, New Hampshire (officially associated with Dartmouth and overseen by their president). Dartmouth is the smallest of the Ivy League schools and is famous for its selectivity, for its nearly 250-year history, and for

Figure 8. Screenshot: Support website interface for the University of New Hampshire EconJourney course. Reproduced with permission of Neil Niman, University of New Hampshire.

serving as part of the inspiration (the Alpha Delta Phi fraternity) for National Lampoon's *Animal House*. The co-writer of the, "To-ga-To-ga" / "Fat, drunk and stupid is no way to go through life, son," comedy, Chris Miller, is a Dartmouth graduate, class of 1963.

In 1891, following the bequeathal of farm and land assets by Durham resident Benjamin Thompson, the college's move to Durham was approved. In 1923 the college's name was changed to the University of New Hampshire. UNH is home for over 15,000 students and runs the oldest endowed sustainability program in higher education in the nation. In 2012, UNH was named the sixth "coolest school" in the country by *Sierra* magazine for its efforts in sustainability. Tuition and fees for in-state students were $17,624 in 2016, $31,424 for out-of-state students, and room and board were around $10,000 for undergraduates. Famous alums include John Irving, Academy Award–winning screenwriter and novelist; Carlton Fisk, professional baseball player and inductee into the Baseball Hall of Fame; three former governors of New

Hampshire; and over 20 professional hockey players graduating from UNH's famous Wildcats team.

Niman studied economics at the University of California, Santa Cruz, and The University of Texas at Austin. He now serves as the associate dean of academic programs at UNH. At the time of the initial course development in 2012 he served as the chair of the Department of Economics at UNH and was preparing for the inaugural launch of a revamped Microeconomics 101 course. His class was typically made up of undergraduate students from a variety of disciplines, many with a built-in affinity and ability with regard to the discipline, but others with no natural disposition toward logic, rules, math, and related concepts. He employed a number of graduate assistants (GAs), one of whom, "StoryCoach" Jennifer Trudeau, a fifth-year PhD student in the same department, described the makeup of the class. She notes that there are a large proportion of students in the class:

> Who aren't necessarily the traditional economics students, a lot of economics students are logic based, number-kind of, applied math people . . . for those students who come in . . . maybe they're in marketing or advertising and they have a more creative brain and they like to exercise those skills, and you wouldn't typically get that in an economics class necessarily because it's logic, rules, math and concepts.

Trudeau's explanation introduces the concept of melding creative individuals and personal flavor to a microeconomics class environment focused on concrete facts, logic, and rules. For students to succeed, these facts and rules must be memorized and reapplied when analyzing and implementing principles of microeconomics beyond the classroom. Niman picked up on this and explained why the "story" has become central to his thinking about creating an engaging and motivating educational experience:

> Stories are the way we communicate; stories are the way that we raise our children; stories are something that we do every moment of our life, especially now with this whole social media revolution. And so, if we've trained people to become storytellers, or storytelling emerges as part of our normal way of life, doesn't it make sense that learning should incorporate those skills?

He sees the role of narrative as a multifaceted communication that develops, as he puts it, "organically," blossoming into "the student's imagination" on a framework that we've constructed. His hope is that in this model the student, with guidance, becomes vested, which makes this a more meaningful learning experience. The idea of co-creation of narrative to illustrate and frame concepts and key course elements became the signature feature of his course.

Niman and Trudeau implemented a form of gamification with elements that are common to other models—competition, collaboration, and rewards—along with another layer that they feel can provide mnemonic traction for learning to persist. These devices, they hope, will not only promote student engagement but also motivate students from a variety of backgrounds to connect with the course material. Trudeau feels that their format provides students "a different way to project their voice" and hopes that they can make what is, for many, a difficult subject more accessible. Niman's personal website, where he has recorded much of his thinking in the genesis of this class, captures the rationale: "We believe that learning best takes place when it is part a co-created process. Students are no different from anyone else; they do not like to be told what to do. Rather, they are looking for assistance in reaching goals that *they* establish along a journey that takes them where *they* would like to go. They need the freedom to explore, a variety of pathways to choose from and the tools needed to help them succeed."

Niman's team developed the course during fall 2013 with user testing scheduled for November of that year. Unfortunately, staff turnover and Niman's competing responsibilities meant that user testing was delayed until 2014. The planned launch date for the class as a credit-bearing undergraduate first-year course was shifted to summer 2014. Student comments (integrated into the sections that follow) came from individuals on the development team who had taken the economics course in its ungamified versions rather than from students currently enrolled for credit.

The Rationale: Why Gamification?

Niman's elevator pitch on the course was that the learning experience is fueled by "the student's imagination on the framework we have created." Co-creation, the idea of story and story elements as used in many games, is the fundamental philosophical pillar to the model. He sees his role as the instructor of the modified course to be helping students develop their stories rather than "spoon-feeding" them fixed narratives or case studies that may not resonate. The idea of mnemonics and even whimsical memory prompts came to them in earlier work on helping students retain critical information. Trudeau recounted how she and Niman recorded a brief illustration of a key economics concept, "We went out and played tennis to explain the law of diminishing marginal returns. So it was very obvious, in that case, that the students' retention of that concept was helped by Jen looking like an idiot while playing tennis out on the tennis courts." Niman and Trudeau began to reflect that it would be more meaningful when the examples were self-generated by the students and then compared within the class. Emerging research into tools students are familiar with, like Facebook and other social media platforms, indicates that perceived value emerges from a co-created process that has the user learning more about themselves and their friends while enhancing feelings of belonging within a community of peers (Marandi, Little, & Hughes 2010). Niman's personal epiphany came when grading final papers for an executive MBA class, which he used as an opportunity to show a prospective MBA student that she was capable of participating in an academically rigorous company environment:

> I said to [student name], "You want to go check these [MBA papers] out." And it was a real learning experience for her, you know, because here are these executives' writing and what's the quality and how different are they? Are they really good? Or are they really bad? And it's by seeing what other people are doing that you say either, "Wow, I thought they'd be awesome and I would be so much further behind," or "I'm right at their level," or even, "I can do better than them." So it's all about relative comparisons, right? And seeing what other people are doing.

Niman framed the course around the notion of *relative position*, positing that people gain motivation, build self-esteem, and learn through their relationships with each other. He speculated that more effective motivators than points or badge systems, which he doesn't particularly see to be of value, would be students posting their thoughts and reflections of a more personal nature, knowing their fellow students would rate or "like" it in a manner that they are very familiar and comfortable with through their social media use.

Perhaps the most transformative element of their model was the idea that students with different skill sets may be able not only to coexist but also to support each other and encourage mutual discovery and learning. Encouraging fuller class participation through the provision of comfort or safe zones may be a key benefit of gamification, whatever the specific means and format that facilitate that end. Theorists such as Schell (2008) and Kapp (2012) perceive failing in games not to be stigmatizing (as is often the case in academia) but instructive. This removal or reduction of "fear of failure," at least hypothetically, encourages student participation and can make competition a more viable element. In the UNH model, Elizabeth Assaf, a sophomore studying business administration with a concentration in information systems management and marketing, illustrated the enthusiasm typical of members of Generation Y when sharing their personal narratives. "If the kid sitting next to you has an awesome story and really gets the concepts because he's made connections in ways that he can understand them and you have not and you know you have to present next week, that itself is competitive and game-like." Again, from the recent student perspective, Abigail Hahr, a sophomore majoring in economics and minoring in political science and justice studies (she is also involved in the development of the course), described her prior experience taking the traditional course in her first year:

> I was a freshman last year . . . it's a really daunting prospect walking into an economics course, but the thought of it being more game-like would make it less daunting. I can think, "OK I can do this, all I have to do is work through this game and I'm creating this and what I decide for my character to do will decide whether they succeed or not." I think it's less daunting—rather than seeing all of the scary concepts come at you all at once in a textbook this is more like working through them and giving you a better chance at grabbing them.

Elements of Gamification

Here is the description of the course as outlined for student participants:

> Learn economics as you write a story.

> Learning economics can be a challenge. Too many concepts are often applied in unrelatable contexts that have little meaning. EconJourney is designed to use the power of story to help students learn how to take complex ideas and apply them in ways that will make them understandable and memorable.

> The course is broken down into 12 stages. Each stage introduces the student to three important concepts. They encounter a challenge that must be overcome and writing prompts designed to help them think about how to use economics to gain insight into key events in their own life. Every four stages create a chapter and their final story will combine all three chapters into one coherent whole where they become the hero of their own story.

> By walking students through a logical thought process, it assists them in building associations between what appear to be a series of disconnected ideas. By

having them apply these concepts within the context of a story line that they develop, they begin to see their applicability toward solving a problem that is meaningful to them. In turn, it empowers them to think about change and the power of narrative as both a thought process and a means of communicating ideas in an understandable and engaging way.

A story-based approach to learning economic principles creates an educational process connected with a student's life and therefore is just one more extension of those daily activities that leads them to consider who they are and how they fit within the broader social fabric. The stories we tell about ourselves help us to establish a sense of self that can serve as the foundation for acquiring the knowledge and skills that lead to personal success both in the here and now as well as into the future.

As Niman reflected in conversation, games and literary narratives have been used to illustrate economic principles for a long, long time. He quotes William Breit and Kenneth Elzinga, who stated, "All good economic analysis is structured like classical detective fiction" (Breit and Elzinga 2002). Niman's twist is allowing the students to personalize the narrative. He refers to his students as "multi-modal consumers of information" and "storytellers who share their lives on a daily or even moment by moment basis." He is convinced that storytelling for Millennials (his current audience for the most part) is more important than for any prior generations, with perhaps the exception of Arthurian troubadours with their oral histories, as means of maintaining and perpetuating legend. Their stories, he postulates, are not merely entertainment or knowledge dissemination; they are actively being used to create a sense of identity and "place within a social fabric consisting of friends, relatives and peers." He feels that co-creation, as built on the work of Prahalad and Ramasawamy (2004), provides a means of encouraging mastery as a means to a more significant (for the participants) end. He encourages the students to take on the role of the hero in their own story. As he explains, "By adopting the role of the hero in the story, the student can establish an identity within the context of a story that can take on epic proportions, thereby contributing to a sense of self-esteem." He continues, "This explains, at least in part, why games are so attractive, relative to other activities, and can form the foundation for self-reinforcing activities." He feels that a more interdisciplinary focus in the class will empower students to achieve more than simply memorizing facts or terminology. If he can get his students to actually write well, utilizing key concepts and terminology, he feels that they will be better motivated to engage and better equipped to retain these concepts further down the line in their education and work life. As he states:

> The *EconJourney* process is about more than just a new way of learning economics. It is also about teaching students how to write, solve simple math problems and become analytical thinkers. It is about promoting creativity and (hopefully) that learning can be fun. It is also designed to place individual action within a social context; thereby helping students understand that a single individual can truly make a difference.

As a final justification, not that he felt he needed one, Niman touches on lecturing as a poor means of instruction. A 2010 survey indicated that close to 83% of class time is still spent lecturing despite the fact that many studies, including one by Walstad and Allgood, demonstrated that there was only a marginal difference in subsequent recollection of key information between a student that had taken an economics course and one that had not (1999). College seniors who had taken a class in economics scored 62% on a 15-question test, only 14% higher than students scoring 48% who had never taken an economics class in their life. The bar is disappointingly low.

Turning Students into Stakeholders

The development process for Niman's team was initially theoretical and therefore, by definition, platform-agnostic. Their early focus was on the elements and rationale rather than the precise mechanics of delivery. Developing with no fixed platform in mind was a contrast with the other cases in this study, where the realities and restrictions of available tools and platforms were uppermost in most teams' minds. Not being tied to a specific learning management system provided the team with the freedom to think more creatively. Niman fueled the development team with his assimilation of, and enthusiasm about, prior work connecting economics with mnemonic narrative. The distinguishing feature of the UNH project is that the model encourages student participants to develop their own narratives to better personalize the key elements that they need to remember. In his paper "The Hero's Journey: Using Story to Teach Economic Principles," Niman quoted Savitz and Tedford to provide more context on this perspective, "If you read between the lines, you'll discover that the entire Facebook platform is organized around the generation and amplification of stories" (Savitz and Tedford 2012, 21). This concept of going beyond the instructor-provided, culturally dated narrative is clearly captured in the succinct statement by Trudeau, Niman's (by most standards, young and connected) GA: "I'm 26 and my references are dated." Niman elaborates upon the need for personally resonant narrative, referencing Hawtrey: "It is about empowering students to identify pertinent content in order to create their own stories that are both relevant and meaningful for them" (2007, 143).

The Journey/Narrative

The UNH microeconomics journey, or EconJourney, involves a 12-step process with a challenge in each step (see figure 9). To overcome the challenges, the students need to use economic concepts explicated by "helping applications," "helping utilities," or other cues that help them learn to understand and apply the concepts. The process proceeds in two parallel lines, with one developing the story and the other the concepts. The gaming incorporates both the journey and sharing within the group through discussion forums. In these forums, students can compare stories and characters, voting for best, most creative, and the like.

Structurally, the story develops through a series of challenges. Meeting these challenges requires the students to develop an understanding of critical economics concepts. The system is organized in two synergistic tracks. In one the students are supported in developing a story or a narrative while, in the other, they are presented with explanation and illustration of key economics concepts. Niman, like many before him including George Lucas (*Star Wars* director), was influenced by the work of Joseph Campbell, the American mythologist, writer, and lecturer (1904–1987). In his most influential and most widely cited work, *The Hero with a Thousand Faces*, Campbell identifies the common features and plot similarities that are evident in hero narratives across the millennia, from ancient times to the present day. While there are many versions of the template for the "hero's journey" (with stages or steps ranging from just over half a dozen to three times that), Niman employed a format proposed by Christopher Vogler, author of a famous guide for screenwriters (*The Writer's Journey: Mythic Structure for Writers*) that lists twelve distinct stages. As figure 9 shows, the challenges are subdivided into specific, thematic categories bundled into three broad bands. After each band, stories are shared, and encouraging feedback is given.

The Journey consists of twelve stages. It has been broken down into thirds so that you can share your work and get feedback along the way. You can start by clicking on the first stage, or if you have already started, just click on the stage where you left off.

Figure 9. Screenshot: Initial draft interface for the UNH EconJourney course. Reproduced with permission of Neil Niman, University of New Hampshire.

Band one is bracketed under the heading "Setting the Stage." The four categories within this band are:

1. The Ordinary World—the hero is described in a familiar environment where they have been living, to a degree, in a state of ignorant bliss. Think Luke Skywalker on Tatooine in *Star Wars*, Simba as a baby lion in *The Lion King,* or Woody as a child's favorite toy in *Toy Story.*

2. The Call to Adventure—some shift occurs. Some catastrophic, or potentially catastrophic, event happens that really shakes up the blissful content of their (now former) life. The hero realizes that sitting back, doing nothing, is not really the right thing and starts to "overcome their ignorance," as Niman puts it, becoming a positive force for change. Think of Skywalker (*Star Wars,* again the obvious analogy) or Po the Panda in *Kung Fu Panda* (for the younger readers).

3. Avoiding (or Refusing) the Call—cold feet. In starting to understand the magnitude of what needs to be done, the hero develops dread and actually starts to step back from the challenge. She or he attempts to hold on to the past and wishes it had all never happened.

Think of any sports hero movie where the training is tough, the opponent is scary, or the odds against are high.

4. Acquiring Skills, Tools, and Knowledge, Meeting with the Mentor—the desire in the previous step to walk away is overcome by further recognition that if nothing is done, everything will be lost, and the future will be untenable. The scale of the problem and the understanding that there is no other option allows the hero to overcome his or her fear and persevere, through training and hardship, to acquire the skills to ultimately succeed. Traditionally an older, wiser mentor figure appears, sometimes by magic, and commits to training and educating the younger, naive hero. Think *Rocky*, Bruce Lee, *The Karate Kid*, or Winter the dolphin in *A Dolphin's Tale*.

The second band within the journey is titled "The Journey Begins."

5. Crossing the First Threshold—having got around all the prevarication and committed to saving (or finding or killing) something, the hero typically travels to a new environment to train and study the challenge while starting to hone potential solutions. The location provides a fresh perspective but reinforces the sense that if he or she doesn't act, everything, including this new place (not just the hero's own home base), will be destroyed. Thor coming to earth in the movie of the same name comes to mind without much specificity as to what he does or why.

6. Friends, Enemies, and Challenges—*Captain America: Civil War* has now defined this category for a new generation of cinemagoers. In this stage, as the hero continues preparation, friends become rivals or threats to his or her mission to save/find/kill someone or something. The hero has to persevere and keep learning, training, and developing ideas to eventually meet the ultimate challenge (often referred to in gaming parlance as *the boss battle*—more on this later).

7. Uncovering New Knowledge (or Approach to the Innermost Cave)—having made it through the preceding stages with much existential angst alongside tangible challenge, the hero develops a sense that the answer was somehow there all along. The veil of ignorance begins to fall away, and the hero begins to see that a solution and ultimate victory is possible after all. George Lucas cultivated his *Star Wars* characters so that they came to see the power of The Force and realized that all was not despair and doom.

8. Facing the Ultimate Challenge—typically something will come up that will threaten the whole episode—a late twist, a re-emergent threat or challenge that was considered already vanquished. The hero has to overcome this, hopefully, final challenge.

The third and final band is titled "The Road to Victory."

9. Formulating a Solution—having faced and conquered that ultimate challenge, the hero is now fully empowered and ready to return home and address the key threat.

10. Encountering One Last Challenge—as the hero nears home, one final challenge arises that produces one final seed of doubt as to whether the solution/training package is actually pointing at the truth and/or whether her or his solution really solves the problem. This confirmation check is often thought of as the final piece of the puzzle—the last lingering qualm assuaged, the certainty of a hero set in noble bronze.

11. Mysteries Revealed—an opportunity for reflection on how far the hero has come, how his or her doubts and insecurities have been peeled away, leaving a sense of certainty and a resolution to complete the task. Frequently a sense of "this is why I was chosen." A final girding of the loins before going into battle.

12. Celebrating Victory—in a magnanimous, calm sort of way, demonstrating humility and a suggestion of reluctant hero-hood, the hero returns home, slays the monster, and changes the world for the better.

Niman gives examples (beyond the pop culture *Star Wars* / *Kung Fu Panda* / *Toy Story* examples given) where authentic, real-world challenges could frame a hero's journey, including

- Climate change suddenly getting very serious, making the Earth basically uninhabitable;
- The exhaustion of all fossil fuels and conventional energy sources.
- Population explosion to an extent that the Earth cannot feed its inhabitants;
- A sudden dictatorship or emergence of megacorporations that enrich themselves at the expense of everyone else on the planet; *and*
- Some form of cyber-attack rendering all electronic devices inoperable (imagine the panic for the 19–22-year-old with this disaster).

Despite these examples, Niman still hopes that students will use the guiding framework to support the development of their own personal narrative stating, "We always intended to create some sort of forum where students will be able to share their writing initially within a smaller team then more widely with other students in the class." Despite this very student-centered nature of the activity, he obviously also wants students to be afforded the opportunity to share their narratives with their professor. Alongside the instructor's more considered, or academic, feedback, he hopes to generate more peer interaction asking questions along the lines of, "OK, so who had the best character?" Since the journey is broken into thirds, at the conclusion of each band there is an immediate opportunity for the students to pause on the core memorization of economics and instead, using the concepts and terminology they have reviewed, construct a story in three main sections (or twelve steps). These stories will get them feedback on both their grasp of the key terms but also on the excitement and vividness of their writing, their creativity, and their imagination. After each band, each student will award gold, silver, and bronze rankings to the three stories they thought were the best. The instructor, or his GAs, will convert the awards to points and post the leaders to a leaderboard under the hero's (rather than the student's) name. Through this format both social interaction and a degree of competitiveness will be built into the model.

At the end of the course the students will be directed to put the whole story together and will receive comprehensive feedback again on both aspects. Niman hopes that this social element, blended with supportive and constructive instructor feedback, will provide a richer source of encouragement that translates to increased student engagement and time-on-task. As an extra support, Niman employs "Storytellers" in the build. These recent graduates of the class provide culturally relevant, age-appropriate sample narratives so that, encouraged by their examples, the enrolled students will overwrite the provided examples with their own fully personalized narrative. The final, hyper-personalized context ultimately will serve as a mnemonic tool to help students weave economic concepts into a framework that they can recall when needed. After all the students complete their journey and share their full story with their "Journey Team," the top hero/ story from each subgroup will be labeled "Superheroes," and their stories will be shared via a blog that the entire class will review before voting to determine the class "Ultimate Hero." The professor will retain the authority to elevate stories that he considers of special merit to contend for the final recognition.

Trudeau connected their model to a direct gaming format, contextualizing the Millennial student's comfort with the evolving story format: "There are many different types of games. There are the massive multiplayer role-playing games (MMORPGs) that are story-based. The story is evolving and you have to do these tasks within the story and eventually there's some outcome that you get to at the end, which is, I think, very much what we're trying to do except that we're having them create the story that is evolving."

Her own illustrative example comes from current pop culture, "The *Hunger Games* trilogy has a lot of economic underpinnings in it so when I read it I sunk my teeth into it . . . it's politics and economics and we're dealing with scarcity and how people are fighting with it. If you sit down and read it, you can make the connection."

Niman is comfortable with this construct, when many other instructors perhaps are not. Certainly, students in this kind of environment have a greater degree of autonomy than would be seen in a didactic lecture environment. As focus in academia has sharpened on student-centered learning (SCL), his work seems well aligned with the core principles of this approach:

- Students solve problems, answer questions, formulate questions of their own, discuss, explain, debate, or brainstorm throughout the learning experience.
- Students are presented with or collaboratively formulate big-picture challenges for themselves that frame and motivate their learning. These are real-world-applied, significant challenges that require a multifaceted approach to resolve.
- Active involvement and participation are necessary for learning.

Niman again quotes Prahalad and Ramaswamy, "Co-creation as a part of learning is not about ceding control of the educational process to the student, nor is it about joint knowledge creation, rather it is about creating an experience environment in which students can have an active dialogue and co-construct personalized experiences that will facilitate the learning process" (2004, 9). Summarizing, Niman adds, "It is about creating an environment where a student can take abstract constructs and turn them into relatable concepts that have meaning for them."

Cooperation

In the EconJourney class, each student is randomly assigned to a team termed the Journey Team. Each team will consist of at least six students, with each working independently on their story, completing initial elements including their hero character and their own unique context. Following every fourth step of the journey (see figure 9), students will upload their work to a Journey Team blog and will be required to review the progress of their teammates. In this collaborative phase, each team member will be asked to award gold, silver, and bronze rankings to the top three in their team. Niman conveyed the possible value of class participation by noting, "What might be the most effective piece of the learning experience is not necessarily creating your own story but seeing the other stories that students in the class have created."

Competition

Niman's personal philosophy on the value of competition is captured in this quote, "Whether it is against other players, some performance standard or an imaginary opponent, competition often brings out the best in each of us." The narratives in the class are posted to the class leaderboard under the individual hero's name. Positions on the board are not directly grade-related and so run no risk of violating federal privacy guidelines. When all heroes have completed the journey and shared their stories with their team, the highest-ranking individual narratives will be labeled "Superheroes" and will be posted to the main collaborative area where the entire class will review and vote for their "Ultimate Hero." Individuals whose heroes did not make it to the final competition can submit their completed narrative to the professor, who may choose additional contenders, thus ensuring that those who thoughtfully connect narrative and key economic concepts can get recognized. This kind of in-class peer competition is not intended to produce grade pressure (or a pressure to succeed) but rather to lead to the development of self-esteem when stories are shared in a safe environment and other students like or recognize each other's work. Although there may be students whose work is neither graded well nor upvoted in the narrative/journey side of the equation, the extra means of recognition suggest that all students have a greater range of possibilities for gaining esteem through either their economics understanding, their creativity, or other elements that the instructor chooses to recognize.

Technical Build

In fall 2013, Niman's team was empowered (but also arguably limited) by the lack of platform and technological specifications that they had in place. UNH, as part of the state system, runs the Blackboard learning management system. Even as the course was always likely to be connected to the larger institutional system, Niman was comfortable linking out to other development platforms they might end up using. He consciously encouraged thinking outside the box, and so his team's language was creative yet lacking detail in terms of concrete implementation:

> We'll have some sort of notes section where they can type notes to themselves and dump that into a database, and then they can pull that up at any time so they don't have to remember these things. So at the end of this sort of brainstorming stage we're talking about, they'll have a button that will call up the choices they've made. We had started with Wordpress, the blog developing software, but for the ideas we had [as a team] we felt that it wouldn't support our needs—we wanted to have a database behind a dynamic site.

Student Reaction

Samantha-Jo Virga, a junior economics major at UNH, commented on the importance of personalized content in the hero's journey model and the potential that it may have for retention of information. Her comments were based on her own academic experience and the development team's discussions, "That article that your teacher says, 'Read this'—am I going to retain it a year later? I doubt it. But if you're making your own story that's kind of cool so you're going to . . . I would assume, remember it—bits and pieces at least." She wondered whether the instructor role would change in this less instructor-didactic, more student-centric environment:

> That's hard to say—it could change a lot of things. As it stands, I feel like unless you get to know your instructor well the roles are really separate. They're the faculty, you're the student. In this model I would hope that the student gets more passionate about the materials and maybe . . . you would get more discussion and debate about the stories. So perhaps the instructor does become more of a coach—more of a guide—rather than throwing information at you and then just seeing if you do well on the exams.

Elizabeth Assaf, a sophomore who acted as pilot tester and "Storybuilder" on Niman's team, reflected on the potential for the model to allow participants to go beyond their usual classroom persona—something that is particularly useful if they are labeled, either by themselves or institutionally, as an under-achiever. "It's the concepts of gaming, creating that experience where you're playing that character that might not essentially be who you are, but it might be who you want to be. So if you're striving academically to be the person you want to be, academic standards-wise, and you're creating that experience to get there then it could be completely different from the usual pass or fail in this classroom." As a self-declared high achiever, Assaf is self-aware enough to know that she does not necessarily represent all students who will be tak-ing this entry-level economics class. This was a theme shared by almost all of the student-developers: that there will be students in the EconJourney class who are there because they have to be rather than because they want to be. Although aware of differing student types, the team did not manipulate the design for particular subgroups, feeling that all students would benefit from the gamification. According to Assaf, "Some students are there because they have to be there. We want to take that and make it so every kind of student finds some type of interest in this program and is willing to put in even a tiny bit of knowledge and work. Even among the high achievers there are a lot of students who think, 'I'll memorize this and then forget about it.'"

Outcomes

Niman is comfortable speaking of the EconJourney model as a gamified course while distancing himself from what he perceives as the norm for gamified courses. He distinguished between courses that have some added game elements versus those that have been fully gamified, stating, "The whole approach is sort of a gamified approach where, just as in a game, I cre-ate an avatar, I develop a character, the character builds skills, the character has experiences, they overcome challenges, they see how they are growing and progressing, and they feel good about themselves. I mean, that's gamifi-cation more than just giving someone a badge or something like that."

When discussing elements such as cooperation, competition, and recogni-tion, the UNH team conceives of these coming as embedded elements in the course rather than as the instructor granting awards or badges. This approach fits with the open nature of their narrative (student-led) and their idea of co-creation to engender buy-in and mnemonic retention of information. Recognition by virtue of social/peer approval also reflects mechanisms such as "liking" in Facebook, accruing approval from peers on platforms and implementing tools used by the target demographic for this course. Millennial students tend to be, in Niman's experience, more comfortable sharing informal feedback in a social media–like environment than they are formally assessing their peers academically.

A third part of the model that Niman feels could have great value is the potential for social support to reduce failure anxiety. He feels that reducing fear of anxiety could be of particular value for less-confident learners, such as first-generation college attendees or fragile learners: "Many students seem to be more interested in managing risk than achieving success. Whether they are trying to prevent losing points on an exam, looking foolish answering a question in class or selecting easy rather than difficult courses to take, it is more about averting losses than gaining success. The EconJourney process is designed to build students up so that that they are more willing to take a risk and try to learn something new. It is about replacing fear with achievement."

The development team hopes that the blend of mnemonic aid and additional student-generated context will stimulate dialogue, encourage sharing, and allow the fun context of the activities to counteract the more typically daunting atmosphere of the economics environment for non-economics/math majors.

Although the team emphasizes encouraging creative, non-logic/non-math-minded students in the milieu of economics, an associated benefit is that their model is likely to encourage logic/math-minded economics majors to think and write creatively. This serendipitous bonus is something that may help science majors whose only writing training typically comes in general education English and social studies classes that are often forgotten when students get back to their science or math-based coursework.

Niman summarizes the potential for his gamified format to develop competencies beyond those usually emphasized in an economics or STEM course, "We're trying to do more than just teach economics. So there will be a lot of critical reasoning to overcome these challenges and certainly to develop the students' stories. There's also a big focus on writing and communication skills so we're trying to sort of cover all of that. Writing isn't an add-on in the class, writing is an integral part of the class."

As institutions face increasing pressure to confirm teaching effectiveness and tangible student output competencies, the cross-disciplinary, interwoven nature of Niman's format merits encouragement. If he is able to increase the presentation skills of economics majors, develop the capacity of non–math majors to grasp central concepts of microeconomics, or even just generally improve student engagement, then his model will be validated. This potential is certainly uppermost in Niman's mind, as illustrated in his paper, "The Gamification of Higher Education: Designing a Game-Based Business Strategy in a Disrupted Marketplace," in which he comments, "We are failing our students. Some think it is because the material we teach is not very relevant for today's economy. Others think it is because something fundamental has shifted and, as a result, learning styles are no longer in step with the way higher education is delivered. I think it is because we have not engaged students in a way that has made their educational experience a personal one with demonstrable benefits and a clear rationale for how it is going to make them more successful."

When asked about the motivation and need for a new model such as this, Trudeau stresses the potential long-term value, "There are not many jobs now where you go and sit in a room by yourself—it's very much collaborative and working with others—so if you need to get your point across, this may be another way to articulate the numbers story in a different way." In a final reflection, Niman alludes to the potential for extension of his concepts to wider audiences:

> I could see this format as an add-on to a traditional class or it might be a substitute for a traditional class . . . might be something that somebody just wants to do. Our thought is just to build the site and make it available to anybody and everybody. In future iterations, we may target someone who is sitting in their living room who is not part of a degree program at all. They may be attracted to one, any or all aspects of the project, "I'm creative, I'd like to write a story and I'd like to learn a little economics in the process."

Given the low completion rates of online courses—particularly MOOCs—a hero's journey model such as the one being developed by the UNH team would have to fulfill only a small portion of its potential to merit further study. Trudeau's summary is appropriate in its scope and encouraging in its conviction, "I think if you can get students more interested [in academic content], be it through competition, self-discovery, better examples or whatever, you can only make the learning experience a better one. I've stood in front of the class and seen the people who are enjoying it and getting it and comparing that to those who just don't care. Finding a new strategy to get those students to care is . . . attractive. I'm hopeful that it will kind of make the subject matter more accessible to a broader population."

Where Are They Now?

On May 17, 2016, I spoke with Niman to see where he had got to with the EconJourney project. My questions were, How has the project evolved? Has it grown or atrophied at the institution?

BELL—So Neil, thanks for taking my call. I'm wondering if you could fill me in on the two years since we reviewed the EconJourney project together back in 2013–14.

NIMAN—This past year we were doing EconJourney 2.0 and we've got some really interesting ideas we're going to implement over the summer to create version 3.0. With EconJourney we did it in a single class. We focused more on sort of telling a story rather than learning economics, we didn't really implement any of the games stuff well, and we didn't really know what we were doing, so it was sort of a disaster.

Then we sort of cleaned it up a little bit and ran it again and had a lot more success. Part of it was we knew what we were doing, and we'd made some pretty fundamental changes and restructured the content. The students were really receptive to it, and that sort of spurred us to come up with version 2.0. We did a total site redesign, so the look and feel was entirely different, and a lot of the content was different. You know, we had gone into the project design with great enthusiasm but didn't really think of it from the student perspective. They didn't want to read anything, and they don't want to click on anything. They just want to do as little as possible and the key question became, "How can we better engage them?" Version 2.0 is focusing on changing the way we presented the material, by creating a more linear design in the site and better specifying what our expectations are and what they [the students] need to do.

And so now we're doing version 3.0. We've been focused on getting the content down, and now we have a better idea of what content we need. We're going to continue to refine the content and add game elements that don't exist. We redid the challenges so now they tell a story and serve as an example of what it is we expect the students to write. We're creating a more engaging story, but now we're going to add some agency where the students can pick different forks in the story so that they feel more part of things. Then at the end of the story, they're going to be able to pick what happens and choose (we haven't figured out what we're calling it yet) a talent or a skill that the character in the story develops. This will earn the equivalent of a badge, and they'll be asked to use that in their stage writing. Then at the end it's sort of like a personality test, where we'll tell them the twelve character-istics, traits or talents that they identified and what it means. So that it's sort of this New Age, self-help kind of thing, while at the same stage [they] sort of learn economics . . . and we continue to hope that they draw a better connection be-tween the character that they're writing about and their own perceptions of them-selves. This is getting back to that "changing mindset" stuff that we were working on a couple of years ago. We are embracing that and looking at the semester (and at each stage) as a series of interventions that hopefully at the end empowers them to think that this validated their character make a difference so that they can make a difference too.

BELL—What you're saying is that the original (1.0 version) was too loosely structured? Allowed the students too much freedom of choice and movement?

NIMAN—The first version we took kind of a sandbox approach, "Here's a sandbox and a bucket and you go build a sandcastle." The students were like, "Well I've never seen a sandcastle and don't know how to do a sandcastle," or "I can't decide." We dis-covered that they need more guidance than that, so we put more structure into the site, but we're still trying to slip things in without them realizing it. And the content we redeveloped and rewrote to try to make it more engaging, snappier, and briefer. We're trying to give them a little more structure, so now we give them writing prompts. In fact, we went [in 2.0] too far the other direction. We gave them very specific writing prompts, and all they did was take them and essentially turn them into a series of essay questions. The students shifted to, "well I'll just answer the writing prompt," rather than thinking about how the writing prompt was intended to nudge them and to get them to think what to write. So in version 3.0 we're throwing away all the existing writing prompts, and we've come up with a new way of envisioning how we're going to get them to pull out concepts and use the con-cepts in their writing.

The part I forgot to mention is this past year we've used version 2.0, and we have had a tremendous amount of success. In the fall we used it in a class of two hundred, and I had an instructor teach two sections of a hundred students in each. One sec-tion used a formal publisher's e-text and support materials, and in the other section he used EconJourney. The lectures were exactly the same, the exams were exactly the same, everything was the same except a difference in the electronic learning platforms. What we discovered was that students didn't perform any worse on the exams using EconJourney than they did using the formal publisher's e-text and sup-port materials. In terms of preference, students didn't strongly prefer one over the other, and so we were feeling really good about that, as I don't know how many millions of dollars were spent developing [the formal publisher's e-text and support materials], but we spent, I don't know, a few hundred bucks, three weeks of my wife's time, and whatever time I put in developing the content. So it goes to show, we didn't see any difference in learning outcomes whatsoever, and the students were equally satisfied without having to spend tens of millions of dollars. Then we used it again last semester and ran the same experiment, but the professor used a different [formal publisher's] e-text and support materials instead of the previous publisher's e-text and support materials. As far as she can tell (the students just took their final exams on Friday), throughout the semester EconJourney students did equally as well on the standard exams.

So we did this semester to see if hopefully EconJourney is yielding better results on what we really care about because the questions were sort of standard multiple-choice questions, the kind you would see in a mindless economics class—nothing special. It occurred to me that in EconJourney, we're hoping to improve their writing ability, and we're hoping to get them to think critically and to get them to use the concepts in a meaningful and relevant way. So what we did this semester (and we're grading them as we speak) is, in addition to the multiple-choice exam we wrote a special EconJourney question. We gave them a couple of paragraphs of text and asked them to pull out econ concepts and use them in a meaningful way. So we're about to evaluate how the students did in those terms, and what we're hoping is that in the "plain Jane vanilla" economics exams EconJourney students don't do any worse. But [we hope] in terms of something that asks them to use the concepts in a meaningful way, that they do a lot better, and we'll have those results in a week or two.

Something else that we're going to do is we're going to reach back to those students who took the class in the fall semester and ask them to take an exam and to see if the EconJourney kids retain their knowledge of economics any better than they do with the formal publisher's e-text and support materials kids—that's something that we want to test.

And then what's really exciting, or nerve-wracking, is when we roll out version 3.0 next fall we'll have 650 students, using EconJourney 3.0.

BELL—Can you tell me where you went with the tech platform? It was very basic in the pilot, and it was something you had said you wanted to work on.

NIMAN—We're still using WordPress. We've found ways to make the platform more powerful so the students move through levels. They can follow a progress bar, and we've set it up so they can get immediate feedback, so we've been able to do a lot more with the WordPress environment. So we're still staying in the WordPress environment, and, in fact, one of the papers that I'd really like to write if I ever get free time is how WordPress can be used in this way with this whole movement for open educational resources. The one big impediment in the way is, well, if you want some sort of electronic learning platform to support some open resource, you'll find the major publishers have a stranglehold on that. Basically, you move[d] away from the environment where they charge for the textbook and threw the software in for free, and now they're charging for the software and throw the textbook in for free. So what we're trying to do is we're trying to say, "Hey—we'll give you a template, we'll show you how to build your own Journey platform and you can do this for relatively few dollars," and really eliminate the last barrier to entry that the textbook companies have to maintain their stranglehold on the market.

So this summer I've hired a graduate student to develop an Eco-Journey (as in ecology, not economics), and I've hired an undergrad to help him build that and document everything that's done so that at the end of the summer we could basically distribute a guide that says to other faculty and even other institutions, "Hey, if you want to develop your own journey approach, here's how to do it."

BELL—That's great. Before we wrap, I'd like to talk to you about a second project that has sparked off at UNH, something that you described to me back in 2013 as your ultimate goal, and what you saw as an expression of gamification's massive potential on a campus-wide implementation. Can we talk about that?

NIMAN—Well, I think that that might merit a separate chapter all to itself. Do you want to come back to that later—say, chapter 9?

BELL—Sounds great. See you there.

■ ■ ■ ■ ■ ■ ■ ■ ■ ■ ■ ■ ■ ■

CHAPTER FIVE

Ethical Decision Making

The University of Waterloo (UW), established in 1957, is a public research, co-ed university with its main campus in Waterloo, Ontario, Canada. It has a reputation as one of the leading proponents of cooperative education, placing over 19,000 of its 27,000 undergraduate students with over 5,200 employers annually. It was founded with the goal of educating the engineers and technicians Canada needed for its postwar development. UW's second chancellor cultivated the system, blending classroom, academic study with industry training, forming the basis of the co-op program. Its location in a key region, in what is referred to as Canada's Technology Triangle, has provided both opportunity and impetus to support and populate fledgling startups and growing businesses, all in a synergistic relationship with what has been called one of the top economic development organizations in Canada. Through its Research and Technology Park on its North Campus, businesses are granted access to the university's faculty, co-op students, and alumni as well as use of the university's facilities and resources. Among over 160,000 graduates are John Baker, founder of Desire2Learn, and Mike Lazaridis, cofounder of the company that became BlackBerry Ltd. The school is proud of its reputation that its faculty, students, and alumni have formed more companies than any other Canadian university, a reputation that has seen the university labeled "the Silicon Valley of the North." Canadian citizens and permanent residents pay between C$9,000 and C$15,000 for tuition and books, with international students and nonpermanent residents paying more than double that. There is a C$658 co-op fee, and housing and meals have to be added to the above fees.

UW's institutional openness to the possibilities of gamification was publically demonstrated when it hosted the 2013 Gamification conference. This was the second time that the university had hosted this event, a conference that brings together academic researchers and industry leaders to engage in discussions and demonstrations of gamification in health care, marketing, education, and entertainment. All told, around three hundred attendees from all sectors of business and academia participated, including a broad range of nationalities from beyond the United States and Canada.

The Rationale: Why Gamification?

The Waterloo Professional Development (WatPD) core at UW was developed by the faculty to support the experiential learning of the university's co-op students. The format of WatPD, online courses in topics related to their real-world experience, allows students to continue to engage with the institution while they are "out" immersed in their co-op. The central idea is that these fully online, credit-bearing courses will allow students to arm themselves against, or react to, real-world challenges. They provide students with the opportunity to develop skills that UW faculty and administrators feel will improve their subsequent employability and workplace productivity. The courses have always included an element of constructivism—asynchronous discussion areas created to encourage students to reflect on connections between the workplace, their academic courses, and their career path. UW's own literature describes the program as emblematic of "Waterloo's commitment to innovation in teaching, technology, and co-operative education." The overall objectives of the WatPD program are listed as:

- To enhance the overall work-integrated learning experience of co-op students by providing engaging and relevant online courses to improve students' employability and workplace productivity.
- To promote the integration of what is learned at work with what is learned during academic terms through critical reflection.
- To enable peer learning and foster a sense of community among co-op students.

The WatPD program has four required courses and eight electives. Ethical Decision Making PD9 (figure 10) is one of the electives. These courses are designed to be concrete and succinct, intended to take students between 20 and 25 hours to complete including time spent reading, watching, and listening to course content and completing course assessments. Students who self-reported through surveys (with an impressive 75% completion rate averaged across courses) confirmed 20 to 25 hours of work during the 10 weeks that the course runs. The fact that the WatPD courses are available for students to take while they are actually placed at their co-op during a "work-term," as

UW calls it, allows them immediately to apply the knowledge they are gaining to the work environment. The courses include assessments and formative (instructor) feedback on individual assignments, quizzes, tests, and exercises. The final grade in the course is binary, submitted to the registrar's office as either a CR (credit) or NCR (no credit) and appearing on students' transcripts in that format. UW administrators feel that these courses do not require a proctored final exam, as plagiarism is not felt to be a major risk given the clear participation benefits and fairly low academic requirements for the students. The official course description for Ethical Decision Making reads,

> Borrowing from philosophy, game theory and economics, this course equips co-op students with both theoretical and practical knowledge needed to make ethical decisions in an ever-changing and increasingly competitive workplace. How we act will affect others. And insofar as our actions affect the well-being of others, ethics has something to say about how we conduct ourselves. A basic assumption of the course is that interests and incentives drive human behavior. With a clear understanding of how interests and incentives affect the decisions people make, students will be better prepared to navigate the complexities of ethical decision making in the workplace.

Greg Andres is an assistant professor in philosophy and instructional support coordinator at UW. He develops courses for the WatPD program taken by approximately 16,000 students each year. Andres discussed how his interest in gamification developed from experiences in his face-to-face classes and transitioned to his online class Ethical Decision Making:

> In lectures, on campus, I started using i-clickers just to encourage attendance and participation—and it's incentivized so they get—well, this term it's 15% [of their final grade]. If they come to class and answer 75% of the questions they get 15% just for sitting in the seat. I teach a lot of the concepts by just having games, and I have them play against me. They're usually just game theory games, so there are two decisions to be made, two players: here are the outcomes, use your i-clicker, how would you play it? It works beautifully. In the lecture, I ask a question, "How many of you are familiar and understand the prisoner's dilemma?" And they are all very confident (80%), "Yeah, we know how to play." "Alright, let's play a game." And the majority of students play irrationally, so it's like—in what sense? You highlight that disconnect—you think you know how to play, let's talk about it. Then I thought, "That's got to work online," and it was just a hunch, in an online context, this has . . .

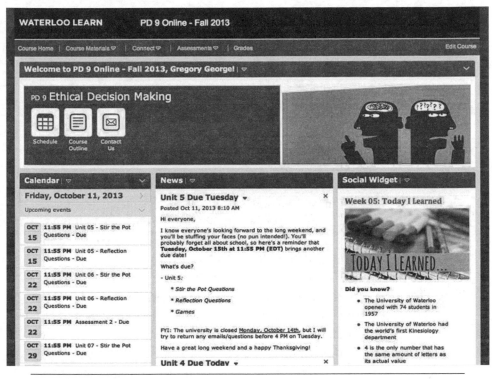

Figure 10. Screenshot: University of Waterloo Ethical Decision Making course. Reproduced with permission of Greg Andres, University of Waterloo.

something similar has to work. We can take the course concepts and not just have them passively, you know, listen to it or read it, but, "Here's a game, let's play it."

Andres explained that the flexibility of games allows him to provide new situations where students can apply course concepts. UW is known for the emphasis it places on co-op programs. On the UW website, a statement on "The Mission of Co-operative Education" emphasizes that the program is designed to "inspire uWaterloo students to connect to the possibilities in a continuously changing world of work; enable them to bridge their academic and workplace knowledge; challenge them to learn, grow, and contribute wherever they go."

Andres believes there are aspects of gaming that clearly motivate and engage gamers and resonate with the goals and aspirations of co-operative education. As students take his course while active on co-op, he is hopeful that the embedded games and game elements ameliorate the jarring contrast between the lived experience of the real workplace and that of school. There are certainly elements emphasized in the literature on experiential education (Kolb 1984) that would seem to overlap with skills needed to perform well in a gaming environment. The need to think quickly in rapidly changing situations, the ability to make informed decisions, and the opportunity to receive immediate, corrective feedback are all key elements of experiential learning that gaming advocates would find familiar. Other elements of experiential environments, including competition for rewards and penalties or stigma for failure, are also not uncommon in both real-world and virtual games.

Ethical Decision Making: The Gamified WatPD Course

The objectives of the Ethical Decision Making course specifically (as opposed to the general WatPD program aims mentioned earlier) include building an understanding of ethical issues in the workplace and fostering students' ability to take personal responsibility in group contexts.

The course has three types of assessments. Nine units with short-answer questions are worth 27% of the final grade. Three long-answer assessments are worth 55% of the final grade. This leaves 18% of the final grade that is carried by the gamification elements contained in the nine units, for a total of 45 games at five games per unit. The gamified elements are designed to be nonpunitive, rewarding participation rather than success (e.g., "the right answer"). To pass the course, a student must receive an overall grade of at least 50%, meaning that any student could hypothetically skip the gamified elements and still receive a CR grade. Notably, none of the students does.

Elements of Gamification

Andres's course applies the term "to gamify" quite esoterically, based primarily on the instructor's personal interests rather than through any sustained analysis of game elements. Andres uses subject-related quiz games and gamification elements, including a leaderboard, and is considering other elements to increase student engagement. The games are actually scenarios based on quite traditional course content, with no heroes or narratives layered on top. The instructor discusses the games that are embedded in the course content:

> The games are the type of games that you would find in any game theory text. Each game consists of a brief setup (a scenario or some type of story), a description of who they are playing against, two choices and the outcomes of their choices. They are then asked to make a choice based on their ethical values (worldview, or what-

ever you want to call it). They play against me in most of the games (well, against a programmed version of me). There is also a leaderboard. Each student sees their individual ranking, but only the top 10 are displayed for everyone to see.

The Centre for Extended Learning (CEL) team at UW supported the build of the platform as envisioned by Andres. As Mark Stewart, the CEL instructional digital media developer, described it,

> Greg worked with an online learning consultant and a course developer here at CEL to flesh out his request. Once the concept was nailed down, the development team was brought in to work out the technical details and start the build process. This process took a long time as both teams had to educate each other on what was needed and what was possible, especially in the time frame. This was a custom build that would have to be done from the ground up. We used MySQL, PHP, Javascript, json, and HTML to bring these games to life.

The Leaderboard

Andres built the leaderboard so that all participants retained the option to remain anonymous or have their name displayed based on personal preference. The nature of the course, the way the game elements are graded (that is, students receive points for any sort of serious attempt), and the ability for students to remain anonymous, Andres felt, would protect the UW team from privacy concerns. Figure 11 shows the leaderboard distinguishing students who chose to remain anonymous and those who elected to be visible in the course (their names are blocked out here to protect the innocent).

Game Scenarios

The games are related to course content, but they can be taken independently and do not need team or cohort synchronicity (i.e., everyone doing the same thing at the same time) to complete. The students are presented with a scenario directly embedded in the Canvas LMS (figure 12), and are asked to make an ethically informed judgment call based on their understanding of readings and materials provided by the instructor.

As an example, the dilemma presented in figure 12 raises a question of whether the student in a job-hiring situation would allow a potential employer access to his or her Facebook profile. The student in this scenario has a fairly clean profile, with few embarrassing posts or pictures. Another job candidate, known personally to the student, has a Facebook profile with evidence

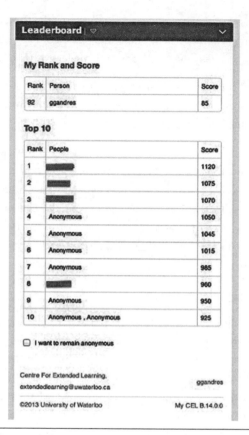

Figure 11. Screenshot: Leaderboard for the UW Ethical Decision Making course. Reproduced with permission of Greg Andres, University of Waterloo.

of a more hedonistic lifestyle. The question is whether the student would make the ethical decision to grant the employer access to his Facebook page. She knows that in doing so, she would be making it difficult for the other candidate to say no, hence exposing his personal foibles. Having made their choice in the scenario (figure 13), students receive immediate feedback that is intended to provoke further thought and discussion rather than simply stating that a choice was right or wrong.

Instructor Feedback

As suggested in figure 14, Andres rarely provides an absolute response, preferring to encourage discussion with the aim of getting the students to continue reflecting on the issues after the coursework is complete.

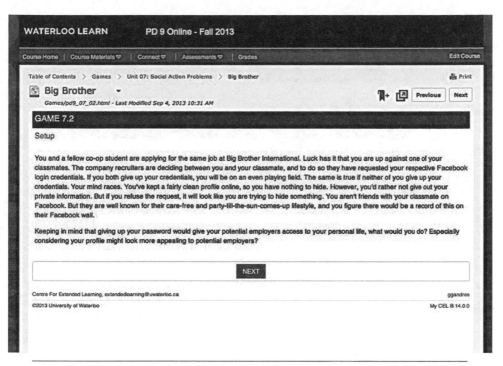

Figure 12. Screenshot: Game 7.2 setup in the UW Ethical Decision Making course. Reproduced with permission of Greg Andres, University of Waterloo.

Given the way the course content is built out, individuals can overzealously race ahead and complete all game elements. Doing so provides the short-term boost of topping the leaderboard—the "look at me!" factor, as Andres terms it. Yet this phenomenon of racing ahead also limits the opportunity to build peer interaction in the games and game elements. Conversation on discussion boards in online education tends to flag if students are not moving lock-step through the materials. Andres recalls the lack of high-quality discussion about the scenarios as a disappointment. "So they play the game and there's a moral in the story (usually conveyed in his feedback) and I was hoping that this would translate into discussion board discussions, but not so much."

One exception to the general lack of discussion-board activity was in connection to one game scenario where, ironically, a lack of clarity (arguably, poor instructional design) provoked interactivity. Andres explains, "There was some discussion on the discussion boards—not as much as I'd wanted. There was one particular game that they were annoyed with. They were like,

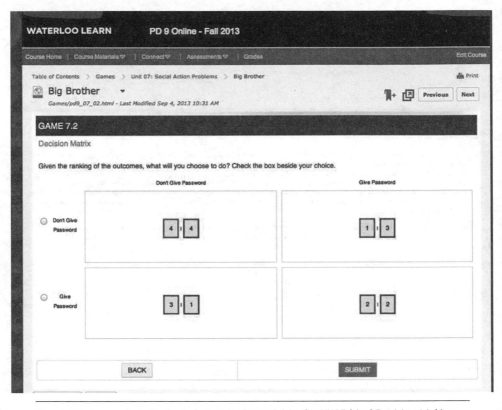

Figure 13. Screenshot: Student choices in Game 7.2 in the UW Ethical Decision Making course. Reproduced with permission of Greg Andres, University of Waterloo.

'What's the point of it?' So I was like, 'Here's the point,' and they were like, 'Oh, OK.' But of course I made the games so that they are kind of vexing, so it frustrates some, and it's like, 'Now you're irritated and frustrated, now you're ready to listen.'"

Andres felt that the leaderboard could be a solid motivator for some students but would have worked better if the activities and events that generate points had been sequenced to prevent "reading ahead." Andres dug into this issue when he asked the students for feedback after the course had been completed. "Within two weeks of the course, four people had played all of the games, and I asked them, 'Why? Why is this?' And they said, 'So we'd be top of the leaderboard.'"

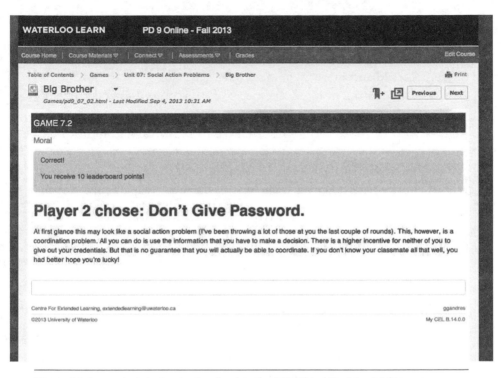

Figure 14. Screenshot: Instructor feedback in the UW Ethical Decision Making course. Reproduced with permission of Greg Andres, University of Waterloo.

Outcomes

The students playing the games are briefly engaged (for 5 to 10 minutes) by each game scenario with no real sense of progression or suggestion of increasing degrees of difficulty. Even though student engagement on discussion boards was spotty at best, Patrick Laytnera (a former student in the class) referenced the leaderboard as a motivator to monitor progress among peers in the class. "For the most part it's you against the system, the system being Greg (the instructor). Usually it's just . . . you pick your answer and it has its answer tucked away and based on your answer you get points or not. The games add a competitive element so you get more involved in the course. Since it's an online course, you don't have any interaction other than computers, so this pulled you into the course."

When asked whether this kind of course might work better for certain types of students, Laytner replied, "I think especially (for) students who aren't engaged in the content. Professional development courses tend to have a fair number of students who just want to do the bare minimum, get the credit, and then drop it (or not drop it but stop working on it). I think that the games could encourage them to stay engaged."

It is worth bearing in mind the specific nature of Andres's class population: working students looking for resources and hoping (or having) to stay engaged with the university while distanced from the campus in real-world co-ops. Laytner suggests that there is a real temptation for students to do the bare minimum to get the *CR* (credit received) box checked without a great deal of effort or learning. Yet none of the course participants skipped the gamified elements. Andres believes that the game elements—combined with, I would say, his experimentation and enthusiasm—increased engagement with the course. Also noteworthy is the fact that Andres won the Waterloo Arts Teaching Award for 2013, thus earning institutional recognition for his energy and creativity.

Andres reports that, from the course that ran in September 2013, the majority of the 38 students responding to the survey (out of 221, an admittedly low survey-completion rate) stated "We find these games engaging and fun" (62%) and "These games are helping us understand the course core concepts" (71%).

Andres realizes that the experiment is in its early stages. He is confident that "with over 200 students per term, there will be a lot of data for me to mine. My ultimate goal is to analyze the data to see if the games actually succeed as a teaching tool."

The games and the leaderboard provide a rudimentary gamification theme to the course, although Andres' interest in the field means that he is always primed to add features that he reads about in the work of practitioners. At the 2013 UW gamification conference, he informally shared his interest in implementing a *spotlight* feature in the course as a contrast to the exclusively meritocratic leaderboard so as to highlight a qualitative achievement of the instructor's choosing. Examples of spotlight awards could be the student who improved the most during the past week or someone who suddenly has achieved something particularly challenging. This approach, he hopes, will help build community and encourage the class as a whole to work toward a common goal.

Institutional Embrace of the Gamified Course

Having decided to gamify his course, Andres pitched the concept to both his academic supervisor, the vice provost of academic affairs, and the UW tech team. The concept was received enthusiastically on the technical side in the form of eager agreement to help him build his game elements. As he describes it, when he discussed his ideas with the manager of the CEL, his enthusiasm was palpable, "He sat back in his chair and he said, 'If we can pull this off, it'll be brilliant.' They had never done anything else like this before, so they took it on as a challenge too."

In terms of the academic, rather than the technical, permission to develop the course, Andres reflects, "I asked my boss, Anne Fallon (the vice provost of academic affairs)—I pitched it to her and she loved it, and she said, 'Just run with it.' So I ran with it, and later she did come back and said to me, 'Um— can you just explain for me the rationale—just so that if the associate provost does come back to me then I can say, yes, this is the motivation.' But no one at co-op, no one in the provost's office has come back to us . . . So now it's just pure academic freedom!"

Fallon describes some initial trepidation but indicates general institutional encouragement of Andres's initiative in the form of technical support and public endorsement:

> I wouldn't say that I had concerns with including gamified elements in the course, but I did have concerns about how they were implemented. It was important to me that the games included some sort of reflective piece and that students were clear why the games existed and how they were augmenting their learning. I also had concerns with the leaderboard. I didn't want students to feel the need to compete with each other. The compromise for the leaderboard was to implement a feature that allowed students to earn points while playing anonymously.

As with many gamification projects, the elements have been infused into what is, to all intents and purposes, a "regular" catalogued course. Andres's course seems to have been protected by the blanket coverage of academic freedom to teach a course as the faculty member sees fit. Fallon further comments, "The course was not vetted at the senior academic level. The catalog description does not include reference to games. The games evolved as the course was being developed." Clearly, Fallon and UW's interest in gamification as a concept and their desire to demonstrate UW as an industry leader supported Andres's desire to experiment with the format. UW is unique in this study, as it is the only example among the four cases that supplied any level of institutional academic endorsement for the instructor's project.

Next Steps

In terms of extending the experiment to other courses, Fallon comments, "The gamified elements would need to be adopted on a course-by-course basis by instructors who are interested [in] or passionate about the potential for games. It would only work as an organic process and if a body of literature existed to support the benefits of gamification." She also thoughtfully presented her concerns that this initiative might be misperceived as frivolous. "I think there is a reputation issue, too, and I believe it extends to students and faculty. I'm not sure if there is research that has been done on this, but in my experience many students—at our school, at least—react negatively to learning situations/assessments that fall outside the parameters of stereotypical academic exercises like essays, exams, etc." Fallon's comments illustrate sentiments I heard at the conference, including support of faculty experimentation:

> Games fall neatly into the category of unexpected assessment, and I think students tend to dismiss the learning experience because it isn't deemed academically rigorous. I believe that students can be persuaded of the benefits of these less traditional assessments, but that the challenge of doing so is exacerbated in an online environment. I think some faculty members share similar perceptions to their students. Academia falls into the box of lectures, labs/tutorials, midterms, and finals. In their mind, games are for fun, not for academic credit.

She does, despite her caution, conclude with a degree of positivity and optimism, "I think there is great potential in gamification but that there is much work to be done. We need research to provide a strong pedagogical underpinning. We need significant resources to build games that are engaging and that have enough finesse to actually meet the intended aims. Last but not least, we need to address preconceived notions about learning and academia."

These conclusions, in combination with Andres's statements and enthusiasm, provide a healthy tension between the desire to experiment and the desire to prove the efficacy of his gamification efforts. UW seemed, in 2013, to be in an excellent position to continue as a leader in both experiential education and gamification.

Where Are They Now?

On May 20, 2016, to discuss the progression of his work and to generally catch up, I spoke with Greg.

BELL—Tell me how it's all going. WatPD9, Ethical Decision Making, is it still running?

ANDRES—Yes, it is still running. It went live fall of 2013 and has run every semester. They have gone to a different model. It will run two semesters, then be off one semester, and then run for two and be off for one. This semester it is not running, so we are doing a program review of it. I hope to address the games, as initially I had envisioned the games to be one way, but the tech people [the web developers] said, "No we can't do that, so here's the compromise." I want to see if I can get it closer to what I had originally conceived the games to be.

BELL—Can you talk a little more to that?

ANDRES—So what I wanted was more akin to a "choose your own ending [adventure]." Have the thing structured so if they played one way in a scenario it would take them to [a certain new] scenario. If they played another way it would take them to a different scenario. The tech people cashed it out as, "we can't do it technically." Right now it's built in Desire2Learn (D2L), and it just uses the [native] quiz function—which is very limiting. I think it was the ease of using that convinced the developers it wasn't worth doing the other way. You'd have to build a much more elaborate engine in the background to actually do what I conceived of doing. I want to push to see if things have changed, to see if they can actually catch my vision this time. I'd be willing to do the back work to make this fly. One of the things we'd need to do is the game would have to be able to track the student's progression through it so we could provide feedback. "How are you playing relative to how others are playing?" More importantly, it's so we could track their progress and assign participation marks for it. So that's why they [developers] used the quiz feature in the first place—so it was obvious if the students had done it or not. So we'd have to build some sort of machine mechanism, some engine, to track their progress to assign participation marks.

BELL—How have you enhanced the game in subsequent runs? You were a little disappointed not to provoke more discussion between the games—has that improved at all?

ANDRES—So one of the things we've done is every week we post an actual news story that motivated and inspired this particular game so the students don't just see this as an abstract activity. You know, "Here's how the game actually played itself out in real life, here's the actual story." It still doesn't generate discussion.

BELL—What else have you learned in the time between launch and now?

ANDRES—That it's really hard, that student engagement in an online context is incredibly hard. It's so much easier to run these games. I do a lot of these games in my game theory course that I teach on campus, and the student participation and engagement there is of a very different nature. It might be just if you're online in a context like this, maybe the students are more inclined just to take the mindset of being a passive observer. These games are intended to make each of them an active learner. But, I mean, that's true of lectures on campus in general also, that it's always a constant struggle to convince the students that if I'm talking you're not learning . . . that they have to actively engage in order to learn. It's possible in a class to do that, but I don't know how to do that in an online context.

BELL—Did your efforts affect the institution in any way? Did anyone pick up on this? What progression did you see? How did your efforts affect things?

ANDRES—I have no idea how to gauge that. The program loves the concepts and has committed itself to making it better. I'm on the radar within the institution itself. We have a Center for Teaching Excellence, and we have teaching fellows throughout the university, and two teaching fellows have put me sort of in the public awareness. One just recently said in a letter to the other teaching fellows, "If you're ever looking for ways to engage students, check out Greg Andres as everything he does is amazing." I was also interviewed by *US News & World Report* and was featured in an article on student engagement and gamification—WatPD loved it.

The Director of WatPD is tasked with bringing the courses [that WatPD provides] to the broader student body. Right now, it's just for co-op students, but they want to make it like a diploma or like a stand-alone certificate. You would do your degree, and then you would take these extra courses, and it would be on your transcript that you've done this extra professional development aspect to your education.

BELL—If you could really enhance and promote gamification at Waterloo, what would need to be done?

ANDRES—I suspect we would need money to do a study in the course. We have a lot of data from thousands of students, but we haven't yet really correlated how student performance [in the course] is affected by how they did in the games. Here's the ideal world: we would do a study and put some numbers behind it, then we would use that, and I would work with the Center for Teaching Excellence at UW to promote this kind of thing within a course. I don't think most professors at UW might be convinced by just the anecdotes I present. Most would probably say, "let's see some real numbers. Can you definitively demonstrate, or at least show, that active learning in this way contributes to student success?" And that's a huge project.

BELL—Have you taken this out yourself? Maybe presented at any other conferences or taken it on the road to other institutions?

ANDRES—No, I haven't. I've been sidetracked by other projects and other ideas.

BELL—Have you seen or heard of anyone doing good work?

ANDRES—Actually, other WatPD courses in development now have taken the interactive "choose your own ending" type elements into the course itself. I hope that the Center for Extended Learning has been able to construct this, and my hope is that it's just a jump now so that this can now be applied to my games. I think they have already built a partial engine to do what I want. Seems like other courses are taking that aspect of student interaction and engagement much more seriously.

BELL—Does this differentiate per student type?

ANDRES—I noticed that some of the science-y students are much more uneasy with the moral gray areas of the games and subjects that are foisted on us. They want the answers to be clear yes or no (or black and white) where these games are forcing them to go, "you're dammed if you do, damned if you don't."

BELL—Do the kids that come up and say, "This is great" or "This is cool"—are they a particular demographic?

ANDRES—I have no idea. Thinking of how it plays out in class, I think that the older students definitely grasp the point of the games quicker than first-year students. You know, in class, sometimes the point of the game is just completely lost [on younger students]. We have to go back and either play the game again or go step by step and just explain [what was] the point of the game.

BELL—Any employer feedback from the perspective of the co-op providers, perhaps?

ANDRES—There was a study as to the effectiveness of these courses on employers' attitudes towards students who had done it. There was a sense that there is value to the courses that was the conclusion of the study.

BELL—Any other reflections now that you're older and wiser?

ANDRES—I would totally do it again, and I'm looking forward to putting down version 2.0. I think it's totally worth it.

BELL—What was it like from your perspective as a faculty member? Did implementing it enhance or undermine your position?

ANDRES—It was a labor of love, a lot of work. But like in class, it pays off in spades. The kids seeing the connection between the theoretical concepts and how they actually play off in real life.

I've done two PD courses, one for engineers and one for the general population of students, and I'll get every semester two or three students who have taken my PD courses online and have sought me out to take my on-campus course—specifically my game theory course. This is a self-selecting group so not representative of the campus, but they report they loved the games or they felt bad about how they have played the games. One woman this past fall told me, "I didn't think that Ethical Decision Making would make me feel that bad." So the students that have cared to comment have quite enjoyed the games.

BELL—Are you still a gamer? Do you play games? I seem to remember that you were more of a fitness fanatic—biking, running?

ANDRES—Ironman in 2014.

BELL—[*Worst follow-up interview question ever*] You saw *Iron Man?*

ANDRES—No, I did one [the triathalon] in Quebec. That's where I injured myself—on a bit of a break right now.

BELL—That's great. Thanks so much for your time.

■ ■ ■ ■ ■ ■ ■ ■ ■ ■ ■ ■ ■ ■ ■

CHAPTER SIX

Dungeons and Discourse

Massachusetts College of Liberal Arts (MCLA) is located in North Adams, Massachusetts. With around 1,500 students and a student-faculty ratio of 1:13, 76% of students agree that professors put a lot of effort into teaching their classes (25 respondents), while its party scene gets a sanguine B– (Niche.com). Founded in 1894 for teacher training as North Adams Normal School, by 2014 MCLA had expanded to 19 majors and 35 minors with a focus on critical thinking and communication skills. It is known for its quality, affordability, and Berkshire Hills Internship Program—coolest acronym in this book award goes to "B-HIP"—through which students gain hands-on experience with cultural venues in the area. Notable graduates include urban fantasy author Anton Strout, writer of *Dead to Me, Deader Still, Dead Matter,* and *Dead Waters* (influenced by the party scene at the college?); Cleveland Indians World Series pitcher Ken Hill; and "Barstool Sports" blogger Brian McGonagle, a.k.a. Rear Admiral. In 2015 its in-state tuition and fees were $9,475 and out-of-state $18,420. Room and board were assessed at a smidgeon under $10,000.

Gerol Petruzella is a humanities instructor who also teaches ancient languages, philosophy, and ethics. He has taught philosophy at the Massachusetts College of Liberal Arts (MCLA) since 2007 and served as the coordinator of academic technology since 2011. His areas of specialization include ancient Greek philosophy, ethics, and Greek and Roman language and literature. Further areas of interest include the ethics and social implications of open-source culture. When the coordinator of academic technology at MCLA left her position, Petruzella was asked to cover the position in an interim capacity. As a faculty member, he was committed to learning the newly implemented Canvas LMS and thought that, in taking the new role, he would be able to learn the new tool and support other faculty in doing so. Although not from a formally trained technical background, he was comfortable with computing, and he since has grown into the role.

Having taught his regular philosophy class (PHIL 100) between 2007 and 2010 in a standard format, he wondered if his new technical skills would allow him to develop a gamified course inspired by his own gaming interests. The specific idea came from a web comic titled *Dungeons and Discourse,* which grounded discussions on philosophy in scenarios based on the role-playing game *Dungeons & Dragons. Dungeons & Dragons* was developed in 1974 by Gary Gygax and Dave Arneson and is explained to neophytes on the official homepage: "The core of *Dungeons & Dragons* is storytelling. You and your friends may tell a story together, guiding your heroes through quests for treasure, battles with deadly foes, daring rescues, courtly intrigue and much more. You can also explore the many worlds of *Dungeons & Dragons* through any of the hundreds of novels written by today's hottest fantasy authors, as well as engaging board games and immersive video games. All of these stories are part of *Dungeons & Dragons.*"

The *Dungeons and Discourse* comic produced by Aaron Diaz, an Oregon-based Internet cartoonist also known as Dresden Codak, fueled Petruzella's interest in experimenting and attempting to tie his academic and social/gaming worlds together. His gamified three-credit course PHIL 100: A First Course in Philosophy (Dungeons and Discourse) ran in MCLA's spring terms 2012 and 2013. The first time the course ran (with 15 students) no one was informed that it was to be gamified prior to the class. By the time the course started its second run, the campus was aware that the instructor was experimenting with gamification, and 20 students enrolled.

The Rationale: Why Gamification?

In 2012, having spent a year familiarizing himself with basic responsibilities in his new role as coordinator of academic technology, Petruzella decided to explore his own creative ideas to enhance student engagement. His empathy for students who have traditionally struggled to engage with higher education was apparent when we spoke. "Our campus has a reasonably high population of students who are first-generation students coming out of personal backgrounds . . . there are not necessarily a lot of folks in their backgrounds who have done college, so this is a potentially strange and new and intimidating, kind of environment." Close to half (45%) of the students at MCLA qualify as low income and are eligible for federal Pell grants. As became clear in our conversations, the motivation behind Petruzella's gamification work is directly tied to his efforts to engage and encourage students from disadvantaged backgrounds. MCLA, according to its own literature, strives to promote excellence in learning and teaching, innovative scholarship, intellectual creativity, public service, applied knowledge, and active and responsible citizenship. The school, in its own words, "prepares graduates to be practical problem-solvers and engaged, resilient global citizens" (MCLA 2013). The environment at MCLA seemed comfortable with creative instruction and supportive of instructors such as Petruzella.

Petruzella revealed his interest in the realm of student engagement and his notion of gaming's potential to reduce the separation between study and play. "I think, across the board . . . it's unfortunate but true, that there are a lot of students, whatever their backgrounds, coming out of high schools where there is not a lot of playfulness associated with education." His focus on the introductory-level course captures his interest in pulling students from what he sees as K-12 thinking to practical problem-solving, producing the engaged, resilient global citizens that are referenced in the MCLA values. "I see a gamified intro course as the opportunity for a freshman to break some of those habits or expectations that students may be coming in with, that might negatively influence their attitudes towards education—their own perception of how to go about being in class, being a learner."

Elements of Gamification

Under the banner of gamification, Petruzella implemented elements to deliver his take on a *Dungeons & Dragons* course reimagined to capture and convey key concepts of entry-level philosophy.

Personalization

Recognizing the role of personalization in role-playing games such as *Dungeons & Dragons*, Petruzella built out a personal page for each student. He did this by embedding a spreadsheet produced through Google Docs into the Canvas LMS. On a basic level, this approach allows the students to create their own biography, adding a photo and a personal quote or mantra. Figure 15 illustrates Petruzella's own personalized page. The interface also keeps track of students' gold (awarded for participation in class discussions), quests completed, skills accumulated, and any bonus objects found. The personalization element had the secondary effect of introducing competition for at least

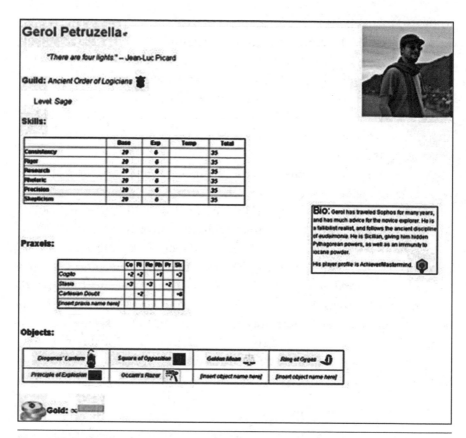

Gerol Petruzella

"There are four lights." – Jean-Luc Picard

Guild: *Ancient Order of Logicians*

Level *Sage*

Skills:

	Base	Exp	Temp	Total
Consistency	29	6		35
Rigor	29	6		35
Research	29	6		35
Rhetoric	29	6		35
Precision	29	6		35
Skepticism	29	6		35

BiO: Gerol has traveled Sophos for many years, and has much advice for the novice explorer. He is a fallibilist realist, and follows the ancient discipline of eudaimonia. He is Sicilian, giving him hidden Pythagorean powers, as well as an immunity to locane powder.

His player profile is Achiever/Mastermind.

Praxeis:

	Co	Ri	Re	Rh	Pr	Sk
Cogito	+2	+2		+1		+3
Stasis	+3		+3		+2	
Cartesian Doubt		+2				+4
[insert praxis name here]						

Objects:

Diogenes' Lantern	Square of Opposition	Golden Mean	Ring of Gyges
Principle of Explosion	Occam's Razor	[insert object name here]	[insert object name here]

Gold: ∞

Figure 15. Screenshot: Instructor's personalized page in the Massachusetts College of Liberal Arts Dungeons and Discourse class. Reproduced with permission of Gerol Petruzella, Massachusetts College of Liberal Arts.

some of the students. As Ross Betti, a student from Petruzella's first gamified class, describes it: "The competition for me was pretty important. If we had the opportunity to have competition—I like a good, healthy competition—it helps me excel in courses. If someone next to me has a better character than me, I'm going to redo that assignment. I wanted my character to be the best—I was like, 'I'm going to have the coolest tricked-out wizard in Logos.'"

The Quest

The metaphor for learning in the Dungeons and Discourse class is a journey, or quest, through realms where philosophical concepts are presented and explored. Five realms in total represent six theories of thought. Students spend approximately three weeks in each realm discovering scrolls left by former travelers that they have to analyze and be ready to discuss in the face-to-face class meetings. Petruzella developed the scrolls using open educational resources, some from the Creative Commons (a peer-reviewed repository of resources) and others from the University of Adelaide collection of classic texts. These scrolls replace a textbook, a change that has the benefits of reducing costs for the typical MCLA student and allowing Petruzella to add supplemental content when he discovers it through his ongoing research. Nate Stanley, another student from Petruzella's class, reflected on the decision to move away from textbooks:

> If there's no book you actually have to listen, you have to pay attention. I'm one of those students where the day before an exam I can write all the notes from the text and I can ace the exam, but does that mean you learn anything? It means that you have the ability to remember a few words and regurgitate them. I think that by taking textbooks out of the equation and putting people into unfamiliar situations; I think that is going to make them succeed much more than they would just in a normal classroom environment.

The scrolls and information lead to quizzes with short answers, correlating to concrete skills and outcomes that ultimately map to learning outcomes in the traditional versions of the class. Given that Petruzella has had no formal technical training and lacks technical support from MCLA beyond his own capabilities, a map simplistically illustrates the realms without any technical or tangible ability for the participants to track progress through the land.

Participation Rewards and Incentives

Although the class was designed to be potentially run fully online, in early iterations Petruzella has hosted face-to-face sessions to discuss progress and offer what he calls the "marketplace." On each student's personal page in Canvas, three gold coins are subtracted every day during the term, accounting for living costs and equipment maintenance. Through evidence of learning and thoughtful discussion in the marketplace sessions, students are awarded additional gold coins to augment their supply. Petruzella developed the participation-incentive system in a gamified format. The merchant (Petruzella) purchases good questions, and students have to barter to replenish gold that "expires" as the class proceeds. Petruzella adopted this approach with the goal of encouraging class-wide inclusion. One of his students, Nate Stanley, describes the format: "Every week, we met two to three times. We called each class the marketplace, and we'd have readings called scrolls that were by Socrates and the other philosophers and we had to decipher what they were trying to say and put it into our own words. When we'd go to the marketplace, the teacher would bring up these questions and when we answered them correctly, he'd say, 'I would buy that.' Which means you're getting through participation, you're earning gold."

A second student, Ross Betti, compared the experience to participation in other classes, noting that all individuals felt compelled to participate to continue in the game. "The key was to keep participating in class, which kept everybody involved, which is more than a lot of classes do where there are three or four people who talk all the time and there are a lot of students who don't." He elaborates: "If the (student) question was the right question and it was something that would strike up a discussion not only between you and the teacher but also among the students . . . you would earn gold that way, not only by giving the answers but also answering to other students, and it just makes the whole thing essentially a bazaar. You get everybody trading ideas, trading theories, and it made it a very productive environment."

When reflecting on the experience of delivering his gamified course, Petruzella describes a recent conversation at the faculty center where class participation of all students was discussed as a concern in traditional (non-gamified) courses. The conversation made him reflect further on whether his gamified approach might promote greater engagement than a traditional course.

He explains:

> Faculty are concerned about making participation the sort of thing that's available to all students on a fair basis. The topic was implicit around recognized bias in how you interact with students and whether that's in terms of gender—privilege male students in certain ways—or students of color or whatever . . . "How do I carry on a classroom discussion in ways that are fair towards all participants?" when students are not coming with the default, "Yes, I'm going to speak up and I have something to say very confidently." So what are the ways, the techniques for pulling those folk in and giving them a space and an opportunity and mechanism for participation?

Although not a key driver of Petruzella's work, the possibility that gamifying a course might democratize participation, thus compelling all students to participate irrespective of an instructor's conscious or subliminal prejudices, could be a valuable outcome of his approach.

Collaboration

Many successful role-player games incorporate teamwork, and many games that are played online are now team-based. One of Petruzella's students describes his online gaming experiences, emphasizing the social nature of what is sometimes considered a solitary pursuit. "I play games where you can really get to know the people that you are playing with; you're not just interacting through a microphone. I mean, these people I play games with on the computer I have been playing with for six or seven years, and I've been playing a sequence of games with them that are made by the same company, so I know how they play, and they know what I am capable of."

Cognizant of the importance of teams, Petruzella has built numerous opportunities throughout the course to collaborate and promote the benefits of group work in the Dungeons and Discourse model. Although the initial exploration of the realms is individual, for the activities and assessments students are organized into groups of four or five and encouraged to collaborate to look for details and come to understandings that individually they may have missed. Students who were interviewed reflected positively on the implementation of the team elements. Betti comments:

> As a class we rated higher than average for participation . . . I think it (the teamwork) forced people to get together more—my team got together to discuss things as we needed to. As far as people being apprehensive about asking questions, I think it became much easier as the semester went on and you had to work more and more with each other. When other people weren't sure what the answer was, that forces more people to talk about it. Being a game, it feels like it's not a classroom so you don't feel boxed in pressure thinking. It builds critical thinking; it builds creative skills.

Reflecting on the noncurricular effect of embedded teamwork, he whimsically remarked that, just as during high school, teamwork leading to social skill development is a valid exercise. As he put it, "Let's face it, college is just an expensive version of high school."

The student also elaborated on the effectiveness of teamwork despite his own personal reticence to interact freely in a more typical classroom environment: "I mean, I'm going to make a point to say hello to the person next to me and across from me and maybe move seats once during the term. But the group projects—I had to do two of them. I don't enjoy doing group work, so I'm in an uncomfortable environment where I have to overcome my little

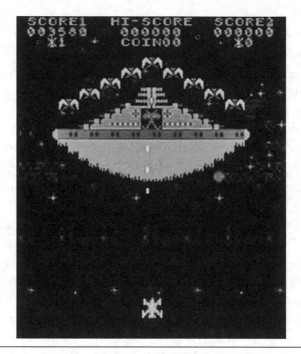

Figure 16. The mother ship from *Phoenix*, an early video game boss.

fears. It helped a lot—we learned a lot because everyone really wanted to learn."

Boss Battles

The *Urban Dictionary* describes a "boss battle" as any encounter or situation that is particularly difficult or challenging (video game example in figure 16). A fight with a boss character is commonly referred to as a boss battle or boss fight. Boss battles are generally seen at the climax of a particular section of a video game, usually at the end of a stage or level, or guarding a specific objective. The boss character is generally far stronger than the opponents the player has faced up to that point (*Urban Dictionary* 2013). Translated to an academic environment, the metaphor lends itself to a final assessment or challenge that tests learning and knowledge accrued to that point.

Petruzella used the Canvas Assignment feature to develop boss fights at the end of a section or realm. He created these elements with a narrative setup where the enemy character in the story presents a speech featuring informal fallacies to which the students have to prepare rebuttals. When he ran the class the second time in 2013, Petruzella ran in-person extensions to the boss fights with former students returning to argue philosophy in character as the "wise, old, hoary boss." As he affectionately reminisced, costumes were worn, and, even more encouragingly, the former students demonstrated retention of knowledge and philosophical arguments they had studied the year before.

Boss battles were referenced by developers and interested faculty at institutions in prior chapters, but at most institutions, no one had found a means of developing anything to approximate the principle. In this respect, despite the lack of any funding and minimal technical support, Petruzella is advanced in his implementation of this element at MCLA. In the battles with the boss figure, students were organized in teams with assigned roles given by the instructor to each team member. Each group was given a specific task. One group analyzed the writing, identifying fallacies (factual and philosophical inaccuracies), while the other group worked on presentation (a rebuttal to be presented to the whole class). The groups shared their work using the collaborate tool in Canvas. A student describes his experience of the boss battle, his enthusiasm apparent:

> For the exams, each realm had a boss—he's the king, he's the mayor, whatever you want to call it. And with the first one, the first city which was Logos, he had arguments about using logic and using research and things like that—you had to debunk his arguments because they saw us as threats, essentially trying to overthrow the nice little cozy pad that he had established for himself. So he's trying to say all these lies from history and everything else and we had to go back in time essentially through research, and say, no this isn't what caused this, this caused this. So we ended up liberating the people of Logos and they were able to go about their lives.

Outcomes

In a class with 15 to 20 students, Petruzella admitted to struggling to keep up with class updates. He was unable to automate a satisfactory feedback process and failed, according to the students and him, to keep up with manual processes such as awarding and tracking gold awards based on marketplace participation. Petruzella's reflections focused less on the incremental gold and more on the assessment elements in the course. He describes his concern about scaling as a limiting factor, stating: "I would say that most of the scaling concern would come dealing with assessment. I guess that's not surprising.

Given the particular subject area that I'm doing, philosophy, there's only so far you can go with auto-graded sort of assessments. You're talking about philosophical discussion and dialog, so the 800-lb. gorilla in the room is scaling assessment."

He had considered peer grading, stopping short of what he calls the "xMOOC idea," where "I create this packaged thing and then just put it out there and let everyone just run through it." He continued, "You know, when I look at these MOOCs and I see, 'Hey let's all 3,000 of us go to this Google Plus hangout on Thursday night and . . .' Yeah, right." He favors more efficient or sophisticated models that could make use of social features in a similar way that Reddit—the self-declared "Front Page of the Internet"—does. Reddit incorporates peer voting and a complex algorithm to encourage participant engagement, weighting new and interesting posts or articles more heavily while letting older posts wane or fade. In a similar manner, Petruzella envisioned students' gold piles fading without their engagement. As he explains: "I'm thinking people surely have gotten further along [than simple peer assessment]—thinking of things like Reddit where there's this really robust—you know, vote up, vote down, and it's not totally random, not just the Wisdom of the Crowds—the notion of, somehow, a privileged user or privileged commenter who has some sort of credentialing with extra weighting."

Students' candid, quite critical but supportive, commentary identified two key areas for improvement. The first emphasized the need for the instructor in a totally manual course to keep up with basic features such as the gold awards. Students described the instructor's failure to keep us as demoralizing, in part because at course launch the system had seemed to hold such promise. Betti again comments: "At the end of the course, if you looked at my gold, I was negative 50-something gold, and it wasn't because I wasn't asking questions. I'm an active participant in class. But it's because questions weren't being recorded or the value of our questions wasn't being recorded or not put in the program. I think it demanded a lot of Petruzella as a professor to keep up with the game."

He reiterated this minimum requirement as the first target for the instructor to improve in subsequent class launches. "The gold has to be better—he doesn't have to do the character profile pages, but the gold, he has to record that and get that in the system. You can't do your assignments if you don't have your gold and if you're trying really hard next class to ask questions and that doesn't get recognized."

The lack of technical sophistication in Petruzella's course build was considered a disappointment for participants, although again they couched this criticism in encouraging and supportive language. After the gold-maintenance issue, the next recommended area for improvement was to provide a means, even a perfunctory one, of visually illustrating and tracking progress through realms.

Stanley commented, "My impression when I first saw the realm graphic was that I would have a character that I would literally move through a little land on a computer . . . but there wasn't any of that. It was like, 'Alright, class, now we're in this land.' So there wasn't actually any gaming going on." He speculates about how greater use of technology could improve the course. "If you could write a program where you could actually take your character and go through this preset little land and you are forced to go in this direction like an RPG [Role Playing Game] kind of thing—then I think it's a great idea. I think it's a fabulous idea, and it could be entirely online."

As a self-declared gamer, Stanley had strong recommendations for an improved second version. He outlined the kind of development that he would encourage:

> The biggest thing would be the visual, the cinematics. If I were to boil down any core—there'd need to be a log-in basis and you'd have to spend some time logged in or you'd lose points or something. There'd need to be some structured communication—you could even use Skype. For gaming online, I use TeamSpeak where you can have 80 people on a server talking. Just for now, I don't see visuals being used effectively. You can use other game- development tools like the SDK gaming program at home . . . I've seen a lot of great games come out of development kits like that. It's literally just walking down a corridor, and you can take [a] left, turn right."

In terms of core academic elements, Petruzella adhered to the content of the traditional PHL 100 course and developed course outcomes to be consistent with those of traditional sections. In a direct comparison with his own former iterations of the PHL 100 class, Petruzella's average grade for the two gamified courses was 78.86 compared to an average of 70.82 for the two prior terms the course ran as a traditional, nongamified course. He certainly leans toward the conclusion that the gamified elements are making a real difference while acknowledging that his small sample sizes make any conclusions about course efficacy, student engagement, and grades tenuous at best. He does not let that uncertainty dissuade him from reflecting on another out-come (or possible anomaly) that he intends to continue to observe in future iterations:

> Looking at some of the numbers, it looks like there is a slightly higher percentage of students who ended up declaring philosophy majors, who took the (gamified) Dun-geons and Discourse version when compared with a couple of years ago when I taught it as a standard. Because it's a PHL 100 course we get a wide range of majors taking it, and, because it's a freshman-level course, we also get a fair number of first-semester freshmen and, in this case, second-semester freshmen who may or may not have declared a major at this stage.

Petruzella feels that the gamified format is best suited to introductory courses, where students lack what he calls the intrinsic motivation of prior success. His working hypothesis is that MCLA students, who include large numbers of first-generation college attendees and students from low-income families, need a boost to get on board with the concept and practice of higher education. Petruzella asserts that if these students can get through entry-level classes and start to dig into a subject area, the content of the course it-self intrinsically may motivate them to persist. Prior to that state, he feels that any means of encouragement—including gamification—must be worth exploring.

> My suspicion is that gamifying might have a disproportionate effect with respect to 100 and 200 level "Intro to" sort of survey courses and maybe less so as you start to get into the upper-classman seminars, at which point you are dealing primarily with majors who are committed to a field of interest and have, sort of, developed a mature interest [in] a discipline and are ready to really engage deeply in a way that freshmen are not necessarily. So I sense that a lot of the value certainly does come from the engagement—grabbing a student's sense of curiosity and playfulness and doing a bit of a transition.

As noted in the case study of the gamified course at UW, while competi-tion and meritocratic reward may be a valuable tool, gamification seems to have the potential to encourage students who are not near the top of the class in terms of traditional achievement. Betti suggests this benefit, stating:

> I think everybody learns differently. Because of the fact that there are the visual cues, it levels the playing field—there's no smart or stupid person in the game. I think it

helps all students. I'm a straight A student anyway, but I know a couple of guys in the class . . . I mean—everybody's smarter at something than someone . . . And it allows people to relate to each other because, you know—this guy's really smart, but if he's stuck on this, maybe we can figure it out. So, there's involuntary teamwork there . . . there is going to be some part of it that's going to advance somebody.

Petruzella wants to add further means of encouragement and affirmation in future versions of his gamified course:

I'm thinking I would like to add badges. I would have some that are sort of serendipitous, you know, the idea of someone happens across a hidden component or someone follows a path further than expected or further than required and discovers some sort of bonus. So I'd have the badge for the going-above-and-beyond kind of phenomenon, but I'd also want some sort of core badges available just for most students who just got through and accomplish the quests as explained, as presented, rather than necessarily going off on their own.

Finally, although at times critical, students' conclusions were constructive and gave the sense that they really want to see this kind of model succeed. Stanley describes this potential: "Class was less like class; it was more like playing a game, and it made it very easy to fall into it . . . at least [for] me. I looked forward to every time I had philosophy." Attempting to compare like for like in terms of his own experience in Petruzella's course, Betti concludes, "I wish I had something to compare this against, I really do, but this is my first philosophy course. I wish I could say, 'In my first philosophy course, where it was all books . . .' I know I learned a lot and I retained a lot—I can answer . . . a lot of questions about Socrates and about Plato. I'm all about it. I was just so interested in the topic."

He describes how the class was motivated in a way that was novel to him compared to what he had experienced in other, nongamified courses: "There was very rarely a day when we went in tired in the morning and were like, 'Oh, we don't want to do anything.' I don't know if the incentive came from the game or our participation. We'd go in, we'd say our next challenge is the dread relativist and were talking about whether this applies or that. Ask our questions—'How can we arm ourselves better against him?'—that kind of thing."

His takeaway from the gamified class was that his learning would persist longer than in his other classes. "People on the outside may say, 'Oh they're just playing games,' but they're going to be learning something from it, which is more than I can say for many normal classes where you have that normal class [routine of] cram for the exam, pass the exam, and then forget."

Despite quite candid feedback on the shortcomings of the Dungeons and Discourse course format, the student interviewees were encouraging and interested enough to summarize the potential of gamification in a format such as Petruzella developed. The student excitement at the potential for gamification and gamified courses raises the question of whether Petruzella's work might be extended or better supported at his institution. Petruzella noted that one challenge is the relative isolation in which faculty tend to construct their courses: "It seems to me that there is a growing number of people [at multiple institutions] doing really good things with gamification. I think generally a barrier is that everyone is working in his or her course. I'm working in my Philosophy 100 course, and it's all well and good and I have the freedom to do whatever I want in that context, but my students next semester are going to go and take Philosophy 200 or 240 or they're going to take History 100."

He speculates that these experiments may remain isolated for some time to come, in part, because the institution has not formally embraced this model while at the same time, faculty tend to operate in isolation with few opportunities to collaborate effectively: "We don't have an infrastructure as a college within which a gamified course has any significance beyond itself. From the point of view of MCLA, Dungeons and Discourse is still just PHIL 100, which amounts to three credits, and students get an A, B, C, D, or F in it, and that meets certain graduation requirements and major requirements as PHIL 100—that's what the college sees, no matter what crazy things I'm doing within the guts."

Petruzella believes that gamification has a potential role within higher education at large but describes a middle-ground scenario where gamification is established but not widespread. He feels that the best-case scenario would be if gamification could carve itself out a place as a viable path in higher education. He clarifies that he doesn't think gamification needs to be the standard or needs to replace credit-based higher ed. "I would be happy to live in a world where there are colleges that do a game-based bachelor's [degree] or even a game-based major. I would be happy to see those exist side by side with these more traditional models."

Where Are They Now?

In a follow-up conversation I discussed how far Petruzella had got with his gamification interests in the two years since we last compared notes.

BELL—Since we talked around 2013–2014, where are you at? Where did you get to?

PETRUZELLA—Since that point, I'm in the situation where I'm full-time doing this academic tech thing and teaching one course over that in a rotation. I've taught the Dungeons and Discourse course one time since then. In spring 2015 I ran it again, and I [am] on the books to teach it again in fall [2016]. So it's quite firmly established in the college catalog now. The course this coming term is part of our college's first-year college experience.

BELL—Did you modify it at all?

PETRUZELLA—Yes, but I didn't mix modifications. Some were merely structural, responding to the platform [Canvas] developments as they introduced new features over time. I also made a conscientious decision to develop the character of Del the Oracle. I had a placeholder when we last talked—another persona representing another person, another voice beyond my own for students to interact with. So I actually gave that role to my TA, to represent Del the Oracle as another point of access into the game world. I remember that I did that this last time I taught, so that was an addition—an expansion of the game world, another non-player character, as it were.

Another piece that I added in was when Canvas rolled out a plug-in for easy badges, so I started to assimilate some. It wasn't systematically, just the occasional 'you get a badge for discovering an Easter egg' or something like that. I didn't roll out badges as a systematic part of core piece of the game—just as an additional experience in the game play.

The third thing I remember I developed was basically kind of a store. I had developed a method for students to acquire gold pieces through class discussions by coming into the marketplace and earning gold pieces. And at that point, the first couple of times around, there wasn't any structure around use of the gold pieces. It was sort of a bare placeholder, and you couldn't do much with them. So what I ended up doing was pretty straightforward. I threw up a Google form representing the store with several options associated with certain numbers of gold pieces that students could choose to cash in by submitting a request through the form. So that was something I wanted to try out . . . low-level, if you had five gold pieces you could cash them in for a twelve-hour extension on a particular deliverable—things like that.

BELL—So more academic constructs rather than game elements?

PETRUZELLA—It was a mixture. Some were explicit to the course environment, some were more fun, like a free download of a song in the course. There were probably about 10 different options representing difficulty and levels of challenge. The fourth change that I made was again not really within the game play but more the structure of the course itself, and I did contract grading with students that semester. At the beginning of the term I offered them three different paths, essentially, and they selected what kind of effort, what kinds of things they wanted to do, and what sort of final academic grade that would get you for the successful completion of this path versus [another path]. So they chose one at the beginning, and just about a third to half of the way through the class, around midterms, we revisited it, and I said, "OK, think back as to what you selected at the beginning. We are about halfway through what we need to do, half our time together. Does that still feel accurate to you? Is this still the path you want to choose? Do you want to change it?" So I gave them a midpoint opportunity to renegotiate the path they had created. Those are the four things I remember doing differently this past time round.

BELL—Back to Del the Oracle—was that a typical GA/TA mentor sort of role? Were they guiding or were they cheerleading?

PETRUZELLA—A little of this and a little bit of that. Certainly, the core responsibility of the TA was student support. In the character of Del, the access point was in a course discussion. It was a dedicated discussion area where students could ask for help on anything over the course of the semester that they were encountering, whether it was a difficult scroll or a challenging quest or whatever it was, and the TA (as the character of Del), would respond in this typical cryptic oracle/oracular kind of way. So their persona in this response was intentionally mysterious and was intentionally not in the business of giving a direct answer. It was my intention, in explaining the role, the TA was to be helpful but not to give direct answers, but to hint, to direct, to nudge in a direction, to encourage the student to reach out to another resource that would be helpful in finding the answer. So that was the model of the oracle, and it helped that the TA for that particular semester was very familiar [with] classical models of oracles so almost immediately got what I was after with that.

BELL—These sound like great enhancements. So what did you learn? What worked? What changed with these enhancements?

PETRUZELLA—I would say one thing I immediately learned, one strong lesson I took away, is that building [the game] in itself does not make them come. Mentioning Del the Oracle as an example, I had to mention Del the Oracle almost on a weekly basis to remind students that Del was available and a good resource. And this is just a particular example of a more general observation, I suppose—you can mention to students as many resources as you like, but mentioning them is rarely enough. You need to, I needed to, prioritize them myself through constant reference to encourage the students to internalize that importance. So that was sort of a process lesson for me. I'm not sure, but I think the contract grading was useful to students, but that's just based on my own observation. Looking back, I know that relatively few students, a small handful of students, chose the midterm semester opportunity to change or to revise their contract.

In most of those cases students chose to revise upward. Some students who had chosen the C [grade] path chose to upgrade and said, 'I'm ready to tackle the more challenging path and go for the B.' So that was encouraging—but the majority of the students stayed with what they initially chose. I'm not sure how to interpret that or what that means.

BELL—When we first spoke you had sensed, rather than quantified, a slight upwards movement in student grading and engagement, and you had reflected that a greater proportion of students had declared philosophy as a major. Did those patterns persist, and did you see a net effect of your efforts?

PETRUZELLA—I did get a little bit more insight into more quantifiable elements of the project. One of the improvements in the platform was the development of an analytics dashboard at the course level for the faculty. Through that I could see engagement over time, aggregated over the course, and generally I saw strong patterns of engagement. I'm doing a side-by-side analysis of the gamified course versus the traditional. I would say that those initial observations did persist, and now I'm getting more numbers to back that up. But we're still talking really small sample sizes. This past term we had around 20 students, so again small numbers but clearly more engagement.

BELL—One other thing that stood out was your extension of your work to a more general discussion around unconscious bias. I recall you had fostered discussions at faculty senate or curriculum committee around equity and removal of bias and that this had resonated with faculty. Did your work in this area gain any further traction?

PETRUZELLA—Directly, not so much. I haven't, for example, convinced the philosophy department to convert a bunch of their courses to incorporate gamified elements or anything like that. That would be pretty spiffy if that happened—but it didn't. What has happened is that I have incorporated a lot of the lessons I have learned, the insights I have gained, into my work in academic technology. Just in general I work with faculty a lot one-on-one in terms of course development and design, and I make sure as part of those conversations I bring up and suggest some of these considerations that have been meaningful in my experience. When faculty are working with me to develop a course, whether it's hybrid, online, or face-to-face, I may out-line and say, "Well, this is a very interesting discussion topic." I try to appeal to fac-ulty's own experience with this because there are a whole lot of access points, "So you know there is always this risk of discussions being dominated by some very strong voices, so here we are developing this discussion in a new medium for you so let's think about it. Are there tools available to us that could offset some of that risk? Have you thought about defining specific discussion roles?" By way of example, a lot of people will create a discussion and expect everyone to give the same type of response, be it analysis or reaction. So instead of that, what if you tap certain types of people and say, "Your role in this discussion is to play a devil's advocate so your responses should be geared that way." Then you create other subsets whereas your role in this discussion is, say, a researcher, so your only role is finding further links to support the reactions that people give. So something like differentiating roles in a discussion. This is not directly coming out of the Dungeons and Discourse experi-ence, but it is very much resting on the same principles and the observations that have been formed to what I do. So that's connected to my part of work doing the instructional design stuff.

I probably mentioned when last we spoke that there was another faculty member in the philosophy department who was interested in including some gamified ele-ments in his course. He teaches a logic and critical thinking course pretty regularly. He wasn't interested in doing a top-to-bottom restructuring as I did, but he wanted to include what he called 'Gladiator Logic' games as a unit (at least within the broader context of his traditional course structure). He's not necessarily thinking about gamifi-cation as pedagogy. He's using this as a general engagement type of choice, but it is something that has latched on a certain bit. His practice has at least been encouraged by what I've been doing. It's a sort of a team completion sort of model. He teaches this face-to-face in a kind of *Jeopardy*-style, time-restricted sort of competition.

In terms of other paths of influence, my course has been designated a first-year experience course. Mine will be the gamified one, so students will be exposed to this early in their experience here. Our digital librarian is interested in developing virtual campus tours, etc., so she tends to be quite involved in the first-year experi-ence also. She's another promising person on campus that is interested in a sort of augmented reality tour with QR codes around campus—that kind of thing.

BELL—What would take it to the next level at your campus? What's needed in your opinion?

PETRUZELLA—I don't think politics is one of our bigger issues. I would say our culture here is pretty receptive in terms of trying things like this out. The biggest issue that

I could identify right now is lack of support resources (insofar as gamification is not tied necessarily to technology), as a lot of the most evident and accessible points of access do tend to be related to technology, and right now our Center for Academic Technology is me—I'm it. I had a half-time colleague who retired this past semester, so right now any and all faculty who have any sort interest in learning something new (be it developing a project, doing instructional design, doing course redesign, learning how to teach online, troubleshooting issues with LMS or e-portfolios) that's all on one person at the institution at the moment. So it's a bottleneck, is really what it is. I will be out connecting with other people in academic now at conferences and places and I always think, "Ahh, you have six people in your office—how nice that must be."

BELL—What about the changing demographics, etc.? Other higher ed challenges? Do you have any other reflections? Is it worth the effort?

PETRUZELLA—I still think that it's valuable, and I think it's a good pedagogical path. I do still think that. I think that in the intervening time I have noticed some more of these issues getting a bit more mainstream in the educational conversations. So that's interesting because some of the ideas that may have been new-seeming several cycles ago have been a bit more taken for granted, a bit more taken as common wisdom in certain circles, and I think that recognizing the value of play and the value of allowing students the space to fail without penalty—those are a couple of the particular, general ideas that have gained more traction over the intervening time. And since those are core to a lot of what I was thinking and have been trying to do with this—that's encouraging to me. That makes me think, "Alright, so these things are starting to be recognized as useful and valuable. They are starting to have proven their merit a bit more in practice." So maybe initially it was an exciting idea that seemed like it would work, but now it seems like people have been trying it for a while now, and it seems to have worked. So there's that reinforcement cycle, I think, going on broadly. I do think that institutions, including my own, are starting to get a bit more serious about strategizing to reach out to expand the population we are trying to reach. We have seen some of the hype cycles reach their conclusion around things like MOOCs and whatnot, but coming out of the other side of that we still do have a core of things that we want to commit to.

We definitely want to commit with outreach to disadvantaged students—that's always been a part of the mission of certainly what my institution is doing. We're starting to get a lot more technically literate staff and faculty as we start to hire new people. We're seeing that shift happen, where I'm finding I need to make the case less. Newer faculty coming in are like "Yeah, of course" rather than "Oh, what is this?" So to cycle back to your question—yes, I'm still committed to pursuing gamification as a method that does, I think, at least two really important things.

One is to provide new and/or disadvantaged students an opportunity to learn from mistakes or failures or not quite coming in with all the tools. Gamification does that, and that's been shown to be really a critical piece of what we're after. I think also there's that element of games as presenting the experience of higher ed as an experience that students come to want for its own sake. And that's always a constant worry in conversations that I have and that I hear. The worry, the commodification of higher ed—that students look at it as an experience that's just as a means to an end, whereas having a gameful kind of experience challenges that. You don't play a game just for the sake of having a high-paying job at the other side of it. The game experience is its own reward in that way, so insofar as we can present learning to students in a way that is intrinsically enjoyable, I think that's a second really important advantage to pursuing gamification.

BELL—Do you still play games?

PETRUZELLA—I do, yes indeed. Certainly less than I would like given pesky things like work get in the way. I still play board games and online. I have to say it's been a bit since I've logged into Steam. There's a really cool tabletop game that I just backed on Kickstarter based on a book that I really loved. So I'm still in it a little bit. I still try to practice what I preach.

■ ■ ■ ■ ■ ■ ■ ■ ■ ■ ■ ■ ■ ■

CHAPTER SEVEN

Threat of Crime and Terrorism

Founded as the Farmer's High School of Pennsylvania in 1855, via a spell as the Agricultural College of Pennsylvania, Penn State College became The Pennsylvania State University (Penn State) in 1953. By 2003 it had grown to the extent that it had the second-largest impact on the state economy of any organization in Pennsylvania, generating an economic effect of over $17 billion. The mission statement of this research-intensive university emphasizes teaching, research, and public service. With an annual enrollment of close to 100,000 across its 24 campuses and online, it is one of the biggest universities in the United States. Famous alumni include Kelly Ayotte (former US senator), William Perry (former United States secretary of defense), John Aniston (actor on *Days of Our Lives;* Jennifer's dad), Immortal Technique (political activist, rapper), Hugh Edwin Rodham (Hilary's brother), and a multitude of football and baseball players. On the fictional side, Dr. Abby Lockhart (of the TV show *ER*) and, in a nice piece of symmetry with the University of South Florida's Hulk Hogan (who is real and mentioned in chapter 3), Dr. Bruce Banner, whose alter ego was The (Incredible) Hulk, are Penn State alumni. It is not documented whether The Hulk played football for the Nittany Lions—he would have been a heck of a nose guard. Penn State's student body is 75.4% White, 5.5% Black, 4.3% Asian, 4.4% Hispanic, 0.2% Native American, 0.1% Native Hawaiian/Pacific Islander, 1.7% two or more races, 5.8% international, and 3.1% unreported. Undergraduate annual tuition and fees in 2016 were $17,514 for in-state students and $31,346 for out-of-state students, with $12,000 to $14,926 estimated for additional costs (room, meals, books, and supplies) for all students. Graduate costs vary by program; the MBA goes for $23,708 annually for in-state and $38,068 for out-of-state students.

Fred Aebli is a former major in the United States Marine Corps, where he worked aviation logistics. He joined Penn State in 1999 and worked on both the two-year and four-year curriculum in the information sciences and technology

(IST) degree. Based at Penn's Worthington Scranton campus, he teaches online courses for their World Campus, is the IST program coordinator, and manages IST internship and community outreach programs. His recent non-teaching work has included an analysis of distant synchronous information systems courses and, at the annual Online Learning Consortium International Conference, a presentation on gamification techniques parenthetically titled "Turning an International Terror Plot into a Classroom Game."

Aebli grew up as an only child in Scranton, Pennsylvania. His father passed away in the summer of 1977 when he was nine years old, and, as is so often the case, the loss cemented many events around that time in his mind for perpetuity. He was supported through the love of 12 aunts, uncles, and cousins and clearly managed to glean a happy childhood despite his father's death. One member of this family support team, an uncle in Arizona, informed him of the upcoming release of a movie that seemed to be worth seeing based on rave reviews in the media. It was called *Star Wars*, and, as Aebli recalls to this day, it was like nothing he had ever seen. When young Aebli finally got to see the movie, he was blown away. The adventure and his imagination allowed him to mentally leave behind his own challenges, replacing them with a journey to the stars and beyond, roleplaying different characters and creating new storylines in which he was central. The technology underlying the *Star Wars* movie fascinated him, and he latched on to all things related to space travel and science fiction. He lived and breathed all things *Star Wars* for many of his formative years and recreated that world through toys, models, and, as he grew older, through the fledgling world of computers. Play had always been a means of escape for Aebli, and, prior to his *Star Wars* exposure, his mom had fed and encouraged his imagination buying him action figures and construction kits. It was, however, his discovery of the Atari 2600 in the early 1980s that put him on the path of true creativity and creativity with an end product; he began to learn how to make (or code) "his own stuff."

When playing with these early home video games, Aebli became intrigued and challenged himself to learn how to get under the hood hacking and writing new code, putting him on the path to software development and programming. As this interest grew, his relatives realized that this was a hobby to be encouraged. He was given first a Timex Sinclair 1000 and later a Commodore 64 on which he taught himself BASIC programming. Moving on to high school he found like-minded friends within the *Dungeons & Dragons* crowd, and he, perhaps to impress these new friends, started to challenge himself to develop *Dungeons & Dragons*–like role-playing games. With 8-bit graphics and his newly acquired skills he managed to create simple path-based games developing the twin sides of his interests in real technology and creative fantasy. Progressing through high school, still walking this middle ground between reality and the stars, Aebli decided that he wanted to become an astronaut. As a first step on that path and to help secure his own education, he decided to serve his country in the military. A long-time family friend of his mother suggested he shoot for a pilot career in the marine corps (again, one step closer to the stars). Aebli attended marine corps Officer Candidate School, graduated from Penn State with a computer science/math degree, and received his commission as a second lieutenant in the United States Marine Corps. However, the giant leap to becoming an astronaut proved beyond him because of his lack of a terminal science degree. Not allowing that disappointment to blunt his energy, after a rewarding career in the marine corps, he entered service in the US Army and went back to school as an active-duty soldier to receive his Master's of Informational Systems Resource Management degree. In a clear summary of Aebli's humor and never-say-die attitude, he has a news clipping on his home refrigerator reading "Astronaut Applications Being Accepted." Nothing gets this man down.

On discharge from the US Army, Aebli was determined to further his technology experiences that he had begun when on active duty. The Internet was now a thing, and he realized that his experience to that point meant that he could build new things for this new environment. Proficient in HTML, Flash, graphics, and coding, he was hired by Bell Atlantic to lead a software project before leaving to work for an Oracle consulting group at a nuclear plant in Berwick, Pennsylvania. While there he started to teach night classes, and, after a round of corporate downsizing, he explored the possibility of teaching back at his alma mater. His former computer science professor told him of a new degree that the university was starting called information sciences and technology and encouraged him to apply. He has now been teaching there for over 16 years. Over that period, he has created many courses from scratch, coordinated the IST internship program, and engaged the campus in what he calls a "pre-incubator business startup hub" to foster new ideas and innovations. Uppermost in his teaching philosophy has been the sentiment that got him through and beyond his own personal challenges: "Learning should be fun."

When the university developed a security and risk analysis (SRA) curriculum as a minor for the IST majors in 2012, Aebli was assigned SRA 211: Threat

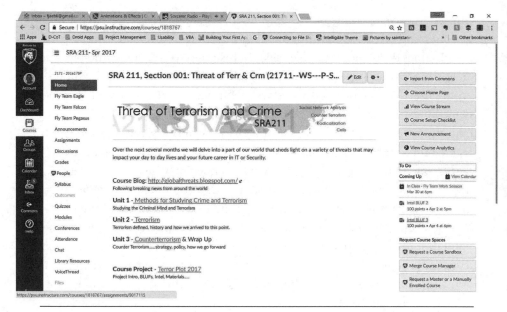

Figure 17. Screenshot from the Penn State Threat of Terrorism and Crime SRA 211 course. © Fred Aebli, Penn State University; used with permission.

of Crime and Terrorism (figure 17). The university website describes this minor as "intended to familiarize students with the general framework and multidisciplinary theories that define security and related risk analysis . . . providing a grounding in analysis and modeling used in information search, visualization and creative problem solving."

Students typically take SRA 211, Aebli's course, as rising sophomores, and it is offered once a year in the spring as a resident course. It was initially developed and delivered in Penn State's Angel learning management system (LMS) but was ported, as were all institutional courses, to Instructure's Canvas platform when the university transitioned in 2015. The program target demographic, and indeed the student body generally at Penn State, consists of technology-comfortable students of traditional college age with some nontraditional and active-duty US military personnel and veterans alongside them. Most of the students are familiar with video game play, but there has also been a developing vibe around more traditional board games. Aebli himself recognizes this and serves as an advisor to both the IST Club and to the League of Extraordinary Gamers Club (LEG). This latter LEG group has had recent near-exponential growth. Aebli oversees rooms filled with young people engaging directly with many different types of board games, eschewing, at least for a short period, cell phones and related technologies.

Aebli's first attempt to gamify SRA 211 was driven by his desire to create a more engaging experience in and out of the classroom. Thinking back to his time in the marines, he reflected, "Turning anything into a game automatically makes it more engaging . . . You definitely see it in the military. You see engagement go up when you train Marines in realistic scenarios, so I thought, why wouldn't it work for my students? Why should they have to learn solely from listening to lectures and reading textbooks?"

Aebli's version 1.0 of this project was developed as a role-play game that represented the structure and format of the G8's counterterrorism working group. The G8 (at time of the course actually the G7) is a governmental political forum that has evolved from an initial group of six member states (France, Germany, Italy, Japan, the United Kingdom, and the United States) in 1975 who got together to debate and formulate mutually beneficial local and international policies. The G6 became the G7 in 1976, when Canada joined; Russia also signed up in 1997, making it the G8. When Russia was suspended in 2014 on the basis of their annexation of Crimea and intimidating behavior toward Ukraine, everyone arrived back at G7. Doubtless that will change again soon, but let's leave it at that for now.

Within the G8 there are many subgroups, and one of them, the Roma-Lyons group, established in 2001 under Italian presidency (countries rotate and switch the leadership role), looks at strategies around terrorism and transnational crime. Roma-Lyons meets three times a year when members debate and develop prevention and mitigation strategies. Roma-Lyons members are drawn from the member countries and are typically foreign or interior ministry representatives of their respective nations. The group, in simplistic terms, develops a shared approach, recommendations, and best practices for the safeguarding of public security. The results of this subgroup's work are passed on to the G8 group's interior and justice ministers at their annual meeting, where they are reviewed and, in many cases, adopted as national policy for the constituent member countries.

Aebli's idea for the central project for his fledgling SRA 211 course was to base the class format on the workings of the G8 Roma-Lyons Group. He assigned groups of students to specific countries whose national security agencies were to be analyzed and reported on to the class. The team assigned to Great Britain had to analyze and review MI5's organization, policies, and practices, while the team given Canada had to do likewise with the Canadian Royal Mounted Police (the Mounties). With class sizes between 15 and 24 students, the average team size was small—only three to four students. At the start of the project the Roma-Lyons players had to elect a country to chair the group (or to serve as president) per standard G8 protocol. The members of the chair country were tasked with running the classroom meeting as an assembly, organizing the other members, and overseeing the production of critiques of their countries' security agencies. These reports, titled Bottom Line Up Fronts (BLUFs), are a format common in US military writing, following a protocol where conclusions and recommendations are laid out at the beginning of the text, with the goal being to expedite decision making. One member of each team, rising from desks with their country name displayed, reported on their team's BLUF to the whole class. The BLUF content was made more authentic and vital through intelligence reports, provided by Aebli via a password-protected folder in the Angel LMS. The students were given one week to collaborate in their teams and prepare their analyses.

During larger group meetings, students were encouraged to ask questions of one another while the instructor, representing the United States, would "inject thoughts or questions in the event [he] didn't see them making the progress that [he] expected at that point in time." The project culminated in a final project presentation developed collectively as a full 24-member report with each country assigned different aspects of national security and/or political nuance to report out on. One group led the discussion on financing of terrorism, another on weapons procurement, and a further team on logistics and risks. Final presentations were public, and Aebli typically invited guests. He encouraged the students to dress in professional, business attire, and so, with an extra sense of gravitas and one final dose of authenticity, they presented in a large auditorium on campus.

Aebli felt that this version (1.0) of his immersive SRA 211 class, the Roma-Lyons G8 format, was effective. But he was concerned that too many students were disengaged; as he put it, "there was a lot of coat-tailing going on." He realized that the small team sizes did not generate much in the way of team competition or group dynamic. He also had a hankering to go beyond authentic role-playing to more recognizable gamification, leveraging his imagination and perhaps recalling his engagement with adventure narrative and the value of creativity as a motivator. Besides, the original format was not producing significant results in terms of student grades. He hypothesized that he needed to develop more tension and a more competitive environ-ment via team challenges and narrative. He started to formulate ideas around fewer teams competing with more challenging materials, a more pronounced narrative, and a clearer sense of a tangible achievement or reward. Version 2.0 began to take shape.

The Game

For version 2.0, working with limited support staff at the terrorism center, Aebli revised his central project for the SRA 211 course. In the new version, students are assigned to project teams, known as "FBI Fly Teams," tasked with responding as counterterrorism units to intelligence about attack threats. Fly Teams really are "a thing, defined on the FBI website as: small, highly trained cadres of counterterrorism investigators—including special agents and intel-ligence analysts—based at FBI Headquarters who stand ready to deploy any-where in the world on a moment's notice."

A Fly Team's mission (also from the FBI site) is "To bring the FBI's strategic and tactical counterterrorism capabilities to bear in partnership with other U.S. government agencies and foreign partner-nation entities in critical over-seas locations to detect, penetrate and disrupt terrorist networks." To be enlisted onto a Fly Team, along with multilingualism, advanced medical training, and weapons training members must have the following skills:

- Digital media exploitation and forensics expertise;
- Explosive post blast investigations;
- Advanced tactical and force protection skills;
- Tactical evasive driving;
- Hostage survival and resistance training *and*
- Advanced surveillance techniques.

In recent years, FBI Fly Teams have been deployed to the Boston Marathon bombing; the US consulate attack in Benghazi, Libya; the Westgate Mall attack in Nairobi, Kenya; the World Cup bombing in Kampala, Uganda; and the Boko Haram kidnapping of schoolgirls in Abuja, Nigeria.

Aebli described the SRA 211 Fly Team core competency as being able to "analyze and critically assess a large volume of threat intelligence indicating the formation of a possible terror plot at some location around the world." The ultimate goal is to fully "unearth the plot and make recommendations as to how to neutralize the risk." With this overview articulated, he set the stage for teams within the class to compete with one another to determine the terror plot and acquire points to improve their grades. In a manner similar to that of the board game *Clue*, teams were told that it was their goal to learn all the terror plot details and then report out to the FBI director (Aebli) their team's analysis. The target for the students preparing the analysis was to include the terror event location, an estimate of when it would happen, and the nature of the attack (what kind of kinds of weapon were to be used and the scale, including number of potential casualties, etc.). The course/game was structured over a 12-week period. At the beginning of the project, Aebli took the solution, including all pertinent details, and, in front of the class, placed it in a large manila envelope. This was sealed and secured in his office until the last week of the project, to be opened after all the student teams had given their solutions.

Each week the students were assigned (a lot of) readings before they took a weekly online quiz assessing their comprehension of key details and principles of the investigation. The instructor recorded their individual scores and then calculated an average team score. On completion of the quiz reviews, the instructor published an "intelligence batch" made up of fictitious police reports, e-mails, satellite images, and other intelligence artifacts (figure 18). However, only the teams that scored higher than a predetermined average quiz grade (or, as Aebli put it, cleared that level) got access to the intelligence batch.

Teams that scored, on average, below the required level were allowed to keep taking the quiz until they got their scores up and could move on. Clearly, though, prompt access to the intelligence reports allowed a group to get ahead and get closer to the solution faster. The students reacted well to this form of motivation. One commented, "Having the intel batches released after the completion and average score of quizzes was an interesting way of bringing the group together for another purpose rather than just chatting about the project. It helped us all realize that relying on others to complete their work was essential for the group to advance further in the project."

Aebli experimented with other means of providing information by placing intelligence in a variety of campus locations—an aspect he would like to develop in future iterations. Some of his course or project enhancement ideas center on devising puzzles to unlock those locations. "I've also been trying to do some geocaching. I want to actually plant items on the campus and have [the students] find them. So what I want to do is create a video that would contain a puzzle, and from the video it'll generate a URL that will take them

Figure 18. Sample intelligence batch from SRA 211. © Fred Aebli, 2015; used with permission.

to a webpage, and they'll be able to find a map. It's basically just that next level of engagement, outside of the classroom, and they seem really receptive to that."

Students who completed the course in prior sessions were encouraged to come back and act as Special Agents, often peppering the active Fly Team members with misinformation, false leads, and information intended to detract from their ability to focus on the actual solution. Aebli would actively reach out to the most engaged students from prior course iterations and ask them to act as his moles. Aebli comments: "We have a very small campus setting, and within the degree program the students all kind of see each other, and they are aware—these are all upperclassmen, and they'll play this up. They'll literally walk up to a student and they'll say, 'Are you doing Aebli's terror plot now? I'll tell you the answer,' and they'll say the wrong thing, intentionally giving misinformation, and they take it all very seriously. They're great guys and girls."

Another Penn State student who was originally a business major, hearing of the class and learning that it was available as a minor in security, enrolled and served as another "plant," as Aebli calls him. One of the pieces of intel in the course is a map with some Arabic writing on it. Penn State doesn't offer Arabic, so while many try to use Google, it is of great value for them to work with a genuine Farsi speaker. Aebli's plant, Johnny, is Middle Eastern and works part-time in the Penn State cafeteria. When current students need to have the map deciphered, they have to figure out who Johnny is in the cafeteria and approach him to request his help. Johnny gives Aebli feedback on how the students are doing, providing a live element to the experience and thus allowing Aebli to tailor the flow of information. On occasion when Aebli was traveling off campus, he would require students to provide a "proof of life" by taking a team selfie holding up the current day's newspaper. In another authentic twist, active student Fly Teams were penalized when "agents" or the instructor discovered intelligence artifacts left behind in public spaces. These "security breaches" were treated as grading penalties toward batch releases, slowing team access to subsequent information. Reflecting on the class and the intelligence batches, one student commented, "When the project started, it took a while to start making sense of the intelligence batches. It wasn't until the fourth batch of intel when our team started putting the pieces together. It made me like doing the readings, and I felt addicted at some points reading the intel batches because it was so interesting. I really felt like we were solving a major terror plot."

Reflecting the importance of data visualization in modern crime and terrorism study, designated groups of students as a subproject were tasked with building a social network map to represent and then review data, looking for threatening trends. The data representation/visualization team was tasked to report out at the team meetings and would often lead work sessions, plugging in other countries' data and helping analyze the results. Of their own volition, students with a more technical background developed or found tools to aggregate and collect data. Some used Google spreadsheets integrating a macro that allowed them to color-code cells and then tracked color frequency, analyzing trends in the data to help uncover the plot.

At the conclusion of the project period, each active team had to present their plot analysis. If a team demonstrated that they had correctly uncovered one or two elements of the plot, they were rewarded with points to be applied elsewhere in the course, such as to a previously scored test or assignment. Teams deciphering all components of the plot were given points that could be applied to their final individual course grade. For the class session when the students presented their plot analyses, pulling on his connections and his former career, Aebli welcomed FBI agents, National Guard intelligence officers, local law enforcement, and campus security officers to the class presentations. Many came in uniform, adding an extra sense of authenticity to the proceedings. Aebli's military background combined with his access to the terrorism center at Penn State presented him with access to real-world practitioners who gave concrete and motivating feedback to the students. These professionals provided, according to Aebli, "very supportive and constructive feedback on how to present the information in a concise and meaningful way."

Outcomes

The instructor reported success with this approach in terms of accentuated student engagement and retained knowledge at the end of the course. While class participation numbers remained low, rendering quantitative comparisons moot, his qualitative take was quite clear and confident. He and the assembled experts felt that the students were better able to apply principles and techniques (or competencies) typical of counter-terrorist experts in authentic activities and particularly the "plot" project. Aebli reflected, "At the end of the semester we had a feedback session where we just talked, and they said some things that really meant a lot to me because I do strive hard to get this project together. They were saying, 'We've never had a project'—especially the seniors—'never had a project like this ever,' and I think this is how they should all be run."

One student elaborated, "The project was unlike any other I have ever done. The way Aebli designed it made it feel like you were really trying to solve a terrorist plot. Piecing together the evidence over the semester was challenging and fun, and he did a great job at getting us motivated to solve a problem that counter-terrorism teams work on in the real world." Aebli's long-term ambition is to extend the model to related courses and then even to courses in other disciplines.

The Canvas LMS, according to Aebli, worked well at a fundamental or "pilot" level of complexity. Aebli said, "Canvas has a really interesting feature that lets you create modules. Picture a series of boxes where when you're done with the one box and you've achieved all the predefined elements, you can then have access to the next box or module." He used Canvas to facilitate his management of the project, particularly the announcement and communication tools, while also developing individual Fly Team work spaces. As the students leveled up and were cleared to access the next batch of course intelligence, based on their average quiz score, Aebli dropped documents into these individual team spaces. His actual technical build was minor, as he set up all of the LMS work himself with minimal instructional design team support. The only more complex aspect, more of an enhancement than an essential, was the development of a database that allowed him to amend dates and time stamps throughout the course documentation. His original documents featured static dates that required updating, without which they would lose context and authenticity. He noted that he still needed to manually amend names of key figures, and related information, illustrating an awkward aspect of the authenticity of the courses: a lot of those named in the documents were living people whose roles changed over time or who, in some cases, ceased being living people. Aebli commented with a degree of sangfroid, "I guess that's something that somebody's proud of somewhere. It means we're marching forward on this, but I now have to think about who are these actors going to be now and, subsequently, changing the names or finding new names." The increased automation of updates along with, he explained, finding better ways of automating the leveling up, quiz averaging, and intelligence batch releases in future versions are Aebli's priorities for platform development.

In terms of more ambitious enhancements, he remains interested in developing a new digital dimension and has been considering the Analyst's Notebook software (the class currently uses MS Visio) to assist in the tracking and analysis of social networks. This critical aspect of terrorist plot discovery, tracking what is often called "chatter," can provide intimations of impending action. On an even longer and more ambitious timeline he can see the project's potential as a multiplayer video game and has discussed this possibility with the student-led gaming commons group at Penn State.

Reflections

Aebli felt that in his most recent run of the class he "gave away too much" in terms of points and their impact on grades. At Penn State, in a recent session with the chief academic officer, the topic of grade inflation was discussed. The discussion was wide-ranging, general, and generic (not targeted at Aebli or his class), yet he felt that "[he] had contributed to that trend." Aebli elaborated:

I think it's where I placed the points. So what ended up happening—there was a team this last time—they were the first team ever who got all three—the who, the what and the where. It was funny. The week was during what we call "Threat Week," and at 5 a.m. on Monday of Threat Week you were allowed to submit your assessment. They got up at 5:00 a.m. and submitted it with the timestamp at 5:01 a.m. They were clearly overachievers, and a mistake I made with this—I've been doing team-work a lot, but I assigned the teams, and, specifically with this particular team, I didn't evenly distribute my seniors (and they were great students). I just got an e-mail from one of the team who interviewed with Booz Allen, and at interview they discussed the terror project, and I was like, "Wow, that's cool." So this team was really good at analyzing, reading, and assessing, and they were really competitive. These were the seniors; this is the team that just got it. The sophomores were still like "Hey, we're in college?" Then there were two other teams where one team got two out of the three correct, so they got extra points on an exam, and the other team just got one right, so they just got extra points on a lab grade average. But the winning team, that correctly assessed the threat, they got extra points added on to their final grade. I think it was five points, which is a *lot*. That was the winning team. The other teams didn't get so much of a boost. So I think if I were to do it differently, I would back off the total points I was awarding and redistribute it a little bit differently over the exams and the quiz.

Aebli frames his work in a bigger and more significant metaphor. He likes to explain to the students and their parents that college life and education generally are not only about memorizing and regurgitating facts. He tells the students that the biggest advantage of their college life is the opportunity they are given to make better versions of themselves: more articulate, informed, effective, and discerning critical thinkers who question and really ponder the world around them and their place in it. He tells them that they can only do this if they really engage with their classes, their instructors, their classmates, and the materials they are given to review. When he speaks to parents at new student orientation he shares with them this observation, further illustrating his point by indulging his Disney fandom. As he puts it:

When you go to Walt Disney World, you get engaged with an experience. If you were to go to another amusement park that has a roller coaster (well, Disney World has a roller coaster)—but when you go to another park, it's just a ride. At Disney it is an experience. I think when you go and you get engaged in an experience, it starts to elevate and it takes on another layer or level of significance. It starts to be the experience that will stay with you, not the ride that lasts a minute or two.

This is what he hopes for not only with his class but also with the whole student experience at Penn State: making it an experience and motivating the students intrinsically so that they research and learn beyond the minimal class requirements. His goal is to produce students who, after the class is done, will keep reading and listening to the news with a critical ear, students who will keep discussing the issues with friends, colleagues, and family members, getting beyond infotainment and into the substance. His biggest reward in delivering the class is seeing students focused in the classroom, especially certain students who have really engaged with the materials, who go on to widen their world, listening to podcasts and paying more attention to the news. He values the heightening of intrinsic motivation, where they are not studying to pass a test anymore but because "it's cool to know about stuff." He reflects further, "Maybe it's a sense of awakening—they start to realize what they are passionate about, and then they go that route."

Aebli's own personal motivators clearly go beyond the target of simply getting students to earn a decent grade and complete his course with an above-average GPA. His personal incentive is grounded in a belief that while his subject matter is of great value, the life skills that students take away may be even more important. His students may not become international terrorism experts in the same way that he did not (yet) become an astronaut. He wants his students to do well in the class to help them to become better citizens. He stresses in the class that that terrorism doesn't belong to one country or religion and pushes them to question all the intelligence, including his own. As he puts it, "I want the students to come out of the course more engaged in current events and with a better idea of analyzing what's going on in the world. Sometimes students come in with assumptions and stereotypes about what terrorism is, and I want them to be more informed and able to think critically about things."

His use of gamification techniques certainly appears to have motivated and encouraged students to go well beyond cramming for the test and then immediately forgetting their learning. One of his recent students commented, "Overall the project was fun. It helped me advance my analysis and critical thinking skills, and I wish there were more experiences like this on campus." With Aebli's enthusiasm and energy and the attention he is getting at Penn, there doubtless soon will be.

Where Are They Now?

Aebli's course was run more recently than the other cases, but I did ask him to reflect on the evolution of the course and the feedback he had acted on regarding gamification generally.

BELL—I know that you have not had a great deal of time between class sessions, but what did you learn, or what have you perhaps tweaked about your gamification principles?

AEBLI—On the administrative side, I felt that I needed to review where we were at regarding possible FERPA [Family Educational Rights and Privacy Act] issues. I was concerned because even though I was not sharing grades in any way through the platform, the students were discussing their performance on the quizzes and their grades with each other. When they take the online quiz, which becomes available for a 48- or 72-hour period, they are shown their individual grade, which I then collate and report out to the team as a whole. Then when they receive their team grade, particularly if they haven't made the level needed to progress and requiring them to take the test again, they immediately start saying out loud, "Well I got 100 on that quiz, what did you get?" I talked to my academic officer about that, and he said if they are freely giving that information then it was not a concern from a FERPA perspective. With that resolution, I reflected on how interesting it actually was that when they were doing the comparisons and asking how individual team members had done it wasn't in a badgering sort of way. It was quite the opposite—in a fun, positive, peer-pressure but encouraging kind of way. The whole student group was like, "Yeah, let's get out there—let's go." They would hit it immediately, really encouraging and supporting each other. They wouldn't put it off or say, "I have to get to next class." They would say, "Hey, give me fifteen minutes, and I'll go back and take the quiz again." As the quiz was designed to pull from a question pool, it wasn't the same quiz over and over.

The other thing that I have also noticed was the pace. Technically there are four batches of intelligence information that get released, but the vast majority of the students don't get a sense of urgency and engagement until right around batch two. At that point the mountain of intel went from *this* big to THIS big, and most of them get it then, that, "uh-oh, the third batch is going to be massive—let's move—let's go." And the team that correctly assessed it this year (just [based on] observing them and hearing their conversations and seeing them work together), they got it very early on and were hugely motivated. The team that didn't get it didn't do those things. They hesitated more and seemed unsure of how to proceed. When all is said and done, I think the one thing to my advantage, though, is the material. It's contemporary and authentic. My only real disappointment about this class, a bit of a sad commentary, was that it still is disproportionately homogenous, having had 22 students in it with 21 men and only one woman. The [lack of] diversity is definitely problematic for us as a discipline (not only or specifically in this class). Right now, that's what we see in tech—not enough females. The one woman that was in the class was actually from Russia, and she thought it was very intriguing and told me that she got a lot out of the class. For the most part, though, when you see the participants in this format, those who really grab this material, they do tend to be first-person-shooter kind of gaming guys. It's certainly great that they immediately related it to that and they love that. I don't want to lose that, but I am hoping to engage and interest a wider pool of participants if at all possible. What inspires and motivates me the most about this class is when I start off the first class session by saying, "If you make it through this class, I guarantee you're going to be a different person by the time you're done." I'm confident in saying this, as what we do in this class is we look at this whole issue of radicalization from a much different angle, and we look at it critically. What we end up with is not the typical knee-jerk reactions of, "Oh, you know . . ." the stereotypical conclusions that they will even see in the mainstream press and in mass media around them at times. The students start to realize that there is more to this issue than what is often portrayed in the media. All the analysis and, I believe, the authenticity of those factors act as kind of a steroid input to this project. The students really get into it, and I think they really like the competitive piece—so it's really something that I am proud of and that I know has great potential for this and other classes.

BELL—What would take this project or the concept of gamification at Penn State to the next level?

AEBLI—I was invited up to The University at Buffalo where they were hosting a Meaningful Gaming conference, a really simple, early-stage conference. At that event there was another professor who came off as very combative and provocative. The first presenter who spoke was very open-minded, wanting to try new things, and he made some great comments. Then I got up, and I was sort of the applied guy, and I made my comments about what I had attempted, my preliminary successes and so on. Then the third guy got up, and he was very hard-edged, and he didn't like a lot of what we said. To be fair, he warned us ahead of schedule, saying, "You know, when I do this kind of thing I don't get paid a lot of money, and what I like to do is to pick fights." I thought it was a strange thing to say, and I've spent a lot of time around guys like that in the marine corps. I started to pick up on the fact from this guy that he was dismissing this and viewed gamifying a course as being just this month's new thing or a fad like the hula-hoop. I started to even question myself if this is just a fad—this year's MOOC? I think whatever we do, we have to make sure that we document and demonstrate it has good results and show that the barrier to entry is surmountable. I have shown a number of faculty that it is easy to set up and doesn't require a great deal of technical support. So that's the thing I'm finding that everyone comes up to me to ask me: "Well, how did you actually do it?" and "What did you really do?" When I show them that it's, you know, taking quiz scores and averaging them to show a team average, then often my colleagues will say, "What, that's it?" I've concluded that there's sort of a mystique to it, whereas in reality, it's about implementing some creative ideas, not necessarily with expensive or high-cost build-outs. With those elements conveyed and illustrated I think it is possible to get buy-in from the university. At my institution, one of the things I know they are hoping to do is create some easy-to-follow steps that show other faculty members how they might take their first few steps to give it a try, to usher it in.

One of the things people don't realize is that gamification is already around them in many formats and that it is part of our lives even in relatively mundane ways. Those little key-fob things from the gas station or cards from the coffee shops (the tags that you hang on your key that you swipe and get points), well, that's gamification, and people don't make that connection. I think that so many people are locked into thinking that it's got to be a *Warcraft* strategy, virtual or board game, with serious metaphors and high build costs. Thoughtful, creative teachers have been trying this kind of work for years and years. The gamification is an added flavor to spice up [already] good, or even great, instruction. It doesn't have to be this whole, massive, scary production.

BELL—So you're moving towards a platform of changing student behavior, getting people more engaged in current affairs and informed in how to find resources, etc., and not just academic performance for a test or a quiz?

AEBLI—Right. So I was thinking about this. Should I try to capture some survey data from the students who have taken the course and ask them a simple question like, "Are you watching the news more?" or "Are you understanding the issues more?" I think that intrinsic motivation is a very important thing for higher education in general. There is too much discussion going on about the cost of education, so everyone's talking about doing something, and we're all aware of the fact that the next financial bubble is the financial aid bubble that is going to burst if students keep defaulting. So parents, not all parents but most, shop by the course cost not by the experience. I had this interesting discussion with some parents the other day. These were parents of kids who are very hyper-athletic (travel team and everything else) who are looking to get a scholarship [at] any costs. I said to them, "Did you ever think what you would do if you got the scholarship but it is for a Division III school with a very poor alumni base, or it's for a liberal arts degree where they will certainly make it through the program but they won't get a job?" Clearly I'm being anecdotal, but if you get people to understand that when you're looking at an educational institution you must look at the full breadth of it as best you can and ask yourself what kind of experience is it going to be both in and out of the classroom? I think, I get the sense that, that's getting lost. So I keep trying to tell people, to help parents when they're shopping junior year and senior year of high school, that these are the things you should want and that's what you should be looking at. You know, the last time a lot of these parents were in school was 20–25 years ago, and now, all of a sudden, they are shopping for their kids, and they're thinking it's still 1986, and it's not. It's a lot different and a lot more expensive. Their kids need to come out with clear, marketable skills and, even more importantly, behaviors that will stand them in good stead for the next three to four decades of their career in this changing world. Getting people to be motivated—the Indiana Jones spirit, I call it—I want them to be seekers, to be ready for change, to be able to analyze and deal with uncertainty. To be motivated even when you don't know all the answers.

BELL—Generally is the tactic to use the game element to get them through fear of failure then get them to engagement with the subject matter?

AEBLI—There is the weird academic notion that it must be rigorous and, to an extent, not fun because that's what we do and if it's not hard and challenging and superserious (you don't get a C or a D) . . . you know, it's like that . . . I started out one of my talks with, "Why can't learning be fun?" I know certain things are hard, but even things that are hard can be fun.

The one observation I made in my class as we debriefed at the end [with the students] is that the authenticity of the subject matters of the activities is critical. To illustrate how they respect this aspect, recently a professor who left our institution, an expert in terrorism and the psychology of terrorism, made himself available for a live interview session. The students were asking him whether there might be a way to use predictive analytics in a similar way as they are used in the business world to identify or predict the likelihood that an individual is, or might become, a radicalized person. My former colleague was adamant about the fact that it was not a feasible application. He said, "No, there are far too many risk factors and you can't come up with a complex enough equation that would accurately do that." So my students heard that talk and we discussed it, and they somewhat begrudgingly accept[ed] his opinion. About two months later, near the end of the course, the White House announced out that they're going to spend $500 million on a new program called Gecko. This is a new browser-based advertising program that's going to be dropping banner ads on select individuals' PCs who they think may be potential radical candidates. The students were like, "So if all this data over here is saying you're not going to be able to do that yet the White House is going to go out and spend all these millions of dollars to do this, then who is out of alignment here?" I was really proud of them at that moment because they picked up on that before I did, before I recognized the contradiction. So I pulled out a bunch of material in class that day and said "Let's look at this, talk about this." And it was that moment where I saw most clearly how comprehensively they were engaged in the material. It was a really cool discussion, and it wasn't just two guys sitting in the class holding the whole discussion. They organized into groups enthusiastically arguing different sides of the story. That engagement piece arrived through the project, so that's cool. It's a fun, fun approach, and I wish I had learned it sooner.

BELL—You're making critical thinkers of your students—that's a dangerous path you have started on.

AEBLI—Yeah, so it makes you walk out saying, "What have I done?" In my formative student days, as an undergrad, I took discrete math, a philosophy course on existentialism, and a Pascal programming course all in one semester. The result was I came out thinking that I couldn't believe in anything. I had just proved $1+1$ equaled 2, while I had read Nietzsche pretty much proving that I didn't exist. Then I had the programming class, which was challenging of its own merit. In it I had to create a game of solitaire, but I had never played solitaire. So I had to sit down with my grandmother when I got home so she could teach me solitaire—so my life was complicated. I was on pretty uncertain ground at that stage of my academic life, but it forced me into critical thinking and reflection. I think that's part of what inspired me as an educator—get the students outside their comfort zone. It's a really cool journey to take students on, and I believe it makes them better students and hopefully better members of society.

■ ■ ■ ■ ■ ■ ■ ■ ■ ■ ■ ■ ■ ■

CHAPTER EIGHT

Assessing Gamification

CONCLUSIONS AND IMPLICATIONS

The cases and practitioners analyzed to this point have approached the question of gamification in quite different ways, from Easter eggs and hero's journeys through games exploring ethical decision making, fighting bosses in the realm of Logos, and solving threats of international terrorism. The range of implementations makes direct comparison and even relative assessment a challenge. None of the cases have the longitudinal or quantitative data to proclaim significance in a true statistical sense. We should certainly be wary of seeking to unequivocally say which works better or even forming a template for interested educators to follow in these pioneers' footsteps. So much is dependent on the energy and enthusiasm of the instructor that these examples may not be replicable without the specific personality and/or circumstance of the person who dreamed up the example. In these early stages, with beta versions and low-tech implementations, the instructor's passion for what he or she is doing (with acknowledgement of the homogeneity of the sample set of instructors) is crucial for getting students on board. Any instructor who tries to implement a system or model of a gamified course in a mode that he or she does not feel passionate about is not likely to succeed. My candid and simple advice to instructors interested in gamifying a course should probably be to just go with whichever version/chapter spoke most clearly to you and made you think, "Wow, that's cool!" If you are not a *Dungeons & Dragons* fan or a former player, as I'm not, then a Dungeons and Discourse (or a Dungeons and Anything) course is likely not for you. If you like hunting and puzzles, then you could probably carry off an Easter egg–based model.

Having said that, and having stressed that there are clear differences between the models, if we are able to strip away some of the window dressing to get to fundamental principles, then I believe that we will start to see similar traits and underlying concepts. When we start to look for commonalities, rather than differences, we can then contemplate moving to a position of re-

Figure 19. Gamifying math study—subject: author's (second) daughter.

view against some form of consistent criteria. Starting from the point of the instructors' motivation behind the builds, why they chose to pursue this work, we see obvious common ground. The goal of improving student engagement and boosting low completion rates is a strikingly resonant and consistent aim of all five practitioners.

To facilitate cross-case comparison and provide valuable feedback on gamification choices and effects, we really need to be able to apply some sort of a framework or a structured rubric to review and compare the example courses. The goal of this chapter, then, is to provide a form of cross-case analysis, a means of getting beyond "this is cool" or "I don't like that idea" to something more scientific. I would like to see if we can discern why these courses, to the extent that they do, succeed in producing encouraging results by increasing student engagement and, in a variety of ways, enhancing student outcomes. With some means of better breaking down and analyzing what is happening in the five cases, we should be able to develop a means of assessing possible future courses' plans and ideas, determining possible enhancements, and suggesting foci for practice and future research.

Before we get to the analysis, let's review exactly how gamification is incorporated into these courses. The findings from the five examples we have suggest the need to consider three underlying elements:

What technological skill set is needed to implement a gamified course?
Who can or is doing this kind of incorporation?
Why are they doing it in this way?

The individual cases illustrate how specific and distinct elements can be used to deliver gamification in a variety of flavors. Let's look at these three criteria in order.

What Technological Skill Set Is Required?

In the examples, gamification runs the gamut from specifically defined and discrete elements, leaderboards, and Easter eggs to faculty behaviors (providing timely feedback, recognizing effort) and conceptual, comprehensive narrated scenarios. These scenarios, of course, include the student as a hero (University of New Hampshire, UNH) and as an explorer across mysterious lands (Massachusetts College of Liberal Arts, MCLA). The practitioners/pioneers have implemented gamification elements through a can-do blend of basic programming skills, good intentions, and individual effort. In the University of South Florida (USF) and MCLA cases, faculty practitioners who had branched out to academic technology-support positions utilized basic HTML and LMS features. In the UNH case, the visionary drive of Neil Niman carried a very enthusiastic, but inexperienced, team of developers with limited technical skills. Only the University of Waterloo (UW) course benefitted from external technical team support for what was still quite a basic technical build. The tech team at UW was responsible for some build-out of scenarios hosted in the LMS and the main element build-out of a leaderboard that was able to actually work based on scenario grading, providing an anonymous view of each student's position in the class with anonymized peers above and below. This build, arguably the most complex element of all the course builds, was still a relatively small investment and significantly less than that spent on a typical technical implementation.

Most instructors and students stressed that their experiences would have been enhanced with richer implementations and greater functionality, yet they remained supportive. As the cases illustrate, initial wireframe or pencil and paper versions can prove concept and provide feedback. Given the amount of revisions and tweaks that practitioners made between course runs, I would not advise investing in a costly build-out too soon only to have to deconstruct and start again. However, to support maturing plans to move beyond the pencil and paper versions, and to scale for impact across a wider student body, institutions will need to provide significant technical support and indirect funding in the form of teaching assistants or course releases to allow faculty developers the time and space to develop their ideas.

Who Is Incorporating Gamification?

The development of each of the courses in these cases was driven by the project lead. In my sample, all five project leads were male and all around their early to mid-forties. This demographic (the first generation exposed to large-scale arcade video games—remember *Space Invaders* in 1978 and *PacMan* in 1980) is now reaching positions in academia, and in society at large, where they are established enough to experiment with concepts they find engaging. The maturation of this first video or arcade game generation could be one reason why we are now starting to see serious experimentation with gamification that earlier (or older) educators might not have felt was appropriate in a formal academic or corporate setting. Clearly this is not a gender or age-specific set of principles. In workshops that I have delivered on the subject of gamification between 2014 and 2016, the participants are predominantly female (in classes of 25, typically 21–22 are female) and are a mix of backgrounds and ethnicities. I would expect that hero-centered narratives may be more to male tastes, but the majority of the principles of the cases in this work seem to be demographic agnostic with the possible caveat, mentioned earlier, that midcareer educators seem to be in a place where they have the confidence to try this kind of experiment.

Why Are They Gamifying Courses in This Way?

The relative paucity of communication between each instructor and their institutional leaders may be related to the personality of the project leads and their desire to retain a degree of autonomy. All of them seemed somewhat wedded to being on the periphery of mainstream academe. Adding another level of intrigue might be the evolution of the term *gamification* itself. During my interviews and materials review it became apparent that there is already a double-edged sword element with regard to both the term and the concept of gamification. The term is current and dynamic, and it gains attention quickly.

Yet gamification is frequently dismissed as a fad, like the next massive open online course (MOOC). This mixed perspective seemingly accentuated the practitioners' desire to stay off the radar, at least until their ideas were out and tested. Even when higher-level institutional acceptance was apparently likely (recalling USF's promotional tweeting of the course), so is/was the scorn of those jaded by a wave of recent "next big thing" proclamations. Having been involved in the hype around multiuser synchronous communication and virtual worlds (*Second Life* was once "the future") and, most recently, MOOCs, it may well be prudent of practitioners to initially duck the spotlight and make their errors and tweaks in the shadows. Perhaps once their gamified concept is refined and once their student outcome data has started to prove the efficacy of their work, then they will be willing to emerge from the shadows. This subterfuge of taking on the world in a private battle (initially) could also just be resonant with the gaming mindset. Remember that some of these people were interplanetary warlords in their youth. They need a challenge or perhaps even a crusade—the edgier the better.

The only downside of these lone-wolf innovators, as Gerol Petruzella of MCLA notes, is that their experiments tend to remain isolated and unlikely to impact education more broadly—even at their own institutions. Breaking out of this isolation status is the next challenge if widespread dissemination is the goal. In chapter 9 we will look at the only one of the five cases that does seem to have shed itself of its off-the-radar status and has prompted a much wider institutional adoption of gamification principles. Be thinking, dear reader, about which case you believe is most likely to really catch on, or to catch fire, from the ones you have read (or skimmed) thus far.

Though the five cases are all distinct in the way that they have been gamified, a valuable line of thought is whether we can assess the *degree* of gamification as a means of incrementally encouraging more intentional and widespread implementation at an institution. It is important to clarify that it is not particularly helpful to try to quantify gamification inputs or efforts and certainly not to simply rate them as successes or failures. However, the obvious research questions and pathways to widespread adoption will raise the question of variable correlation between the degree of gamification and, as best we have them, standardized or consistent measures of student engagement and learning outcomes. Any kind of correlation or degree of gamification and student engagement, particularly with larger datasets, could drive wider institutional acceptance—a proposal supported by the practitioners. The fact that gamification has not coalesced into a fixed set of rules may, in fact, be beneficial in that it negates the need to describe a one-size-fits-all package to institutions. In terms of institutional support, the University of Waterloo appears unique given its location (Canada's high-tech belt), its administration's sense of entrepreneurialism, and its faculty's technical experimentation. Nonetheless, their vice provost asserted that she would need more concrete, quantified data on the positive effects of gamification on student outcomes before she would be comfortable advocating for sustained institutional endorsement.

It is unlikely that any of the formats or instructor strategies in the selected courses will be universally successful for all students. Where competition works for some, collaboration or cooperation will work better for others. Even in the small sample in this study, gamification, or certainly elements of gamification, appear to show enough potential to merit further research. My conclusion separates MOOCs from other online courses, as I believe MOOCs have a quite different potential as vehicles for gamification.

MOOCs

MOOCs are still, as of 2016, a relatively new format with audiences and demographics atypical for tertiary education. Under the heading "MOOCs Are Not Reaching the Disadvantaged," a 2013 E. J. Emanuel study drawing from over 34,000 MOOC (Coursera) participants in 32 courses found that 83% of the surveyed students already had a two- or four-year postsecondary degree. Although the survey response rates were quite low, it is likely that MOOCs do not tend to enroll the demographic that most institutions are trying to reach through online program expansion. As Emanuel concluded, "Far from realizing the high ideals of their advocates, MOOCs seem to be reinforcing the advantages of the 'haves' rather than educating the 'have-nots.'"

While MOOC participants are demonstrating through their enrollment an inherent interest in the subject of the course, they do not generally need or pay for credits. It would seem likely, as the instructor of the fairy tale MOOC asserts, that a lightly gamified MOOC course with limited instructor connectivity would not have a huge influence on engagement or completion. As with most MOOC data gathered so far (Emanuel 2013; Perna et al. 2013), Kevin Yee's USF course is typical in that it had slightly elevated, but still extremely low, course-completion rates.

Gamification may promote engagement, but given that only 5% of participants complete MOOCs, they clearly need more work on their basic format and goals. Fundamental MOOC challenges such as instructor responsiveness and the lack of student buy-in need to be addressed before a sustained gamification project is going to be of value. Elements of gamification may well increase completion rates in MOOCs; Yee's course had a completion rate slightly above average. In terms of format, if the MOOCs were to target smaller numbers of participants engaged enough to cooperate and compete, then gamification might have more of an effect. The resultant product could be re-branded as a "Modest [sized] [not so] Open Online Course."

More Typical Online Courses

The UNH and MCLA courses, while covering different subjects, are both targeted at naïve, inexperienced students—that is, students potentially lacking confidence and perhaps motivation around the subject matter. The instructors and developers of both courses suggest that gamification might have the most benefit for entry or introductory-level courses. Petruzella suggests that gamification, or a gamified course, may be a way of transitioning students from an environment of "staid high school chalk-and-talk" to one where participation, critical thinking, and creativity are encouraged. The enhanced participation relayed clearly by his students and their self-declared enthusiasm for the subject and the format certainly seem to bear out that view.

The UNH students involved in the development team felt that adding gamification to a core economics course particularly would help students who were somewhat math-phobic but were required to take math or math-based courses (microeconomics by way of example). The mnemonic value of the personal narrative, in terms of providing memorable metaphor and helping students retain key concepts, suggests that low- or entry-level students whose intrinsic motivation for their subject matter has not yet flourished indeed might benefit most from this format.

Somewhat contradicting the suggestion that fragile learners may be those best supported by gamification was UW's Greg Andres's assertion that his real-world-connected scenario games might appeal more to mature students. Andres's perspective certainly underscores the value of authenticity in assignments or scenarios but does not necessarily speak to the value of the gamified elements in his course or a gamified course per se. The format of the pass/fail co-op class at UW as a means of supporting and keeping students connected to the institution during a remote work experience is unusual, and it is genuinely hard to extrapolate more widely applicable conclusions. If Andres is correct, then there may be a continued or extended role for this kind of approach within the broader area of workforce retraining and serving the learning needs of adult working students. However, the class-wide student engagement and completion of nonessential content and activities in his model was encouraging and suggests possible wider efficacy than he himself suggested.

Applying Frameworks: Cross-Case Analysis

As the analyses of the examples in earlier chapters indicates, gamification or gameful design is not a black/white or on/off feature. In order to better review the effectiveness of principles of gamification in developed sample courses, two antecedents in the field are worth revisiting. The works of Kapp (2012) and Csikszentmihalyi (1975) include their frameworks to evaluate gamification (Kapp) and the likelihood of an experience engendering flow (Csikszentmihalyi). Combined they provide a means of evaluating degree of gamification or the potential to engender intrinsic motivation (a hugely valuable metric if it can be used with consistency).

The Kapp Framework

In his 2012 text *The Gamification of Learning and Instruction*, Karl Kapp describes constituent parts of gamified courses under the heading, "It's in the Game: Understanding Game Elements." His work has great applicability to this study, as he breaks down gamified courses into constituent elements with a view to prompting discussion about the degree, nature, and effect of gamification. It was apparent through interviews and reviews of course materials that the various faculty, developers, and practitioners had directly or indirectly incorporated many of the elements described by Kapp. Instructor preference seemed to drive most design/gamification decisions, although the different formats of courses (MOOC, co-op support, for-credit) and the differing demographic characteristics of their targeted students also may have influenced design choices. I found it interesting to speculate which course format would score most highly when reviewed against Kapp's criteria. I assessed the courses quantitatively against the Kapp framework by scoring the extent to which each course addresses his key tenets on a scale from zero to two (table 1). A concept that is not addressed in any way scores a zero, one that is touched upon perhaps only scantly receives a one, and an element that is clearly emphasized and intentionally included as an integral part of the course by the project lead is marked as two.

Table 1. Analysis of the five gamified courses, based on the Kapp (2012) criteria for assessing gamification

	USF Fairy Tale MOOC	UNH EconJourney	UW Ethical Decision Making	MCLA Dungeons and Discourse	Penn State Threat of Terrorism
Abstraction of concepts and reality	1	2	1	2	0
Goals	2	2	1	2	2
Rules	0	1	1	2	2
Conflict, competition, cooperation	2	1	2	2	2
Time	0	1	0	1	1
Reward structures	1	1	2	2	2
Feedback	1	2	2	1	2
Levels	1	2	1	2	2
Storytelling	1	2	1	2	2
Curve of interest	1	2	1	1	2
Aesthetics	2	1	1	2	1
Replay or do-over	1	2	1	1	2
Totals	**13**	**19**	**14**	**20**	**20**

Note: USF = University of South Florida, UNH = University of New Hampshire, UW = University of Waterloo, MCLA = Massachusetts College of Liberal Arts.

Applying the Kapp Analysis

Yee's USF course does a reasonable job across a number of Kapp criteria. The Easter egg focus scores well on elements like competition and reward. His course's clear goals (finding eggs through accessing content) and the competition this engendered, even though collaboration and conflict were not emphasized, also rate highly. The instructor's time constraints, including the fact that he had to forgo some of the other elements that he had planned, do negatively affect the course's overall score. If he had not dropped his plans for course badges and his analogy for team progress, his course would have scored higher in curve of interest, storytelling, feedback, and reward categories. For a solo effort undertaken on top of other duties and responsibilities, Yee's work shows great promise. However, in the absence of extensive automation and technical build, it is again apparent that the delivery of a highly gamified course—as defined by the Kapp criteria—requires major instructor commitment and/or more extensive institutional support, perhaps via supplemental facilitators or teaching assistants. While this requirement of commitment, especially in low-tech or pilot gamified courses, is a possible barrier to entry and certainly needs to be noted, instructor enthusiasm and advocacy in all examples brought encouraging results. Yee's study was clearly an example of this, with the possible extra caveat that some of the challenges to his connectivity were consequences of his decision to run the course as a MOOC. The enrollment numbers, though not massive, were certainly large enough to make course management, even with his ideas of grouped participants, rewards, and feedback, near impossible. If he were to gamify a fixed-enrollment course, with a more typical enrollment of 20 to 25 students, he doubtless would be able to realize his ideas more fully, and his course likely would score higher.

Niman's UNH course scores higher in a number of areas that Yee did not even attempt in his USF course. The project scores maximum points in categories such as abstraction of concepts and reality, storytelling, and curve of interest. Of all the cases examined in this book, Niman's course made the most concerted attempt to weave gamification intrinsically into course content. His personal lack of conviction for what he called "simple rewards systems" or "feedback structures" explained his focus on tying progress in the course to the students' personal stories. While he had challenges in early iterations of his course, obligating multiple revisions and tweaks to his strategies, his high score on the scale indicates, by Kapp's criteria, an extremely gamified course.

The second takeaway from the cross-case analysis is that weaving gamification themes and elements throughout a course and/or wedding core content to a creative story perhaps provides a disproportionate boost on the Kapp scale. In presenting on this topic, my finding is that people think of narrative development and creative storytelling as the hardest element to conceptualize. My counsel has typically been that very effective, intrinsically motivating courses can be developed that ignore the elements that aspirant developers finding daunting. Again, as the cases show, not all boxes need to be checked to produce a good experiment. Acceptance of an imperfect test model is a condition of all the studied practitioners, reflecting their gameful/techie nature. "Launch then tweak" is their mantra.

Andres's Ethical Decision Making course returns mixed results when mapped to the Kapp framework. This finding was not totally unexpected given the way that the games were isolated from other elements of the course. The content-related ethical games provided instant feedback, a sense of reward (accentuated by the leaderboard), and a level of competition. However, of the five cases, Andres's game elements are the most extrinsic and the least intrinsically woven into the fabric of the course. They serve more as self-checks or enhanced multiple-choice quizzes. The activities absolutely did serve a purpose as a form of relief from traditional course fare (e.g., text and discussion boards). Students, particularly those who consumed them all in one sitting, certainly found them engaging, but the effects are likely finite and only felt while engaged in the games rather than in the course as a whole.

Petruzella's MCLA Dungeons and Discourse course (like the UNH Econ-Journey) scores well across multiple categories by virtue of the embedded game reward mechanisms, a sense of levels (culminating in boss levels), attempts at an aesthetic theme, and notions of conflict, cooperation, and competition. The higher scores on the Kapp criteria would seem to confirm that deeper integration of game elements with more course elements tied directly to games or game principles are reflective of a more gamified course. His course only skips elements of time and feedback, again consequences of his limited availability given other duties and a low-tech build with minimal automated feedback and little support for scale.

Finally, Aebli's terrorism course jointly holds top scores across the Kapp matrix. His competitive nature, his interest in the comprehensive Disney experience, and his affinity for games of all stripes, including basic board games, positions him and his work in an exciting place. The more homogenous class structure of his discipline at his institute facilitates his ability to implement a very game-like environment with quite rigid rules and competitive formats. Again, in quite a low- to mid-tech build, he drives the process through his energy and through a lot of behind the scenes work in preparing materials, updating scenarios and tracking progress. His score is penalized, perhaps unfairly, by the lack of abstraction of concepts in a gameful narrative. It is more likely a weakness of the matrix than of Aebli's work that his authenticity and realism are not fully acknowledged as a driver of student motivation. By all accounts, including student feedback and grades, his model was extremely effective.

In conclusion, while the matrix offers a useful framework for cross-case comparison, the application of this framework is also somewhat limited. In the long term and with greater numbers among the practitioner student pools, we should be looking to directly correlate evaluative scores with student engagement, course completion, or longer-term persistence. Having said that, even this some-what rudimentary assessment is valuable for practitioner discussion around aspects of their courses that are either undeveloped or worthy of enhancement. Research comparisons should compare gamified versus not-gamified (in any way) courses to see if any difference in student engagement and other student outcomes is detected. If one were able to confirm a relationship between Kapp scores and student engagement, then these early models could be made more effective and ultimately more widely disseminated and adopted.

Csikszentmihalyi's Flow Framework

As a second means of evaluating the likelihood of efficacy in the practitioner models, I look to the work of Csikszentmihalyi who, in 1975, described eight components as critical in engendering flow in any environment, be it academic, sporting, or social. As a form of insurance, and in an attempt to provide more of a psychological review of what was happening in the cases, I compared the individual cases against eight components of a typical Csikszentmihalyi flow analysis. My hope was that this supplemental analysis might help assess the relative worth of implementing gamification elements in light of their propensity to engender a state of flow in those accessing the courses. Facilitating flow states could be critical for encouraging students to engage with academic content in a similar way as they do with game content. When flow has been achieved, the only thing the participant is thinking about is the activity (concern for self disappears), and the participant experiences a notable loss of sense of time (hours feel like minutes). Translated to an academic course, the nature or amount of flow might be a key determinant for student engagement. The positive correlation between sense of flow and engagement with materials is more than likely. This is of particular importance given that the correlation between engagement and student success, defined as course completion including passing any exams, has been demonstrated in many studies including, significantly, by the US Department of Education in 2010. Whereas Kapp's framework assesses "how gamified" the course is, the Csikszentmihalyi framework may show "how effective a game is" or how the specific gamified elements add up.

Applying Flow Analysis

The goal of this review was to assess whether any degree of flow is likely as a direct result of an instructor's efforts at gamification. As with the Kapp

Table 2. Analysis of the five gamified courses, based on the Csikszentmihalyi (1975) criteria for assessing flow

	USF Fairy Tale MOOC	UNH EconJourney	UW Ethical Decision Making	MCLA Dungeons and Discourse	Penn State Threat of Terrorism
Achievable	2	2	2	1	1
Requiring concentration	2	2	2	2	2
(Tasks have) clear goals	2	1	2	2	2
Immediate and continual feedback	0	1	2	1	2
Effortless involvement	2	1	1	1	2
Control over actions	1	1	2	1	2
Totals	**9**	**8**	**11**	**8**	**11**

Note: USF = University of South Florida, UNH = University of New Hampshire, UW = University of Waterloo, MCLA = Massachusetts College of Liberal Arts.

analysis, I reviewed each course, using a zero-to-two-point scale indicating lack of presence (zero), nominal presence (one), and strong focus/emphasis (two). The results are presented in table 2.

Selected student testimonials (those who "got it") in the USF MOOC indicate that, for some, participation in the gamified elements (the Easter egg hunts) was associated with time passing quickly. Those individuals spent a great deal of time in the thrall of the class, in a sense, engaging with course materials and, in another sense, simply looking for eggs. In an open or voluntary participation MOOC environment, the Csikszentmihalyi concept of class rules was always going to be difficult to enforce, while the large numbers, even in this midsized MOOC, meant that immediate and/or continual feedback was beyond the instructor's capacity. For Yee's course, these challenges of scale and lack of time or resources to implement automated feedback mechanisms for support translate to a low score on a number of the Csikszentmihalyi elements, as they did on the Kapp scores. Student survey feedback indicates that for the engaged participants, time flowed in the hunts that had clear, achievable goals requiring concentration, so the course scored well in the first few categories. It would be interesting to test whether a more fully gamified MOOC with participants agreeing to rules for participation (akin to an honor code) and with systems in place to provide instant, corrective feedback might further ameliorate persistent MOOC retention issues.

The UNH EconJourney model focuses the learning on a game environment. Niman's deconstruction of his course and his conscious rebuild around key elements of the hero's journey was both complex and ambitious. Applying the Csikszentmihalyi analysis, the course scores lower than others in terms of clarity of goals, immediacy of feedback, and control—all of which could impede students getting to flow. Niman's development team consisted exclusively of highly motivated "overachievers," who perhaps lacked perspective on clarity and high-support needs. Elements that speak to academically high-achieving students may not resonate with fragile learners. As Niman relayed in follow-up conversations, initial (beta) launches allowed him to hone the product. In versions 2.0 and then 3.0 he experimented with variation of guidance and prescriptiveness of course parameters. His course development and revision cycle best illustrated the need to get just right the level of challenge and the support structures when trying to get participants close to flow. If students, including those challenged and lacking confidence when facing economic concepts, buy into the spirit of the game, develop effective personal narratives, and enjoy the comparisons (e.g., sharing and voting up or down their classmates' versions) then the course is well structured to get them to flow. In his initial format, the one reviewed for this study, it was not clear that students were envisioning clear goals or feeling any sense of control over their actions. In later versions, when Niman and the UNH team were able to get more students beyond the early, conceptual stages of the course and engage them in the development of a dynamic, personalized narrative, the course would score higher on the elements in this framework.

In Andres's Ethical Decision Making course at UW, although the games provide rewards they are distinct from the core coursework. When students were immersed in the games, time was clearly deemphasized, as illustrated by the students who ran through all of the games in quick time to top the leaderboard. I gave the course a high Csikszentmihalyi score for its game time rather than engagement with the majority of the other course content. The lack of integration of gamification deeper into the course materials suggests that the course could have lower student engagement in the substantial non-gamified sections. The games accounted for 18% of the course grade, but that score was attained for attempting the game in any way. Students actually could complete the course and gain a passing grade either by ignoring or perfunctorily attempting the games. Andres's course is one of the least gamified per the Kapp framework, but the games that are implemented do induce high-level Csikszentmihalyi flow. The lesson would seem to be that with better integration of the game elements and extension of more sustained feedback throughout the course, the approach would have great potential as a template for a simple non–journey/narrative model. The value of discrete Q&A, multiple-choice, or knowledge-checking "games" should not be dismissed, as certainly they engendered interest among what otherwise could be a passive, perfunctory group.

Petruzella's Dungeons and Discourse implementation at MCLA in some ways received the harshest end-user feedback from experienced gamer students, but it was the only course held to those very high (gamer) standards. According to Kapp's criteria, Petruzella's MCLA course is the most gamified course. The Csikszentmihalyi analysis captures the limitations of his format in that it is wedded to nonautomated classroom sessions where the students barter for gold. Adoption of an interactive interface, where students would be able to control their own actions and receive immediate and continual feedback, would increase the flow score substantially. His student feedback was very specific in this respect, as it identified that the ability to track (or control) their progress across dynamic landscapes representing the various realms would have been a valuable and appreciated enhancement.

Aebli's Penn State Threat of Terrorism and Crime course dropped Csikszentmihalyi points only in the achievable category. In his first few iterations, no students scored maximum points by uncovering the full plot details. Subsequently, as he reported in his catch-up call, one class of overachiever students did solve the whole plot. It would seem that the authenticity and immediacy of his materials engage students to strive for what might even have seemed totally unachievable. He effectively used the tools available to him to provide feedback and to clarify rules and goals. His case may have been a little skewed in that he was, to lapse into the vernacular, pitching geeky guy stuff to geeky guys. However, he deserves praise above and beyond that possible caveat given his efforts to engage more gender balance in his class and even in the decision to work in a subject area that is politically sensitive and to encourage moving beyond knee-jerk journalism to real-world global perspective by fostering critical thinking and thoughtful consumption of wider media messaging. These outcomes, perhaps even beyond his more traditional curricular elements, prove a serious motivator, as students sense they are achieving more than checking a box and moving on with accumulated credits.

Comparison Results from the Cross-Case Analysis

Overall, the cross-case reviews suggest that the UNH, MCLA, and Penn State courses are the most gamified in terms of the criteria outlined by Kapp. The Csikszentmihalyi analysis adds flavor, but in most cases, technical simplicity places barriers that hamper flow state. The high-scoring UW course is inflated by the emphasis on the game scenarios, which are only a small part of the course. If weighted across the whole course, the UW figure likely would be closer to the otherwise quite consistent scores for the other courses. The likelihood of gamified courses getting to Csikszentmihalyi's flow is most impacted by the lack of immediate and continual feedback in these models. Without more technical support and a build that would accommodate greater automation, these courses are not going to achieve maximal flow. Aebli's terrorism course comes closest given that the feedback systems are augmented by well-structured peer support and encouragement). He also has the clearest and easiest to pick up and play goal (solve a plot) and the clearest rules (deadlines, points, and penalties).

The Kapp analysis would seem to suggest that a more substantial alignment of actual coursework and core content with game elements, particularly around a central narrative, is most likely to positively affect gamification and *likely* student engagement. The USF and UW courses have added some game elements (leaderboards, Easter eggs, game scenarios), but both stopped short of an integrated and gamified course in these initial, experimental versions. An amalgamated model featuring MCLA and UNH-like centrality of narrative with added self-checks and UW-like distinct games would, applying the Kapp criteria, be the most likely to approximate the type of engagement that could lead to enhanced student outcomes. From Csikszentmihalyi we take the value of simplicity, clear rules, clear target, challenge, and the value of competition and a chase. Aebli's terrorism case illustrates the value of realism and authenticity as an incentive, which is both at odds and in line with Kapp's narrative need.

Part of the excitement, and also part of the confusion, around gamification comes from the fact that it is a general banner term that can be interpreted by practitioners as they see fit. Looking at this with a glass-half-full perspective, it is also worth noting that students are generally tolerant of any and all efforts to incorporate even rudimentary elements beyond a staid read-post-respond format. Administrators, when consulted, are tentatively supportive, and most recognize that student demographics and expectations are changing. On the downside, there is limited collaboration between academic practitioners and potential supporters, funders, or entrepreneurs. Within the administrative side of academia, there is not yet motivation to propagate principles or get them more widely disseminated. Significantly enhanced student learning outcomes, if shown to correlate to the kind of increased student engagement referred to in this study, may well be the catalyst to wider adoption. Coordinated support in the shape of academic buy-in from peers and academic leaders is necessary for these solo efforts to gain traction. Institutional embrace, touting of enhanced student outcomes, and resource allocation in the form of technical support and investment are essential if the field is to get beyond the auspices of enthusiastic but isolated instructors.

The takeaways from the case studies and cross-analyses are instructive. The time constraints and small numbers involved in this study meant that practitioners are not yet going beyond possibilities and low-level correlations. Nonetheless, these possibilities and tentative conclusions do allow for some suggestions and recommendations. The evolution of a consistent, single framework that could be used to assess a wider swath of gamified courses would make conclusions more robust. Although the Kapp analysis was more immediately applicable to the cases in this study, aspects of flow, per Csikszentmihalyi, incorporated into a meta-framework could produce a solid means of evaluating greater investment in gamified models. In presentations and review of this work with academic faculty, the need to measure against criteria that academics can relate to become apparent. In 2015, looking to develop the motivation aspect and reflecting on the impacts reported on students from at-risk demographics, my team and I at Northeastern University pulled the matrix elements into a single rubric and used this to assess vendor adaptive learning products. On the back of that work, we were awarded significant federal funding for a project designed to increase intrinsic motivation of underrepresented minorities in science, technology, engineering, and math fields. Table 3 presents our results.

Comparison testing of gamified versus nongamified courses at scale, looking at pre- and post-tests (before and after gamification), will confirm whether gamification treatments are having a quantifiable, tangible effect. Correlation between the degree of gamification (measured by a tool like the one above) against student connectivity, frequency of logins, or other activity within the LMS would support engagement theories. The challenge of developing a tool assessing "degree of gamification" is that it is, by nature, subjective. This is

Table 3. The SIMPLE matrix

	Absent (0 pts.)	Arguably / could be (1 pt.)	Established / functional (2 pts.)	A signature element (3 pts.)
Rules clear and effective				
Effortless involvement—pick up and play (think iPod)				
Appropriate level of challenge (white-water rafting)				
CCCP: conflict, cooperation, and competition are all possible				
Clear goals with inherent, clear reward structures				
Immediate and continual feedback from instructor, system, and/or peers				
Leveling up or at least a clear sense of progress				
Narrative / curve of interest—can be "real world" based				
Stunning aesthetics				
Fear of failure reduced (mindsets)				
Student control over actions (they get choices at every step)				

Note: SIMPLE = student intrinsic motivation for persistence in learning environments (Bell 2014).

preferable, however, to the on/off prior suggestion that a course is gamified or it isn't. This kind of scoring system should at least provoke discussion and allow practitioners to consider elements that they are or are not addressing. My hope is that this will encourage practitioners to experiment more methodically, seeking to discern whether affordable and scalable gamification might be applied to online courses given potential implications for student engagement. Implementation and evolution of this kind of gamification matrix, building on the work of the likes of Kapp and Csikszentmihalyi, with development and delivery overheads clearly stated and likely outcomes captured, would facilitate better decision making and support the kinds of pioneers explored in this text.

CHAPTER NINE

Catching Fire

THE MODEL THAT BURNED BRIGHTEST

So, dear reader, this is the penultimate section of the text before it all gets wrapped up with a ribbon and we wait for the movie version. Having made it this far, I wonder whether you are ready for a bit of sleuthery. As a reward for carefully reading the cases, or even if you gamed the system by skimming them, I present to you now a game puzzle in this book on gameful design, an Easter egg of an activity if you like.

My questions for you, based on your (careful) reading of the cases:

Which blend of tactics, politics, and personalities among the projects and practitioners you have just closely studied do you feel had the best chance of setting something serious in motion on their campus?

Who was most likely to get traction?

Whose germ of an idea is on the way to becoming massive?

When I first met the practitioners in 2013, they had similar troves of enthusiasm, roughly comparable degrees of institutional support, similar/minimal funding, and a degree of isolation or "off-the-radar-ness" that they (sort of) relished. In chapter 8, I presented two frameworks and a matrix as means of evaluating three key elements: the degree of gamification, flow, and the cumulative effect of overlapping intrinsic motivators. While the matrix is intended to broker discussion rather than to prove one model's efficacy over another, none of them, either in isolation or combination, can fully predict the likelihood that a project really gets traction and succeeds in inspiring a wider audience, even at the project lead's own institution. Mapping each case to the student intrinsic motivation for persistence in learning environments (SIMPLE) matrix (table 4) provides further insight.

Results
Kevin Yee's Fairy Tale MOOC: 14 points
Neil Niman's EconJourney: 19 points

Table 4. The comparison study table

	Absent (0 pts.)	Arguably / could be (1 pt.)	Established / functional (2 pts.)	A signature element (3 pts.)
Rules clear and effective		SF / NH	W / M	P
Effortless involvement—pick up and play (think iPod)		NH / M	W / P	SF
Appropriate level of challenge (white-water rafting)		SF / W / P	NH / M	
CCCP: conflict, cooperation, and competition are all possible		SF	W	NH / M / P
Clear goals with inherent, clear reward structures		W	NH / M	SF / P
Immediate and continual feedback from instructor, system and/or peers	SF	NH / W / M	P	
Leveling up or at least a clear sense of progress		SF / W	NH / M	P
Narrative / curve of interest—can be "real world" based		SF	NH / W / M	P
Stunning aesthetics		SF / NH / W /M / P		
Fear of failure reduced (mindsets)		W	SF / NH / P	M
Student control over actions (they get choices at every step)	SF	W	NH / M / P	

Note: SF = University of South Florida Fairy Tale MOOC, NH = University of New Hampshire EconJourney, W = University of Waterloo Ethical Decision Making, M = Massachusetts College of Liberal Arts Dungeons and Discourse, P = Penn State Threat of Terrorism.

Greg Andres's Ethical Decision Making: 15 points
Gerol Petruzella's Dungeons and Discourse: 21 points
Fred Aebli's Threat of Crime and Terrorism: 25 points

It strikes me that this does better reflect the efficacy of the cases. The meld of Kapp and Csikszentmihalyi elements produces a better balance of elements, and I think that the ratings do capture the strengths and weaknesses of the models. Yee absolutely acknowledged that he struggled to keep up with the feedback and rewards of the system. Andres's project featured engaging games, but they were a little separate from the core of the class. Petruzella and Aebli really worked on the narrative, rewards, and sense of progression, while Niman's first instance of the course (when we assessed it) was challenging and somewhat confusing for the students, who found it hard to think creatively to create their own narrative.

Though I'm confident that we can get closer to an effective assessment tool, running formats against actual retention in massive numbers would be the goal going forward. No SIMPLE matrix score will guarantee institutional uptake and proliferation. It will likely take years of quantified data and concrete correlations between inputs and outputs before that level of certitude sets in. In the absence of that concrete support, my question becomes, "What sets of circumstances or what practitioner behavior that we have seen in the cases make wider uptake possible? Or feasible? Or even likely?" To further investigate that question, we can return to the cases, reflect on the practitioner commentaries, and see whether the work of Niman, Petruzella, Yee, Andres, and Aebli did have longer-term or wider ramifications. If we are to go with the assertion that proliferation of this kind of model is worthwhile and of potential benefit to a wide community of users, then it is of value to ask, and where evidence exists to review, what makes that happen?

As I noted in the interview updates to each chapter, one or two of the models definitely had (or have) a shelf life. Subsequent iterations have been supported and even successfully received without really sparking wider institutional propagation. While Yee's MOOC has stayed mostly in its packaging, he has disseminated elements of his learning to other instructors at his institution, who look to him for support on technical and pedagogical issues. Petruzella's Dungeons and Discourse was certainly given an audience at the Massachusetts College of Liberal Arts, and his work has provoked helpful discussion at his institution around equity, instructors' inherent unintentional bias, and support for first-generation and low socioeconomic status students. Andres, professor of the year winner and all-round great guy at Waterloo, inspired a lot of conversation and review of teaching practice at his institution. Aebli at Penn State engaged his provost and others in significant dialog around media bias and critical thinking. Pushing him, by a nose, into nominal runner-up in the "did the project grow wings (or legs)?" category, Aebli has been asked to lead orientations at Penn State, where he has pushed students to embark on their studies with grit and determination while stressing that they should be using their time in higher education to evolve as collegial, critical, contributing members of society. His language and persona help, as do his general worldview and ethos, but I suspect that his institution feels comfortable encouraging him to take on this kind of critical role after witnessing his students' rapt engagement with his (gameful) teaching. My admiration for all these practitioners is substantial; I hope that that has come through in the chapter descriptions. They have cumulatively touched the lives of many hundreds of students fortunate enough to be exposed to passionate, challenging instructors who clearly are themselves motivated by the process of motivating. While, like the indulgent parent, I feel general pride and have no favorites, one (over)-achiever stands out even in this exalted company.

With his resolute confidence and calmly effervescent personality, Niman at the University of New Hampshire (UNH) drove his team to redesign the EconJourney experience numerous times between 2013 and 2016, learning from each iteration and listening to feedback. The revamped course features carefully calibrated levels of support, reward, and challenge and has benefitted by high usage and high frequency of scheduling (it was used in three courses in the final twelve months of my work with him). Results have been incrementally, but increasingly, positive, while Niman's willingness to support his design principles with solid, academically rigorous notation and reporting has provided a platform for him to gain significant credibility at his institution. While I have categorized the gamer educator as a somewhat edgy disrupter who prefers to dwell on the outskirts or off the radar, Niman charged straight into the key influencers in his world. His book *The Gamification of Higher Education: Developing a Game-Based Business Strategy in a Disrupted Marketplace* was published in 2014, and each of his projects is supported by highly organized and professional white papers that provide validation and support for his ideas. While the EconJourney course/concept has shown great promise in the realm of student engagement and persistence, particularly for non-STEM majors, a potential game-changer (no pun intended) has also been spawned at UNH on the back of Niman's work. The combination of encouraging early class results, solid research protocols, and polished documentation of his work has combined into this perfect storm. This final development, Niman's promotion to the position of associate dean, cemented the foundation for a wider dissemination of bigger ideas that he had somewhat whimsically (I thought) shared back in 2012 when we first met. He had long held an idea that the needle on better student behavior, not only academically but also in social, health, and community-related contexts, might be moved by implementing intrinsically motivating life-related game dynamics on a campus level.

Fast-forward to late summer 2016, when a specific set of planets seem to have aligned in the case of the UNH, among them the drive of Niman, the work of his enthusiastic graduate assistants, good feedback on his gamification work to that point, and the support of Todd Leach, the UNH system chancellor. What they have developed, led by Niman, is a large-scale, business-school-wide implementation of a series of gamefully-designed activities melded to coursework that significantly impacts curricular and extracurricular challenges faced by business freshmen in their first months on campus. Niman, now working as Associate Dean of Academic Programs and Associate Professor of Economics within the Peter T. Paul College of Business and Economics, has lost none of his joie de vivre or bonhomie.

Paul College, as it tends to be called within the community, enrolls 2,600 undergraduate and 300 graduate students with a 65% male to 35% female split. According to the college website, it "prepares students for future careers in management, public service, research, and education." There is a clear emphasis on rounded individuals, with the liberal arts side of the curriculum actually valued rather than being seen as a necessary evil. It is felt within Paul College, and indeed for all 3,200 undergraduate first-year students at UNH, that a traditional residential campus experience is a key part of the student lifecycle. It is in this firmament that Niman has allowed himself a slightly contrived yet mnemonically valuable acronym to explain his extended gamification project. The Freshman Innovation and Research Experience (FIRE Program, figure 20) is designed to provide a comprehensive framework and inherent guidelines for a *healthy body, healthy mind* initial immersion to college life. It is intended to get new students familiar and comfortable with academic practices and to assimilate college/social culture, couched in a context of healthy, or at least *healthier*, living. Special focus is spent on mental health and well-being.

The program is intentionally outcomes-based, conveying to students the skills, knowledge, and experiences they will need to reach academic goals without falling victim to the vicissitudes of life as young adults living away from home for the first time. It is intended to be a comprehensive, holistic experience that firmly establishes persistent strategies and practices to increase student likelihood of success while illustrating and suggesting to them ways of dealing with the varied challenges they will experience as new stu-

Figure 20. Logo from the UNH FIRE program. © UNH/Niman; reproduced with permission of Neil Niman, University of New Hampshire.

dents on campus. Niman describes the intent of the program as a "dual, broad brush-stroke goal," providing an environment in which development of "social ties among fledgling communities of engaged learners" is encouraged while introducing newly arrived first-years to the traditional residential experience.

From a curricular perspective, students are required to take two foundational courses: First-Year Academic Experience I and II (PAUL 405 and 406). These two courses are contained within the larger general education program that runs across both spring and fall terms. Each class consists of a weekly one-hour face-to-face session, with an expectation that the students will spend approximately two additional hours a week outside of class working on related assignments. Around 700 students of the entering UNH business class were sorted (Hogwarts-style) into teams of 20–25 people based on their major, echoing the dependent hero contingency element that we saw in a number of earlier examples.

In their paper "The Paul College FIRE Program," Niman and his coauthors describe the project as an, "integrated, team-based game-like experience" (Niman, Rury, & Stewart 2015). The game elements are layered onto the academically recognized one-credit core courses as a means of intrinsically motivating participants to engage with the core learning goals. The formal goals are listed as

- Informing UNH students of the resources and opportunities available to them for career and academic assistance.

- Developing skills needed to succeed as a UNH and PAUL College student, as well as in business and professional situations throughout their career.
- Encouraging students to get involved in (healthy) campus activities and pursuits.
- Giving each student an opportunity to stand out (illustrating how each student has individual strengths, weaknesses and differences; and that they can all be celebrated and leveraged).

The embedded academic curriculum is intended to engender students with the ability to

- Approach and solve complex problems using a variety of different techniques.
- Effectively present a business concept and corresponding research.
- Experience and develop the culture of being part of a team.
- Locate and evaluate to potential majors, internship opportunities and the corresponding career paths.
- Recognize the importance of mentorship and the value of the broader UNH community network in a "low-risk" environment.

The above aspects are arranged around what Niman and his team calls the three foundational pillars that organize and categorize the students' learning goals. The pillars are *mentorship*, the *grand academic challenge,* and *gamification.*

To illustrate the value of mentorship, juniors or seniors are selected to serve as peer advisors and support the freshmen participants in their early transitions. The application process for the mentor positions is rigorous, with all candidates interviewed prior to acceptance. Peer advisors are required to take the bespoke two-credit course PAUL 696: Supervised Student Teaching, which is jointly taught by the director of undergraduate programs and the FIRE program coordinator. PAUL 696 is designed to imbue participants with the principles of effective mentorship and student teaching practice. It is fleshed out with case studies and worked examples of prior situations in the FIRE program where students faced challenges and needed mentor support to get through them. These worked examples provide real-time means for mentor trainee participants to share experiences and discuss means and best practices in supporting peers in who may be experiencing challenges. In most cases, these juniors and seniors are based on or near campus, physically close by their mentees (the first year participants in the FIRE program). In this small college town, by virtue of their walking the same streets, using the same gyms, and perhaps going to the same bars, they are indeed well placed to support *in loco parentis*.

Another layer of support and expertise is provided by the involvement of alumni mentors who are invited back to participate and reflect on their experiences. Niman found that this has proven a serendipitous bridge to more recent alumni that doubtless delights his advancement colleagues at UNH. The alumni participants are typically younger recent graduates who want to give back to the institution. As they are not yet in a position to do so financially, they contribute with in-kind time and support. Alumni typically interact with FIRE participants virtually without physically returning to campus. Niman describes these alumni mentors as "a bridge to the real world," supplying practical experience that provides "illustrative context and rationale for many of the concepts that, to the insular freshmen, may seem irrelevant or less important." The "bridge" aspect is the connection from what may well appear to be a less-than-authentic, theoretical academic study of principles and concepts to *applied* real-world value. As Niman notes, for most of us this awareness typically only becomes apparent quite a few years after graduation, by which time opportunities may have been missed and mistakes already made. Alumni mentors typically emphasize skills such as the value of clear communication techniques, teamwork, and professional business etiquette.

The context and narrative of the FIRE program really kick in with grand academic challenges. In the early stages (the first four weeks of the program) students can accumulate points that count towards team totals. These totals provide early competition and camaraderie and lead in to the next stage of the game. Niman refers to the grand academic challenge as the "centerpiece of the experience." The highest-scoring team after the opening four weeks gets first choice between a number of provided contexts for the next stage or level. Recent challenges have included

- Colonizing Mars;
- Living virtually;
- Prolonging life;
- Powering the Northeast; *and*
- Surviving extreme weather.

These challenges are intended to provide a motivating context (in our earlier chapters, Kapp's "narrative" category would be checked) and a milieu in which core skills can be cultivated. The skills are intended to translate quickly and with fidelity to authentic business situations. The challenges are large and ambitious but motivate and foment practice in real-world-applicable skills and competencies. Within each of the teams, students are divided into subteams and tasked with reviewing these challenges through one of four lenses: economic, political, social, or techno-scientific. The initial intent is to have students realize the complex, yet interdependent, aspects of larger issues when viewed from different perspectives. In conjunction with UNH's research librarians, Niman's team produced research guides that provide context and critical information on each challenge area for the participants. Small activities and mini-games are woven in and through the content in the guides to train students in behaviors and skills while modeling how they can succeed in their studies and substantiate their research.

The third key aspect of the FIRE project, the gamification pillar, is accentuated through the cooperation of the team members, the challenge between teams, the narrative that is developed around the challenges, and the feedback mechanisms built into the system. Figure 21 is a screenshot of the team leaderboard showing the scores and positions of the top 10 teams ("dependent hero contingency," again). There is also an individual leaderboard and numerous bonus recognitions and awards that channel Niman's favorite sport (cycling) and its hallmark event, the Tour de France. In the Tour there are a large number of individual and team awards (specialist sprint awards, best mountain climber, fastest team, etc.) that, when converted to Niman's FIRE world, allow for multiple recognitions and opportunities for individuals and teams with what he calls "different strengths" to be recognized and celebrated alongside the eventual winner and the team trophy.

Students win awards and points for academic aspects that count toward team totals. They also win credits and score points for certain behaviors on campus, such as participating in university events and activities (healthy, social community events that don't involve copious amounts of alcohol or pizza). As Niman puts it, "By creating a nexus that facilitates the making of connections that can serve as either a substitute or a complement for what exists in their residence hall, students in the FIRE program are provided with an expanded pool of opportunities for building meaningful social relationships." The game-connected point and incentive systems give students reasons to participate and help get them over shyness and initial inertia by

Figure 21. Screenshot: Team leaderboard from the UNH FIRE project, 2016. Reproduced with permission of Neil Niman, University of New Hampshire.

encouraging them to attend events with fellow team members and adding bonus points for inclusiveness. Point-based feedback is augmented with prizes given at specific events, including FIRE-branded merchandise and what the organizers call *Luminary Awards* for advancing in the game. The latter speaks to what we have seen multiple times in the practitioner examples described as "reduced fear of failure," while the former has engendered a sense of pride, illustrating the value of aesthetics elevating the status of FIRE "merch" at UNH.

On the academic side of FIRE, tangible deliverables include three graded assignments in the fall semester and four in the spring. PAUL 405, the first course, requires that the students submit what is referred to as an *academic autobiography*, a self-assessment piece requiring that they candidly assess their strengths and weaknesses before presenting their work on the grand challenges with their assigned lens or role in the team. The second part of the lens work is a group presentation where they share and meld their findings within the team before presenting to the panel. This challenge culminates in a reality TV-like playoff in front of a panel of judges who assess each team's presentations, which, at a meta-level, outlines a business opportunity in the area of their challenge. These sessions were held at the university's Undergraduate Research Conference and, according to Niman, were extremely well attended and notable for the maturity of the projects and the skills and poise of the presenters.

PAUL 406, the second academic course within FIRE, focuses on the students' choices, looking further out to minors, majors, and extra possibilities at UNH including study abroad and internship projects. The students in the second (spring) term work closely with the alumni mentors, who provide tailored support in areas such as resume writing, networking, and associated real-world skills. To accentuate the importance of these skills and to provide a further element of experiential learning during this term, the university hosts a networking reception and a career boot camp. Attendance and participation at this reception are high, and, as an external metric suggesting validation, first-year student participation at the annual spring career fair was almost doubled in the year after the FIRE launch. Niman was confident of the causality as well as the correlation. The grand challenge documentation included multiple drafts and revision cycles, group work, and self-reflection, all emphasizing the need for polished, professional writing, presentation, and communication skills.

Student Stories

A student who recently participated in the FIRE program relayed her experience of the grand challenge and the team interaction:

> Our group challenge was to create a product or service that could help those affected by extreme weather. After a review of real problems facing the world today, our team decided that fresh water would play an even more critical role globally. Our product, *Oasis,* is a compact water purifier specifically designed for natural and environmental disasters (e.g. floods, hurricanes, contaminants).
>
> I enjoyed the opportunity to be one of our team's five presenters. I recognized the importance of the detailed preparation that went into our business plan. Each of the members of my team played a critical role. No one person can be credited with our team/company success. As previously mentioned, "If it's about the company, then it's about the team."
>
> We made it through the first round with a very relevant product combined with an impactful presentation. I believe we won in the final round because judges found our team to be professional and our presentation well designed. Winning the URC [Undergraduate Research Conference] for FIRE was so satisfying because it was at that point I recognized the true value of the UNH curriculum.

One of the peer advisors reflected on his experience mentoring and supporting FIRE participants:

> My experience as a peer advisor has been very rewarding. Not only have I facilitated student growth and development, I have learned and fine-tuned many skills of my own. Additionally, I have expanded my network to include a variety of interesting alumni, teachers, students and advisors who have provided me with valuable insights and lessons. Lastly, being a peer advisor has been very enjoyable! Whether it was joking around with the advisors in the office or participating in team events, I have had a great time. Paul College has some tremendous people, and meeting them has been both eye opening and fun. Without the experiences obtained as a peer advisor, I would not be the person I am today.

A third student commented looking back on his experience and forward to his and the program's future:

> The beauty of FIRE is that we are being rewarded for taking advantage of these opportunities. It is not another obligation but rather an opportunity in itself. I was able to win the first semester of FIRE because I was not afraid to listen to advice from people who knew more and got involved. FIRE allowed me to see what I wanted to get involved in at UNH and through that what I want to do for the rest of my life. FIRE is essentially an awareness program. We are learning, hands on, all of the skills we need to be successful students and, therefore, successful professionals. We're taught about UNH so we can utilize our resources. We are motivated to get involved to access every opportunity. Most importantly, we focus on professional and personal development so we can excel beyond schooling.

Combustion

The perfect storm of push-pull came into being at UNH when Niman's enthusiasm, his track record, and his mostly successful EconJourney project arrived just as the freshman academic experience course was hitting its nadir in terms of relevance (for the students) and efficacy (per institutional metrics). As with many first-year experience courses, students were dragging their heels, "mailing in" their work, and not really retaining anything they were purported to have learned. The respect with which Niman was regarded at UNH, along with his periodic but effective communication with the UNH system chancellor, Leach, positioned him, his team, and his project to gain enthusiastic sponsorship and institutional support when opportunity arose. The implementation

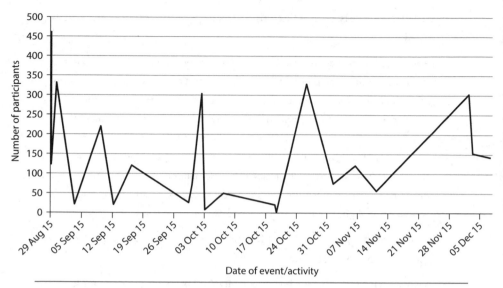

Figure 22. UNH FIRE participation. Reproduced with permission of Neil Niman, University of New Hampshire.

of FIRE has been, by most methods of review, a roaring success. As the team puts it, "Attending class has become an opportunity to connect with friends. By building on each other, assignments have a rationale and reason with an achievable goal at the end. More Paul College students are joining clubs and participating in extracurricular activities. The library guides supporting the grand challenges are the most visited pages at the UNH library."

Figure 22 shows student activity in the LMS, with spikes corresponding to assignment due dates or key times around when rankings were assessed. Student surveys indicated that FIRE participants were participating in a greater number of extracurricular activities than students did back in pre-FIRE years. In the fall semester survey more than half of responding students reported participating in at least five events or activities. Eighty-four percent of students reported making friends within their FIRE team, while 96 percent felt comfortable approaching their peer/mentor with a concern.

In terms of academics, a general census across first-year courses showed upticks in FIRE students' grade point averages (GPAs) (table 5). The improvements were particularly noted in courses where writing and presentation skills were emphasized (table 6). The three courses Introduction to Business (ADMN 400), First Year Writing (ENGL 401), and Ethics (PHIL 430) all reported significant increases in course grades for FIRE participants.

Table 5. Student GPAs before and after FIRE participation

	Fall 2015		Fall 2014	
	Number of students	Percentage of class	Number of students	Percentage of class
At or above 3.0	405	60.72	369	54.03
At or above 3.5	178	26.69	142	20.79
At or above 3.75	95	14.24	49	7.17
At 4.0	28	4.20	9	1.32

Table 6. Student performance in courses emphasizing writing and presentation skills at UNH before and after FIRE participation.

	Fall 2015		Fall 2014		
	Number of students	Average GPA	Number of students	Average GPA	GPA change (%)
ADMN 400	585	3.29	614	3.02	+8.94
ENGL 401	105	3.44	141	3.24	+6.17
PHIL 430	305	3.16	22	2.76	+14.49

Conclusions

The stated goal of the FIRE program was "to strengthen the tie between academics, the student experience and career preparation." It achieved its goal through application of mentorships and gameful design. The game framework allows participants to engender social ties and practice skills with reduced fear of failure in a game-based context. The incentives and gameful cooperation, competition, and reward provide a powerful impetus and remove many of the excuses for not engaging with the college experience.

While not scoring outright first in my SIMPLE review, Niman's model was well placed. He then benefitted more than the others by virtue of his standing, his documentation, his willingness to keep tweaking his format, his empathetic chancellor, and his relentless confidence and humor. Having extended his EconJourney class and the learning and experience therein to the whole first-year experience and the FIRE project, Niman doesn't see a need to stop there. He is confident that the model will work outside of the business envelope. The interdisciplinary nature of the grand challenge work and the ubiquitous skills needed in the vast majority of careers suggest to him that he can (and will) extend the project to all incoming students at UNH. He has even spoken with other institutions and is confident that he could support external installs of this clearly effective program. I have absolutely no doubt that he can continue to achieve whatever he thinks is feasible. His, and indeed all these gamer-educators', adventures are clearly not over.

Captain's Epilogue

The narrative of this text began with *Space Invaders* and *PacMan* (and Ashton Kutcher for a reason that now escapes me). As I come to conclusions and attempt to wrap the text with pithy conclusions, I am going to timestamp and date this with a reflection on the craze of the current day (early 2017). The *Space Invaders* references described the first time technology was added to the mix of gaming on a massive scale and how that, perhaps belatedly, is influencing teaching and learning 40 years on. *Pokémon Go* is an interesting social phenomenon given its gameful elements and the amount of commitment and work being put in by those caught in its spell. It has eclipsed porn, news, and weather in terms of web-search popularity and is, by most definitions, the most successful mobile game ever created. While *Space Invaders* generated similar levels of addiction, GPS tracking (obviously not available in 1978), 4G, and smartphones facilitate mobility, allowing the game developers to accentuate intrinsic motivators and effectively address all of the elements described in chapter 8.

Created by Nintendo, the Pokémon Company, and Niantic (a Google spinoff), *Pokémon Go* added a near-immediate $17.6 billion in market capitalization to Nintendo's stock price, almost doubling its value, when it launched. A subsequent dip when Nintendo clarified that they in fact only had a 17% stake in Niantic did not detract from the sentiment that they made a wise move expanding to mobile gaming from the console base that they had held on to since the eighties. If we assess *Pokémon Go* against the SIMPLE matrix (table 7), it is apparent that they have leveraged almost every means of ramping up intrinsic motivation in their users.

As table 7 indicates, *Pokémon Go* should be a highly addictive, highly motivating activity. And guess what? It is. The aesthetics are not particularly "stunning," and the play, catch, repeat narrative may get repetitive for some players. But even with those caveats stated, it apparently should come with a health warning. A couple in Arizona was recently charged with child

Table 7. The *Pokémon* (high) bar

	Absent (0 pts.)	Arguably / could be (1 pt.)	Established / functional (2 pts.)	A signature element (3 pts.)
Rules clear and effective				X
Effortless involvement—pick up and play (think iPod)				X
Appropriate level of challenge (white-water rafting)				X
CCCP: conflict, cooperation, and competition are all possible				X
Clear goals with inherent, clear reward structures				X
Immediate and continual feedback from instructor, system and/or peers				X
Leveling up or at least a clear sense of progress				X
Narrative / curve of interest—can be "real world" based				X
Stunning aesthetics			X	
Fear of failure reduced (mindsets)				X
Student control over actions (they get choices at every step)				X

endangerment having left their toddler unattended for 90 minutes in 90-degree heat while they played. Another player traveled to Australia to catch a Kangaskhan but was hit by a car while attempting to do so. As he relayed to *Business Insider,* "I thought to myself, I could have died searching for *Pokémon* . . . what has my life arrived to?"—indeed.

It is often said that in terms of looking for means of engaging customers, pornography is streets ahead of any other, ahem, diversion. When a free mobile game, with no tangible prizes and none of the inherent compulsions that drive consumers to porn, outstrips (no pun intended) that commitment, something significant is happening. When a mobile gaming app hits our target demographic right between the eyes and confirms much of what we are theorizing might work in higher education, we can safely say that we are at a nexus, a point of inflection, a watershed, or a defining moment. Demographically, 63% of *Pokémon Go* players are female compared to 37% who are male, 46% of players are between the ages of 18 and 29, and 45% of them make over $50,000 per year. Detractors against gamification and gameful design often talk of the dumbing-down effect—the catering to juvenilia. This *Pokémon Go*–playing demographic is not a brain-dead kid. We could do worse (clearly) than to chase the chasers, but we will have to offer them something at least a little bit engaging in their education.

Technologies like those employed in the *Pokémon Go* game are becoming increasingly accessible for developers and affordable for institutions. Low-tech, "napkin sketch" versions of gamified classes have proven our concept, and the evolution of practitioner work (Niman's FIRE project in chapter 9) suggests that administrators and academics alike are developing a willingness to embrace and encourage even fledgling efforts. The technical and administrative challenges all seem surmountable. How many of us would have identified Niman's EconJourney as the one of the five cases that would lead to such an enhanced and extended implementation? From my engagement with Niman, his team, and the environment at the University of New Hampshire, I would categorize the progenitors of his success in three basic categories. A review of the traits in these categories (below) could well be instructive to future practitioners as they contemplate gamefully designed activities or classes. Here are the key elements that, when aligned, have led to a very successful, institutionally supported, and well-funded implementation.

Practitioner Traits
- Unflappable-ness;
- Gamer traits (fun, playful, determined, no fear of failure);
- Confidence in the value of the work;
- Ability to lead teams and willingness to give it a go with what you have to hand in terms of available, nearly free resources (smart, willing grad assistants, tools that are not so complex they alienate or confuse the community);
- A solid research background for generating academic/institutional buy-in;
- Articulate and good at documentation; *and*
- A level of seniority that provides some degree of autonomy (reduced fear of failure).

Implementation Traits

- Good use of, and integration with, established, familiar institutional technologies;
- Minimal *tech for the sake of tech* add-ons that are not integral to the product;
- Low-threshold apps—all developments able to be quickly launched without too much drama or need for large-scale tech support (at least until proof of concept is in);
- Quick turnaround on incremental improvements; *and*
- Flexible means for students to play (not too locked in).

Institutional Traits

- Leadership that is open to innovation;
- A defined and identifiable need with a concise elevator pitch (in Niman's case, engagement of at-risk first-year students); *and*
- Willingness for, or at least a tolerance of, novelty and ambiguity.

In uniting elements of cognitive science, adaptive learning, learning analytics, and (very simply) inspired and fun teaching, gamification clearly has appeal and real potential for improving student engagement. Further development will be motivated by a societal and institutional need to scale online courses, unparalleled access to learning management system data, and new desires to improve student engagement. Given the extended access possibilities of online instruction, as opposed to traditional campus-based education, advocates for the underserved and legislators in states with ambitious educational attainment goals should explore, or at least support, research into any and all possible avenues for student engagement and retention.

Many of the factors attracting students to traditional institutions are not viable in the online environment. The charisma of engaging instructors, human empathy, and personality are almost impossible to replicate in an online environment. However, incremental adjustments to aspects of the online environment, including the nature and format of materials and the information architecture of a course (how the materials are presented), can be tried and monitored without large investment or extra allocation of significant resources. This low-cost flexibility to change modes of delivery incrementally and monitor the impact of these changes confirms that intentional online course development has great capacity to try out new concepts in the hope that at least one, possibly more, will make a significant difference. If research into gamification produces findings that enhance student engagement or persistence, it could translate into massive benefits to society and the field of higher education given these large and still-growing numbers.

Going forward, it would be helpful to examine whether particular formats and audiences benefit disproportionately from course gamification, as some practitioners suggested. Research should explicitly explore the working hypothesis—articulated in the Massachusetts College of Liberal Arts and, to a lesser extent, the University of New Hampshire case—that fragile learners, first-generation college students, and those for whom education has always seemed a daunting prospect may be helped by less threatening, gamified courses. Emerging disrupted models of education such as competency-based education and direct assessment provide further opportunities to build in rewards, immediate feedback, and other parameters from Kapp (2012), Csikszentmihalyi (1975), and the SIMPLE matrix (Bell 2014). Gamification may provide a means by which newer, disrupted formats for delivering education have an increased chance of success with critical demographics for whom there are few other options.

My motivation in engaging with the practitioners and the cases studied was to dig deeper into aspects of online education that the literature suggests matter for improving student engagement and learning outcomes. It turned out that the most interesting alignment of these elements was manifest in gamified courses. As I have tried to demonstrate, this is not capturing a new cult or a new fad. I have seen SIMPLE traits in many classrooms, and it is my belief that what we are seeing with gamified classes (face to face, hybrid, or fully online) is merely a means of accentuating what effective, motivated instructors do on a daily basis in their classes. I hope that this collection also provides inspiration for institutions, developers, and faculty members who are tempted to have a go at gamified courses in the future. As the practitioners and my own interviews demonstrated, students are bored. Typically their classes are not (almost cannot be) as engaging as Facebook, Snapchat, or *Pokémon Go*. No one is expected to approximate or outdo these sticky apps. Students don't want their education to spill over into their social lives. They are, however, happy to say, "Give it a go. Give me something vaguely interesting that speaks to me and that shows that you have made an effort to meet me halfway." Students who commented on the low-tech builds encouraged more sophisticated (later) versions but did so in a supportive, constructive manner.

Clearly there are, or will be in many institutions, structural issues particularly with regard to the availability of technical support and platform. There are going to be political impediments, perhaps even governance issues, and naysayers to navigate. In the first person, I implore you to take lessons from the wonderful, positive instructors in this story. Give it a go. Be open to failures as well as successes. Learn from the former, and use the latter to further the project. Look at the achievements in this book. Will increased student engagement gain interest at your institution? Will potential inclusion and removal of instructor unconscious bias be noted? Will support and motivation of low-SES, fragile, or first-generation students gain attention? Will it be fun for you? At worst, you'll be a happy, motivated instructor having fun, meeting the students on their level, and learning with and from them—can't be all bad, can it?

Gamification very possibly has a role to play in moving the needle on student engagement, the clearest measurable associate to success that we have. It may be a minor role or a major one. It could be the Holy Grail or akin to one Sokolow wedge in a *save the planet* challenge. Either way, I don't know that the scale of success really matters in rumination over a try/don't try decision. Future work will doubtless unlock more of the keys to engagement and motivation that could turn fragile learners into lifelong learners. If we can focus effort yoked to a *have a go* attitude, we could make dull, impossible courses feel compelling and achievement feasible for those who currently have the worst prospects of success. If this gives anyone a shot at helping any and all students, why would we not? If we can disproportionately encourage underserved and individuals typically "dropped out" by both society and academia, one could argue that we must do so. Motivating and encouraging student achievement is the main reason most of us work in higher education. In engaging students, especially those who are struggling, we will have taken a significant step toward a more educated and inclusive society.

Go ahead: Soar once again. Save the planet. Zap antipathy and boredom. Be the Gorfian Space Avenger you once were. Get to level 27. Game on!

Bibliography

ACT. 2014. "The Condition of STEM." Retrieved from www.act.org/content/act/en
/research/condition-of-stem-2014.html.

Ambrose, S. 2010. *How Learning Works.* San Francisco, CA: Jossey-Bass.

Arum, R., and Roska, J. 2011. *Academically Adrift: Limited Learning on College Campuses.*
Chicago, IL: University of Chicago Press.

Asgari, M. 2005. "A Three-Factor Model of Motivation and Game Design." Paper
presented at the 2005 International DiGRA Conference, Vancouver, British Columbia, Canada.

Auletta, K. 2012. "Get Rich U." *The New Yorker,* April 30. Retrieved from www.new
yorker.com/magazine/2012/04/30/get-rich-u.

Baggett, P. 1984. "Role of Temporal Overlap of Visual and Auditory Material in
Forming Dual Media Associations." *Journal of Educational Psychology* 76(3):
408–417.

Bandura, A. 1997. *Self-Efficacy: The Exercise of Control.* New York: W. H. Freeman.

Blackboard Inc. 2013. "Blackboard Expands Support for Retention Efforts with Early
Warning Analytics." Press release, April 24.

Bloom, B. S. 1956. *Taxonomy of Educational Objectives,* Handbook I, *The Cognitive Domain.*
New York: David McKay.

Bogdan, R., and Bilken, S. K. 2006. *Qualitative Research for Education: An Introduction to
Theory and Methods* (5th ed.). Upper Saddle River, NJ: Pearson.

Boston, W. 2014. Lecture at the University of Pennsylvania to the EdD Higher
Education Management program (cohort 12). Philadelphia, PA, February.

Breit, W., and Elzinga, K. G. 2002. "Economics as Detective Fiction." *Journal of Economic
Education* Fall 2002: 367–376. Retrieved from www.iei.liu.se/nek/730A17/artiklar
/1.283067/Detectivestory.pdf.

Brophy, J. E. 2004. *Motivating Students to Learn* (2nd ed.). Mahwah, NJ: Lawrence
Erlbaum.

Brusilovsky, P., Sosnovsky, S., and Yudelson, M. 2009. "Addictive Links: The Motivational Value of Adaptive Link Annotation." *New Review of Hypermedia and Multimedia* 15(1): 97–118.

Bulger, M. E., Mayer, R. E., Almeroth, K. C., and Blau, S. D. 2008. "Measuring Learner
Engagement in Computer-Equipped College Classrooms." *Journal of Educational
Multimedia and Hypermedia* 17(2): 129–143.

Campbell, J. 1949. "The Hero with a Thousand Faces." New York: Pantheon Books.

Carroll, J., and Olson, J. 1988. *Mental Models in Human-Computer Interaction.* Washington, DC: National Academy Press.

Chandler, P., and Sweller, J. 1991. "Cognitive Load Theory and the Format of Instruction." *Cognition and Instruction* 8(4): 293–332.

Chen, P.-S. D., Gonyea, R., and Kuh, G. 2008. "Learning at a Distance [Electronic Version]." *Journal of Online Education* 4.

Chickering, A. W., and Gamson, Z. F. 1987. "Seven Principles for Good Practice in Undergraduate Education." *AAHE Bulletin* 39(7): 3–7.

Christensen, C., and Eyring, H. 2011. *The Innovative University: Changing the DNA of Higher Education from the Inside Out.* San Francisco, CA: Jossey-Bass.

Clark, R. 2005. "Instructional Strategies." In H. F. O'Neil (ed.), *What Works in Distance Learning Guidelines* (pp. 43–61). Greenwich, CT: Information Age Publishing.

Cline, E. 2012. *Ready Player One.* Danvers, MA: Broadway Books.

Compeau, D. R., and Higgins, C. A. 1995. "Computer Self-Efficacy: Development of a Measure and Initial Test." *MIS Quarterly* 19(2): 189–211.

Cordova, D. I., and Lepper, M. R. 1996. "Intrinsic Motivation and the Process of Learning: Beneficial Effects of Contextualization, Personalization and Choice." *Journal of Educational Psychology* 88(4): 715–730.

Cowan, N. 2009. "What Are the Differences between Long-Term, Short-Term, and Working Memory?" *Progress in Brain Research* 169: 323–338.

Csikszentmihalyi, M. 1975. "Play and Intrinsic Rewards." *Journal of Humanistic Psychology* 15(3): 41–63.

———. 1990. *Flow: The Psychology of Optimal Experience.* New York: Harper.

Dawson, S., and McWilliam, E. 2008. *Investigating the Application of IT Generated Data as an Indicator of Learning and Teaching Performance.* Queensland University of Technology and the University of British Columbia. Retrieved from www.olt.gov.au/project-investigating-application-it-qut-2007.

Deneen, L. "What Is Student Engagement Anyway?" *Educause,* March 3. Retrieved from www.educause.edu/ero/article/what-student-engagement-anyway.

DeTure, M. 2004. "Cognitive Style and Self-Efficacy: Predicting Student Success in Online Distance Education." *American Journal of Distance Education* 18(1): 21–38.

diSessa, A. 1982. "Unlearning Aristotelian Physics: A Study of Knowledge-Based Learning." *Cognitive Science* 6: 37–75.

Dogan, B. 2008. "Association Rule Mining from an Intelligent Tutor." *Journal of Educational Technology Systems* 36(4): 433.

Drucker, P. 2006. *Innovation and Entrepreneurship.* New York: Harper Business.

Dungeons & Dragons official home page. 2013. Retrieved from www.wizards.com/dnd/Feature.aspx?x=new/whatisdnd.

Ecclestone, K. 2008. "The Rise of the 'Fragile' Learner." Retrieved from https://wiki.brookes.ac.uk/display/teachingnews/The+rise+of+the+%27fragile%27+learner.

Emanuel, E. 2013. "Online Education: MOOCs Taken by Educated Few." *Nature* 503: 342. doi: 10. 1038/503342a.

Galarneau, L. 2005. "Authentic Learning Experiences through Play: Games, Simulations and the Construction of Knowledge." Retrieved from http://papers.ssrn.com/sol3/papers.cfm?abstract_id=810065.

Gardner, H. E. 1983. *Frames of Mind: The Theory of Multiple Intelligences.* New York: Basic Books.

Gee, J. P. 2003. *What Video Games Have to Teach Us about Learning and Literacy.* New York: Palgrave MacMillan.

Gentile, D. A., and Walsh, D. A. 2002. "A Normative Study of Family Media Habits." *Applied Developmental Psychology* 23: 157–178.

Greeno, J. G., Collins, A. M., and Resnick, L. B. 1996. "Cognition and Learning." In D. C. Berliner and R. C. Calfee (eds.), *Handbook of Educational Psychology* (pp. 15–46). New York: Macmillan.

Guo, P. 2013. "Optimal Video Length for Student Engagement." Retrieved from www .edx.org/blog/optimal-video-length-student-engagement.

Hart, Hugh. 2008. "Dicaprio to Play Nolan Bushnell in *Atari.*" *Wired* magazine. Retrieved from www.wired.com/2008/06/leo-dicaprio-at/.

Hawtrey, K. 2007. "Using Experiential Learning Techniques." *Journal of Economic Education* 38(2): 143–52.

Hunicke, R. 2009. "Wildflowers: The UX of Game/Play." Retrieved from http://vimeo .com/6984481.

Inan, F. A., and Lowther, D. L. 2007. "Comparative Analysis of Computer-Supported Learning Models and Guidelines." In F. M. M. Neto and F. V. Brasiliero (eds.), *Advances in Computer Supported Learning* (pp. 1–20). Harrisburg, PA: Idea Group.

Kapp, K. M. 2012. *The Gamification of Learning and Instruction: Game-Based Methods and Strategies for Training and Education.* San Francisco, CA: Pfeiffer/ASTD.

Ke, F. 2009. "A Qualitative Meta-Analysis of Computer Games as Learning Tools." In R. E. Ferdig (ed.), *Effective Electronic Gaming in Education,* vol. 1 (pp. 1–32). Hershey, PA: Information Science Reference.

Kolb, D. A. 1984. *Experiential Learning: Experience as the Source of Learning and Development.* Englewood Cliffs, NJ: Prentice Hall.

Krause, K. L., and Coates, H. 2008. "Students' Engagement in First-Year University." *Assessment and Evaluation in Higher Education* 33(5): 493–505.

Kuh, G. D. 2009. "The National Survey of Student Engagement: Conceptual and Empirical Foundations." *New Directions for Institutional Research* 141: 5–20.

Lepper, M. R. 1988. "Motivational Considerations in the Study of Instruction." *Cognition and Instruction* 5(4): 289–309.

Litow, L., and Pumroy, D. K. 1975. "A Brief Review of Classroom Group-Oriented Contingencies." *Journal of Applied Behavior Analysis* 8: 341–347.

McGonigal, J. 2012. *Reality Is Broken: Why Games Make Us Better and How They Can Change the World.* New York: Penguin.

Malone, T. W. 1981. "Toward a Theory of Intrinsically Motivating Instruction." *Cognitive Science* 5(4): 333–369.

Malone, T. W., and Lepper, M. R. 1987. "Making Learning Fun: A Taxonomy of Intrinsic Motivations for Learning." In R. E. Snow and M. J. Farr (eds.), *Aptitude, Learning and Instruction,* vol. 3, *Cognitive and Affective Process Analyses* (pp. 299–253). Mahwah, NJ: Lawrence Erlbaum.

Marandi, E., Little, E., and Hughes, T. 2010. "Innovation and the Children of the Revolution: Facebook and Value Co-Creation." *Marketing Review* 10 (2): 169–183.

Massachusetts College of Liberal Arts. 2013. "Profile Brochure." Retrieved from www .mcla.edu/About_MCLA/.

Mautone, P., and Mayer, R. 2001. "Signaling as a Cognitive Guide in Multimedia Learning." *Journal of Educational Psychology* 93(2): 377.

Mayer, R. 2003. "The Promise of Multimedia Learning: Using the Same Instructional Design Methods across Different Media." *Learning and Instruction* 13(2): 125.

Mayer, R. E., and Moreno, R. 2002. "Animation as an Aid to Multimedia Learning." *Educational Psychology Review* 14(2): 87–100.

Merrill, M. D. 1983. "Component Display Theory." In C. Reigeluth (ed.), *Instructional Design Theories and Models*. Hillsdale, NJ: Erlbaum.

Moorhead, H. J. H., Neuer Colburn, A. A., Edwards, N. N., and Erwin, K. T. 2013. "Beyond the Myth of the Pajama Party: Delivering Quality Online Counselor Education and Supervision." Paper based on a program presented at the 2013 American Counseling Association Conference, Cincinnati, OH, March 23–27.

Moreno, R. 2007. "Optimizing Learning from Animations by Minimizing Cognitive Load: Cognitive and Affective Consequences of Signaling and Segmentation Methods." *Applied Cognitive Psychology* 21(6): 765–781.

Niman, N. 2014. *The Gamification of Higher Education: Developing a Game-Based Business Strategy in a Disrupted Marketplace*. New York: Palgrave MacMillan.

Niman, N., Rury, S., and Stewart, S. 2015. "The Paul College FIRE Program." Retrieved from www.unh.edu/unhtoday/2016/04/catching-fire-paul-college.

Obama, B. 2009. "Remarks to Joint Session of Congress, Tuesday, February 24, 2009." Retrieved from www.whitehouse.gov/the_press_office/Remarks-of-President-Barack- Obama-Address-to-Joint-Session-of-Congress.

Palmer, S. R., and Holt, D. M. 2009. "Examining Student Satisfaction with Wholly Online Learning." *Journal of Computer Assisted Learning* 25(2): 101–113.

Papanikolaou, K. A., Grigoriadou, M., Kornilakis, H., and Magoulas, G. D. 2003. "Personalizing the Interaction in a Web-Based Educational Hypermedia System: The Case of INSPIRE." *User Modeling and User-Adapted Interaction* 13(3): 213–267.

Papert, S. 1997. *The Connected Family: Bridging the Digital Generation Gap*. Marietta, GA: Longstreet Press.

Perna, L., Ruby, A., Boruch, R., Wang, N., Scull, J., Evans, C., and Ahmad, S. 2013. "The Life Cycle of a Million MOOC Users." Presentation at the MOOC Research Initiative Conference, University of Texas–Austin, December 5.

Plowman, L. 1996. "Narrative, Linearity and Interactivity: Making Sense of Interactive Multimedia." *British Journal of Educational Technology* 27: 92–105. doi:10.1111 /j.1467-8535.1996.tb00716.x.

Pollock, E., Chandler, P., and Sweller, J. 2002. "Assimilating Complex Information." *Learning and Instruction* 12(1): 61–86.

Prahalad, C. K., and Ramaswamy, V. 2004. "Co-Creation Experiences: The Next Practice in Value Creation." *Journal of Interactive Marketing* 18(3): 5–14.

Prensky, M. 2001. *Digital Game-Based Learning.* New York: McGraw-Hill.

Randel, J. M., Morris, B. A., Wetzel, C. D., and Whitehill, B. V. 1992. "The Effectiveness of Games for Educational Purposes: A Review of Recent Research." *Simulation Gaming* 23(3): 261–276.

Rankine, L., Stevenson, L., Malfroy, J., and Ashford-Rowe, K. 2009. "Benchmarking Across Universities: A Framework for LMS Analysis." Paper presented at the Ascilite conference, Auckland, December 6. Retrieved from www.ascilite.org/conferences/auckland09/procs/rankine.pdf.

Recruiter.com. 2014. "Career Outlook for Instructional Designers and Technologists." Retrieved from www.recruiter.com/careers/instructional-designers-and -technologists/outlook/.

Reeves, B., and Read, J. L. 2009. *Total Engagement: Using Games and Virtual Worlds to Change the Way People Work and Businesses Compete.* Boston, MA: Harvard Business Press.

Reiff, J. C. 1992. *Learning Styles.* What Research Says to the Teacher 7. Washington, DC: National Education Association.

Rigby, C. S., Przybylski, A. K., Deci, E. L., and Ryan, R. M. 2014. "Competence-Impeding Electronic Games and Players' Aggressive Feelings, Thoughts, and Behaviors." *Journal of Personality and Social Psychology* 106(3): 441–457.

Ryan, R. M., and Deci, E. L. 2000. "Self-Determination Theory and the Facilitation of Intrinsic Motivation, Social Development, and Well-Being." *American Psychologist* 55: 68–78.

Savitz, E., and Tedford, J. 2012. "Facebook Timeline for Brands: It's about Storytelling." *Forbes,* February 29. Retrieved from www.forbes.com/sites/ciocentral/2012/02 /29/facebook-timeline-for- brands-its-about-storytelling.

Scardamalia, M. 2000. "Can Schools Enter a Knowledge Society?" In M. Selinger and J. Wynn (eds.), *Educational Technology and the Impact on Teaching and Learning.* Abingdon, UK: RM Education.

Schell, J. 2008. *The Art of Game Design: A Book of Lenses.* Waltham, MA: Morgan Kaufmann.

———. 2010. "Design Outside the Box." Keynote speech at the Design Innovate Communicate Entertain Conference, Las Vegas, NV, February 17.

Schrum, L., and Benson, A. 2001. "Establishing Successful Online Distance Learning Environments: Distinguishing Factors that Contribute to Online Courses and Programs." In R. Discenza, C. Howard, and K. Schenk (eds.), *The Design and Management of Effective Distance Learning Programs.* Hershey, PA: Idea Group.

Siemens, G. 2011a. "Duplication Theory of Educational Value." Retrieved from www .elearnspace.org/blog/2011/09/15/duplication-theory-of- educational-value/.

———. 2011b. "Learning and Academic Analytics." Retrieved from www .learninganalytics.net/?p=131.

Sitzmann, T. 2011. "A Meta-Analytic Examination of the Instructional Effectiveness of Computer-Based Simulation Games." *Personnel Psychology* 64(2): 489–528.

Skinner, B. F. 1971. *Beyond Freedom and Dignity.* Cambridge, MA: Hackett.

Soares. L. 2013. "Post-Traditional Learners and the Transformation of Postsecondary Education: A Manifesto for College Leaders." Retrieved from www.acenet.edu/news -room/Documents./Soares-Post-Traditional-v5- 011813.pdf.

Song, L., Singleton, S. E., Hill, J. R., and Koh, M. H. 2004. "Improving Online Learning: Student Perceptions of Useful and Challenging Characteristics." *Internet and Higher Education* 7(1): 59–70.

Song, S. H., and Keller, J. M. 2001. "Effectiveness of Motivationally Adaptive Computer- Assisted Instruction on the Dynamic Aspects of Motivation." *Educational Technology Research and Development* 49(2): 5–22.

Staples, D. S., Hulland, J. S., and Higgins, C. A. 1999. "A Self-Efficacy Theory Explana- tion for the Management of Remote Workers in Virtual Organizations." *Organization Science* 10(6): 758–776.

Stewart, P. H., Jones, V. N., and Pope, J. V. 1999. "Learning Styles: Charting with Iconic Learners." ERIC Document Reproduction No. ED 428 403. Retrieved from https://eric.ed.gov/?id=ED428403.

Sweller, J., Van Merriënboer, J., and Paas, F. 1998. "Cognitive Architecture and Instructional Design." *Educational Psychology Review* 10(3): 251–296.

Tsandilas, T., and Schraefel, M. C. 2004. "Usable Adaptive Hypermedia Systems." *New Review of Hypermedia and Multimedia* 10(1): 5–29.

Tsianos, N., Germanakos, P., Lekkas, Z., Mourlas, C., and Samaras, G. 2009. "An Assess- ment of Human Factors in Adaptive Hypermedia Environments." In C. Mourlas and P. Germanakos (eds.), *Intelligent User Interfaces: Adaptation and Personalization Systems and Technologies* (pp. 1–18). Hershey, PA: Information Science Reference.

Urban Dictionary. 2013. "Boss Battle." Retrieved from www.urbandictionary.com /define.php?term=boss+battle.

US Department of Education, National Center for Education Statistics. 2013. *The Condition of Education.* NCES 2013-037. Washington, DC.

US Department of Education, Office of Planning, Evaluation, and Policy Development. 2010. *Evaluation of Evidence-Based Practices in Online Learning: A Meta-Analysis and Review of Online Learning Studies.* Washington, DC.

Vogler, C. 1992. *The Writer's Journey: Mythic Structure for Writers.* San Francisco, CA: M. Wiese.

Walstad, W. B., and Allgood, S. 1999. "What Do College Seniors Know about Economics?" *American Economic Review* 89(2): 350–354.

Wolfe, J. 1997. "The Effectiveness of Business Games in Strategic Management Course Work." *Simulation and Gaming* 28(4): 360–376.

Woodhouse, K. 2015. "Lazy Rivers and Student Debt: Inside Higher Ed." Retrieved from www.insidehighered.com/news/2015/06/15/are-lazy-rivers-and-climbing -walls-driving-cost-college.

Zichermann, G. 2011. Presentation at the For the Win (Serious Gamification) conference at the Wharton School of Business, University of Pennsylvania, August 8–9. Retrieved from www.gamification.co/2011/08/10/lies-damned-lies-and-academics.

Zichermann, G., and Cunningham, C. 2011. *Gamification by Design: Implementing Game Mechanics in Web and Mobile Apps.* Sebastopol, CA: O'Reilly Media.

Index